BLOOD ON THE STREETS

BLOOD ON THE STREETS

A–Z OF GLASGOW CRIME

ROBERT JEFFREY

BLACK & WHITE PUBLISHING

First published 2004
by Black & White Publishing Ltd
99 Giles Street, Edinburgh

ISBN 1 84502 017 0

A CIP catalogue record for this book
is available from The British Library.

Photographs courtesy of Newsquest

Printed and bound by Creative Print and Design

ACKNOWLEDGEMENTS

I would like to acknowledge the assistance in the production of this book of Marie Jeffrey, Ian Watson and the library staff of Newsquest Ltd, Glasgow (Publishers of *The Herald, The Sunday Herald* and the *Evening Times*), the librarians of the Glasgow Room in the Mitchell Library, Catherine Torretti of the *Daily Record*, Stroma Fraser, Grant Jeffrey, Dr Stuart Jeffrey, Rod Ramsay, Robert Kinnear, Samantha Boyd, John Watson, Walter Norval.

RJ
Carradale, Argyll

INTRODUCTION

For hundreds of years, blood has been spilled on the streets of Glasgow – from the beer and bread riots of the eighteenth and nineteenth centuries, to the gang wars of the 1920s and 1930s and on into the twenty-first century with its dangerous upsurge in the culture of knife-carrying and the disturbing rise in the number of murders. The gangs are still with us, albeit in a different form. The Redskins, the Norman Conks, the Billy Boys and their ilk have been replaced by drug gang-lords and mindless youngsters ready to fight over territory or to kill, assault or maim simply for the hell of it.

This book tells the story of some of the villainous happenings in the city. Here, you'll read about murders, bank robberies, poisonings and street fights involving gangs comprised of hundreds of armed men. Some of the most outrageous miscarriages of justice that form a blot on our legal and policing systems are chronicled too. Also spotlighted is the succession of hard chief constables and brave men on the beat who have fought the evil-doers over the years.

According to cliché, newspapers are the first draft of history. And, in its newspapers, Glasgow has followed the deeds of the wrongdoers in detail, day after day, in millions of words. The criminal archives are bulging. Yet, today, Glasgow is enjoying a renaissance in arts and culture. A city has many faces. Wars against crime have been won and lost. There will be more. *Blood on the Streets* recalls just some of the countless stories that form a significant part of Glasgow's history.

A

ACME THUNDERER

Every cop on the beat carried the tools of the trade – a notebook, a pen, handcuffs, a baton and his trusty Acme Thunderer, a heavy-duty police whistle which, when used by a constable with a healthy pair of lungs, could produce an extremely piercing sound. It was said that the whistle was so powerful that, in the right conditions, it could be heard as far away as 500 yards, even in busy streets. For many a young thief and gangster the noise of the whistle was background music to an ill-spent youth, a sort of criminal coda leading to the cuffs being snapped on and a night or two in the cells.

ALCOHOL

Anyone who ever doubted the role played by the demon drink in Glasgow and the city's association worldwide with crime and gangs should spend a little time in the city courts listening to the defenders' pleading. In case after case, from the dawn of justice to this day, the time-honoured phrase 'drink was a factor' and its many variants come into play. Indeed, the phrase has crept into the public consciousness in such a fashion that it is used routinely by many Glaswegians to explain unacceptable behaviour and not just of the criminal kind.

The Glasgow hard man may have moved from a 'hauf and a hauf pint' in some shady sawdust-floored drinking den to Bacardi Breezers, vodka and exotic cocktails in a chrome-plated, minimalist, trendy and highly expensive watering hole. But the booze still plays an important role – even in these days when chemical refreshment is a creeping danger – in the planning of law breaking. Down the years, the pub has played a pivotal role for those hell-bent on nefarious business of all sorts. In the heyday of the old-fashioned gangs in the 1930s, licensed premises often exacerbated the religious divide – the Catholic gangs had their favourites, the Protestants had theirs and it was dangerous to drink in the wrong pub. These pubs had none of the cosy cheeriness of TV's *Cheers* but they were the sort of places where everybody did, indeed, know your name. And, in an era of damp, unheated and unwelcoming housing with tenement stairs to be climbed and outside toilets, the pubs provided some warmth and comfort.

As well as acting as a stimulant for criminal adventures, booze rubbed off some of the rough edges of life in a hard city. The shipbuilders had their favourite bars, as did the dockers and the foundrymen. In this, usually, all-male environment, it was easy for gangs of like-minded and often wrong-minded men to bond into groupings and 'teams'. It was also easy for friends and acquaintances to fall out and for weapons and bottles to be used. Drink was the cause of many of the chib-marked faces in the tougher bars. One solution to the smashing of glasses on to the table and hence in to the face of an enemy might, at one stage, have been plastic bottles and glasses when they became available. Much stitching by surgeons in the city's hospital emergency departments could have been avoided. But, even in the twenty-first century, that particular solution is still just a talking point.

One legendarily infamous place where drink was a factor in the plotting of much villainy no longer exists, having been bull-dozed in mysterious circumstances. The Caravel was a pub in **BARLANARK** and it is believed to be the reason for Tam McGraw acquiring the sobriquet 'The Licensee' in the underworld, even though it was his wife who was the actual owner of the establishment. The chat across this particular bar seldom concerned the latest hot tickets in the art world and nor would there be much polite discussion of cultural events like the reviews that fill so much space in the papers these days. In there, crime, gambling and serious drinking were the things that mattered. Indeed, during the investigation into the murder of Arthur Thompson Jnr, underworld sources suggested to the police that the bar had played a role in the murders of Joe 'Bananas' Hanlon and Bobby Glover, who were suspected of being involved in the killing of Thompson, who was usually known as 'The Fat Boy'. But there was to be no forensic examination of the site. Before the police moved in to search for clues at the pub, a significant east-end landmark, it was demolished in sudden and unexplained circumstances.

Too many pubs in an area can cause problems but, paradoxically, there is also a theory that the lack of pubs contributed to crime in the huge housing schemes. Licensed premises, like other amenities such as swimming pools and libraries, were few and far between in the huge post-war housing schemes that sprung up around the city. Those that did exist attracted any desperate hard tickets in the area, which made such hostelries far from the family-friendly, food-serving bars that are so commonplace now.

Mind you, the old crime-ridden inner-city areas certainly could not complain of a lack of watering holes. Although there were plenty of them, many became known as what the locals call 'stab inns'. Walter Norval, infamous as the city's first Godfather, remembers growing up in the **GARSCUBE ROAD** in the late 1930s and early 1940s. Norval actually lived over a pub – Duffy's – and, within a few hundred yards of his home, there were no fewer than fourteen pubs. He recalls looking out from his tenement flat windows across the road to Scott's pub and watching the blood being spilled. As Friday and Saturday nights drew to a close, violence would erupt as customers fought with each other, mostly with their bare fists. But the bottle and the tumbler also came into play regularly and the scarred faces of fighting men caused little comment among their mates or their women. Scars – or 'Mars Bars' as some called them – were a fact of life. There is the chilling story of a youngster who allegedly slashed a girl with an open razor. The accused claimed in court that the victim had asked him to do it in order to scar her and make her look like a hard case.

In those days, apart from playing a role as the natural HQ for men to hang out in, the pub was also a handy place for the disposal of stolen goods. During the war, it was here that scams involving ration books took place. And it was in the pubs that farmers or farm workers, out to make a quid or two on the side, in desperate times, brought such rare wartime treats as eggs and butter. To the folk in those bleak tenement canyons, such everyday produce was very welcome, no matter where it came from or how it was obtained.

But not all the pubs, even in the 1930s, were criminal dens. Many were honest and cheery places of escape for the working men who toiled hard in the shipyards and foundries. The thirst they developed by day would be slaked in the bars in the evening. And the role of drink in youthful crime, in the early days of the gangs, has also been overstated by some. The fact that, in the 1920s, many youngsters got into a great deal of trouble is undeniable but it was not always booze fuelled. Some commentators at the time thought the city's youths were a relatively sober generation and put this down to the proliferation of movements like the Band of Hope, juvenile temperance societies, kirk Sabbath schools and even the anti-drink teaching of ordinary schools.

A remarkable investigation was carried out by the Scottish Temperance Alliance into what part drink played in the teenage gangs who were clashing on the streets. Their investigator, Robert Spence, reported that many of the young gangs were not formed for criminal purposes but had a religious bias and that often the trouble between them was sparked off by disputes over girlfriends. Most gang members, he found, were unemployed and had little satisfactory outlet for their energy. But drinking, he declared, 'played little part in gang life and in no case was it said that alcohol exerted any decisive influence over lives at the present stage'. Interestingly, Spence blamed lack of parental control for the young gangs. And it was noted that alcoholism played a major role in that lack of control – so, in a slightly indirect way, the demon drink actually *was* guilty again.

Like the unlamented Caravel and most of the Garscube Road pubs, the spit and sawdust howff is long gone, to be replaced by expensively decorated theme bars, wine bars and bars pretending to be airport lounges or wooden-panelled men's clubs. The temperance movement is now at a low ebb and, perhaps as a result, the accident and emergency departments of our great city hospitals are busier than ever, dealing with the headbangers who get blitzed on Fridays and Saturdays in particular. Visit any accident department as a patient after closing time and, before the hand you cut doing a bit of do-it-yourself is treated, you will most likely have to wait in a queue of the injured, smelling foully of booze or ranting and raving in drug-induced tantrums. It is bad enough for the patients but for the doctors and nurses it is an ongoing nightmare, with weekend nights only marginally worse than the rest of the week. So bad is the problem that *The Sunday Herald* could report that, in June 2004, a senior accident and emergency consultant urged police to abandon 'wimpish' treatment of football hooligans, draw their batons and 'knock the f**k out of them'. The campaigning Sunday reported that Ian Anderson, who is based in the Victoria in the south side and who is a former president of the UK's Faculty of Accident and Emergency Medicine, believes society has become 'overly politically correct and wimpish' in the way it deals with drink-fuelled loutishness. He was to have expanded on his views at a conference attended by top policemen (including the chief constable, Willie Rae) and politicians but his outspokenness resulted in his non-appearance at the event. However, he could count on many supporters as well as critics.

Anyone who thought the problems created by abuse of alcohol in the 1920s and 1930s has gone away, or has moderated, is living in fantasyland. Dr Anderson said:

This country has a serious problem with antisocial behaviour and violence. There is a potent cocktail in Scotland – West of Scotland genes, testosterone and alcohol – and it is a potential powder keg. More and more ladies are getting on it so you could include oestrogen as well.

The very fact that a seminar, entitled 'Scotland's Hangover: wake up to the problem', had to be held in the offices of the Royal College of Physicians and Surgeons is dispiriting. Anyone who has read the papers regularly or has made any study of Glasgow's crime archives should be well aware of the problem, even if only at second hand. Dr Anderson was quoted as saying:

> Alcohol is a very useful drug and a valuable tool at social occasions but some of the people we had in the department at the weekend should have 'Don't serve me drink – I am a nutter' tattooed on their forehead. I have been doing this for twenty years and last weekend was as bad as anything I have seen.

He added that the profession was sick and tired of picking up the pieces of drink-related attacks and he believed that west of Scotland men should abandon the idea that our hard-drinking tradition is something we should be proud of.

He went on to say:

> I saw people at the weekend whose lives have been ruined by some nasty little ned who will probably go to court and they will ask for background reports. I would take the neds round the back and give them a good kicking. We have got to sort these guys out. They have got to know there will be consequences to their behaviour.

These forthright opinions, which, no doubt, are also held by many who work at the coalface in the fight against violence, started a media stooshie. Far from being wimpish, the remarks were the kind of medicine that is too strong for some to take.

This tough talk harked back to the days of Percy Sillitoe who, as a pre-war chief constable, encouraged his tough anti-gang squads to retaliate first and had considerable success in curbing gang violence. But, however desirable an option it may seem to the victims, that is not a viable way of operating in today's very different climate. Norrie Flowers, chairman of the Scottish Police Federation, agreed that alcohol abuse was a major problem but rejected arbitrary justice as a solution, saying, 'I am sure many officers would like to do that but we have to work within the law.' And John Brady of Alcohol Focus Scotland said that our drinking culture has to change. For Brady, 'going out to get drunk is not acceptable'. Leader writers, too, seemed unanimous and they reluctantly agreed that, in 2004, the law had to be followed whatever the provocation.

As always, disagreement and differing views on how to deal with the drink dilemma abound, but what there is no argument about is the scale of the problem. Of the record 127 murders in Scotland in 2003, 44 per cent of those accused were drunk at the time of the offence. And more than a third of all accident and emergency admissions to hospitals are drink related. Down the years much blood has been spilled on the streets of Glasgow and much of it was laced with large quantities of cheap liquor. Time to wake up indeed.

ALIBI

This is the defence of being somewhere else at the time when a crime was committed and being able to prove it. It is a staple in the plots of crime novels and B-films but it does not surface too often in real life enquiries – at least not in court. 'I wasn't there when it happened' is a tale detectives hear more often than they want. But anyone with a genuine alibi is usually quickly smoked out by the police and eliminated from the investigation. Occasionally, there is a case where the defence of alibi is heard in court but it is unlikely that one like that involved in the Oscar Slater case will ever be heard again.

Slater was, of course, almost hanged for a murder that he did not commit, having been stitched up by the Glasgow police in 1908. He was sentenced to death but, mysteriously, the sentence was reduced almost at the last minute and he went on to serve nearly nineteen years in prison before being freed. This case is dealt with in some depth elsewhere in this book but a factor that was obscured by all the double-dealing and the police frame-up was that Slater actually had TWO rock-solid alibis. If anyone needed proof of his innocence, there is the fact that Slater didn't even know the correct date of the murder of old Miss Marion Gilchrist, a murder he was supposed to have committed. Slater, who had only read about the murder in the papers, thought it had taken place on 22 December 1908, the day the news of the killing in **WEST PRINCES STREET**, which had shaken the douce west end of Glasgow, became public knowledge. Slater, who was arrested in New York after crossing the Atlantic on the *Lusitania*, was so confident of being cleared that he returned to Glasgow voluntarily. One of the reasons for this confidence was that he said he could 'prove with five people where [he] was the night the murder was committed'. However, that alibi was for the wrong night but, in a strange twist of fate, it was later found that he did have a watertight alibi for the actual night of the murder. That was never brought out in court.

Glasgow's criminal archives also provide a classic example of the alibi that eliminates a suspect in the tale of Walter Norval and the death of his stepfather, the vice king Joe 'The Pole' Kotarba, in the 1970s. Norval, generally regarded as the city's first Godfather and a dangerous and violent hard man, was known to hate Kotarba and, when the brothel keeper was viciously stabbed to death, suspicion immediately fell on Norval, but the gangster had the perfect alibi. He wasn't even in the country at the time of the killing – he was with his glamorous mistress, leading the good life of vodka and sunshine in Tenerife, an island that is no stranger to the criminal fraternity. The cops had to remove him from the number one spot on their list of suspects. Eventually, one of Kotarba's call girls was charged with the bloody stabbing but she was freed after a trial, during which she pled self-defence.

ALLISON STREET

This south side haunt is famously where one of Scotland's best fish-and-chip shops is to be found – it has even been praised by no less than Rick Stein, the culinary sage of Padstow. And, nearby, are the pubs of Victoria Road. But it also has its share of infamy, having been the scene of one of Scotland's most notorious crimes. It was here, in 1969, that a former police inspector, Howard Wilson, shot two police officers after a bank raid he had taken part in. Wilson's attempt to kill the officers' inspector as well only failed because his gun jammed.

Wilson had left Glasgow's finest, soured by lack of promotion. He opened a green grocer's in Allison Street but he was no more of a success in commerce than he had been as a cop. Quickly deep in debt, he joined with two other members of a gun club and started a new career as a bank robber. Desperate for cash, the robbers carried out an ill-thought-out raid on a bank in Linwood which led to them being spotted as they returned to Wilson's flat, above his shop in Allison Street. The shop was close to a police station, allowing the cops coming and going to work to keep an eye on what their old colleague was up to – not the cleverest choice of home base! The police went into the flat but Detective Constable Angus McKenzie and PC Edward Barnett were killed by the cornered ex-cop. Cop killers are reviled but an ex-cop who turns killer is bottom of the heap. Wilson served thirty-two years in jail.

Early in 2004, the street was back in the headlines when a young local was murdered.

B

BAKSI, JOE

Joe Baksi was a famous American boxer who, courtesy of rhyming slang, has become a byword in Glasgow for taxi – 'I'll grab a Joe Baksi home' is frequently to be heard at the end of a night out. Cab drivers ease life in a city where public transport can often be difficult and, on occasion, dangerous. The drivers take old ladies to the shops, make sure drunks keep their licences by whisking them home when they get blootered in a howff some distance from their abode and take relatives to hospitals to visit the sick. Mind you, certain taxi companies have run foul of the law from time to time and have been accused of being a front for criminals laundering money or distributing drugs. But, by and large, they are an important ingredient in smoothing life in the city.

The men and women who drive the cabs, however, often have a lot to put up with. They are frequently subjected to attacks by missile-throwing vandals, a problem that tends to rise and fall with the periodic crime waves that afflict the city. A favourite ploy of the young neds is to attack in areas where some of the roads have been blocked off, making escape easy for themselves but difficult for the driver. The problem was so serious and the Taxi Owners Association was so fearful of injury to drivers that, at one stage, no-go areas were declared. However, this, in fact, is a bit of window dressing and perhaps unfair on the areas singled out. I have been in a taxi attacked by teenagers throwing water filled balloons, a surprisingly dangerous weapon, in a most respectable south side main road – it was no new experience for the driver who had to swerve and narrowly missed solid contact with a lamppost. The thugs are not beyond erecting makeshift roadblocks to make attacking their targets easier. For the record, the danger areas that the TOA listed, some years ago, were **EDGEFAULD ROAD** and **CARLISLE STREET, GOURLAY STREET** in Springburn, **ROYSTON ROAD** in Townhead, **MAYFIELD STREET** in Ruchill, **PANMURE STREET** in Possilpark, **SPRINGFIELD ROAD** in Parkhead and the **TOLLCROSS PARK** area.

Sadly, being of service to the public in Glasgow is no guarantee that you can go about your business in peace and taxi drivers were not the only ones to suffer. In the late 1980s and early 1990s, there was an upsurge in gang violence and an outbreak of the sort of attack that was seldom experienced before, even in the 1920s and 1930s when gangs knocked hell out of each other on a regular basis. Council workers going about their business were attacked. In Pollok, where there was a considerable amount of random violent vandalism, workers even threatened to boycott upgrading work on houses in **LINTHAUGH ROAD** and **CALFHILL ROAD** after a number of attacks. Council employees, tasked with improving life in a tough area, found that the vandals and thugs were more than ready to bite the hand that was feeding them – thousands of pounds worth of damage was done to council workers' cars parked at a local repair centre.

Firefighters are not immune either. There were disgusting reports of fire engines being ambushed by street gangs while they were on their way to fires and even when they were actually in the throes of tackling blazes. Officers frequently met with verbal abuse and worse – bricks were regularly thrown at them. A fireman was even hit by a brick when he was giving mouth-to-mouth resuscitation to an injured man on **GLASGOW GREEN**. There were reports of an officer, wearing breathing apparatus and fighting a fire, being bombarded by stones. In Pollok, one fire officer was quoted as saying:

In the run up to Guy Fawkes, it was murder in here. It has been happening regularly. It used to be that firefighters could go into the roughest area freely because they were helping the community – now it seems we are fair game.

The problem has eased slightly in the twenty-first century although, in 2001, more than 150 attacks on firefighters on duty were logged and many attacks go unreported in the press.

BANISHMENT

This was the hard punishment meted out by cities, towns and villages until around the mid eighteenth century. It was last applied in the Glasgow area in 1755 when James McArthur and his wife Jean were brought before the Gorbals' bailies charged with being proprietors of a disorderly house. Witnesses testified before James Maxwell, Procurator Fiscal of the Barony and Justiciary of Gorbals. The magistrates found the offence proved and:

> adjudged and decerned the defenders to be carried from the bar to the common prison in the chapel of the Gorbals and there to be detained until the sixteenth of September current, at 12 o'clock on which day ordained and hereby ordain that the defenders be carried from said prison, and by tuck of drum, with their heads bare and uncovered, to be banished and hereby banish them from the village and the barony of the Gorbals during the whole of their natural lives; with certification to them that if they, or either of them, shall return after their banishment aforesaid or be found in the said village or barony, they shall be apprehended and imprisoned in prison aforesaid and publicly whipped through the said village of Gorbals on the first Wednesday after their imprisonment; and so often as the offenders return, or be found in the said village during the space of banishment and hereby grant warrant for the apprehending, imprisonment, whipping and banishment of them.

There was no room for any ambiguity regarding that sentence on the errant McArthurs!

This happened at a time when more liberal views were beginning to impinge on criminal matters and reformers were campaigning for the end of the punishment. Indeed, the magistrates in Glasgow itself had almost abandoned the old penalty of banishment. In fact, the legality of the sentence that the brothel keepers received was challenged on the grounds that, although the magistrates in the city itself might enjoy the right of exiling criminals on the strength of it being a Royal Burgh, the same did not apply to Gorbals which was, in those days, merely a burgh or barony. In favour of this line of thought was the fact that an Act of Parliament passed in 1748 repealed heritable jurisdictions in Scotland. Even earlier, when the Barony of Gorbals was transferred to the city of Glasgow in 1647 by Sir Robert Douglas, a special bill was passed confirming to the Glasgow magistrates 'All and hail the six pound land of old extent of Gorbals and Bridge-end with the heritable office of bailiary and judiciary within the said bounds.' This seems to make clear that, from that date, the Gorbals magistrates should have accepted that their jurisdiction in serious cases should bow before that of Glasgow. But the McArthurs were, none the less, shown the door regardless of the legal semantics involved. However, the act did mean the end of banishing criminals 'furth of the Gorbals' and indeed from Scotland.

Whipping through the streets was also stopped though I have no doubt that some of those on the right in Glasgow local government would still make a case for its return. Another rather barbaric form of punishment in use at this time was the stocks. These were for minor crimes and delinquents were only forced to spend three hours at a time, in daylight, in this form of cruel name them, shame them and put them on show punishment. From then on, the guilty faced fines, the jail or the rope.

BARLINNIE

Known on the streets as the Bar-L, Barlinnie Prison is one of the most iconic jails in the world. The building was completed in 1894 and it is now at the centre of controversy and criticism for the appalling standard of its accommodation.

During the early nineteenth century, Glasgow had eight prisons of varying size but, by 1840, only the Burgh at **GLASGOW GREEN** and another jail at **DUKE STREET** were open. To ease prison overcrowding, a farmland site in the east end, Barlinnie Farm, was chosen in 1880 for a new building. It was designed to hold 1,000 prisoners in five four-storey blocks and it has been full to over-flowing ever since it opened. The population is made up of male prisoners on remand, prisoners serving fewer than four years and prisoners waiting to go to another institution with a different category.

Hangings took place in the prison from 1928 to 1960. It is every-one's picture of a grim Victorian jail with little to commend it to penal reformers or modern penal practices. Even the pioneering Special Unit, dealt with elsewhere in this book, closed in the early 1990s.

However, one touch of sanity and an acknowledgement of the fact that the world had changed came in August 2004 when it was reported that the practice of slopping out had finally ended in this Scotland's oldest prison. The authorities had found themselves in a legal corner. Slopping out had ended years before in prisons in England, having been outlawed in 1996. Eight years later a Scottish prisoner, jailed for armed robbery, won a landmark case. Robert Napier was awarded £2,450 because the practice had worsened his eczema. Ministers decided to appeal the decision after Lord Bonomy, the judge in the case, said the practice was degrading. This meant that the prison service faced the possibility of thousands of actions from cons forced to share toilet facilities – in the form of chamber pots – in crowded cells and made to slop out on a daily basis. The rush to provide in-cell sanitation was on. The practice of slopping out in Barlinnie had been planned to end in 2004 but the target date was pushed back to 2008 because of the practical difficulties – which were exacerbated there because of the age and design of the building. The thought of prisoners rubbing their hands at the prospect of suing seemed to have galvanised the authorities and in 2004, after all, one dreadful part of the history of Barlinnie had ended. But, glimpsed from the modern motorway that sweeps past it, the jail can still send a chill through you – its grim history and atmosphere somehow seeping out of the stone walls and over the high fences that cage the desperate men of Glasgow.

BARLINNIE HOTEL

To describe the grim fortress that is Barlinnie Prison as any form of hotel is surprising – just as surprising as the notion that anyone in a cell behind the high walls of this infamous place of incarceration ever had anything to sing about. But, while researching the life of Walter Norval for a biography, *Glasgow's Godfather* (Edinburgh: Black & White Publishing, 2003), of this infamous gangster, the old villain surprised me by giving me a rendition of a song called 'The Barlinnie Hotel'. Walter Norval does not know who wrote it or when but the words are as clear in his head as when he first heard them many years ago. The curiously romanticised refrain must be familiar to many a Glasgow criminal who did time in a building still criticised by prison campaigners. But, for all its unenviable reputation, the 'hotel' is never short of customers!

> In Glasgow's fair city,
> There's flashy hotels.
> They give board and lodgings
> To all the big swells.
> But the greatest of all now
> Is still in full swing –
> Five beautiful mansions
> Controlled by the king.
> There's bars on the windows
> And bells on the door,
> Dirty big guard beds
> Attached to the floor.

BLOOD ON THE STREETS

I know 'cause I've been there
And, sure, I can tell
There's no place on earth like
Barlinnie Hotel.
I was driven from the Sheriff,
And driven by bus –
Drove through the streets,
With a terrible fuss.
Drove through the streets,
Like a gangster at state.
And they never slowed up,
Till they got to the gate.
As we entered reception,
They asked me my name,
And asked my address,
And the reason I came.
As I answered these questions,
A screw rang the bell –
It was time for my bath,
In Barlinnie hotel.
After my bath, I was dressed like a doll.
The screw said, 'Quick march,
Right into E-hall.'
As I entered my flowery*,   [slang for cell]
I looked round in vain –
To think that three years, here,
I had to remain.
For breakfast, next morning, I asked for an egg.
The screw must have thought
I was pulling his leg.
For, when he recovered, he let out a yell –
'Jailbirds don't lay eggs,
In the Barlinnie Hotel!'
The day came for me,
When I had to depart.

I was as sick as a dog,
With joy in my heart.
For the comfort was good,
And the service was swell,
But I'll never return
To Barlinnie Hotel

BARROWFIELD

On dark winter midweek nights, the sky of the east end of Glasgow often shines with the reflection of the powerful floodlights of Celtic Park. The rebuilt stadium is a palace of football, one of the finest in Britain. Celtic's success brings thousands of football fans from the glamour clubs of Europe – Rome, Paris, Milan, Madrid – to see their heroes take on 'The Hoops'. One wonders what these visiting fans make of the neighbourhood or what they know of its history. Almost in the shadow of the gigantic stadium lies the Barrowfield, a housing scheme that is now, at last, showing some signs of regeneration. But, in the early 1970s, this was one of the hardest places in Glasgow and home to two of the most infamous gangs – Spur 78 and Torch, who were originally from Calton. It is not an exaggeration to say that, in this part of the east end, it was like the Wild West. The respectable folk who found themselves in such a place because of cruel fate – and an acute housing shortage – were deposited in a living hell.

The newspapers made regular, if fleeting, visits to highlight the troubles of the scheme and found the locals ready to talk in detail about the way their lives were blighted. What they would not talk about, however, were the neighbours and gangs responsible for such a state of affairs – fear saw to that. Some of the tales were harrowing in the extreme. And reporters visiting the schemes realised quickly enough that it took bravery on the part of people to be willing to talk to them even on a basis of anonymity. 'Don't identify us – we are afraid of what "they" might do to us or the kids,' they'd say. Back in the 1970s, one member of a local family put it this way:

> You take a chance every time you walk down the road. We used to go out every Saturday but now we are afraid to cross the doorstep. There are two gangs in one street, the Torch and the Spur, and, when they are on the prowl, life is just not worth living.

Many families told reporters they would like to continue to live in the area if only the violence was eradicated. But, even if you wanted to leave for a quieter life further out of town, there were difficulties. It was said that a Barrowfield address on an application form for a move to a council house elsewhere often meant automatic refusal, even for those who had lived for years in the area and were only trying to escape the mayhem.

One family of long-time residents told of returning home from holiday to find every window in the house broken. 'They don't care who they do it to. You could have known them for years and they would still do it to you. It's bedlam at times. What can you do?' No wonder that, at this time, **BARROWFIELD STREET** and the streets off it, such as **FRAZER STREET**, **DAVAAR STREET**, **KERRYDALE STREET** and **STAMFORD STREET**, were no-go areas after dark.

The battles between the Torch and the Spur reached new heights in 1977 after the departure of Chief Constable David McNee to London to run the Met. These were dangerous times, when guns were taking over from knives and razors as weapons of choice. Some of the weapons even found their way there from Russia. The gang wars in the scheme made headlines when two Barrow-field teenagers were jailed for having guns and ammunition with intention to endanger life. Led from the court, they were defiant, shouting threats about what they would do to the detectives who had arrested them when they got out. There were scuffles outside the court between supporters of the accused and cops.

The court reports revealed a scheme awash with guns. The arrests had resulted from a raid on a derelict tenement on the outskirts of the scheme. One of the youths had a gun broken down into three pieces and the other had the ammunition. One of the youths told detectives, 'We are getting hammered by the Spur. You know what they did to my brother.' The jury were shown the gun involved which had a swastika on the butt and was engraved with the words 'Torch kill for fun'. The barrel was likewise engraved, this time with 'To Spur from Torch – boom ya bass'. The raid on the house followed the firing of a gun in a taxi in the Barrowfield area and spent cartridges being found lying in the street after gang battles. This gun had been made in Russia and the police were at a loss to explain how it had ended up in the east end of Glasgow.

No wonder the area's reputation was such that stories of washing machines etc. having to be delivered with police escorts! The council did try to put matters right with plans costing millions to refurbish the housing stock of the scheme. But, as soon as the improvements were made, the houses were vandalised, set on fire or otherwise damaged and, although some of the homes were improved, the area was still no safe haven. And it wasn't only because of the guns.

In 1975, Lord Wheatley warned that members of gangs would find their sentences on the increase. Like Lord Carmont before him, he realised that, while harsh sentences may not result in much redemption, at least they made the streets safer for a period. Addressing a teenager accused of a knife offence, he said:

This curse, which is afflicting the country at present and is particularly acute in Glasgow, has got to be wiped out. At one stage in the history of Glasgow, razor slashing was common. To a great extent the use of the razor has been eliminated – unfortunately to be replaced with an equally dangerous weapon, the knife. But, if there is any danger of razor slashing rearing its ugly head again in Glasgow, the sooner it is stamped out the better.

This stern warning was delivered to the youth who had had the temerity to appeal a six-year sentence imposed on him for assaulting a man. The victim, who was permanently disfigured, had needed no fewer than forty-nine stitches in his head.

The name Barrowfield may be writ large in the criminal history of Glasgow but there were some bright moments of hope. In the mid 1950s, there was a successful eight-day community festival, run by social workers. It was an attempt to turn around attitudes to the scheme and improve things for those who lived there, trying to earn an honest crust and bring up law-abiding families. Jock Stein, the Celtic manager who made his name immortal when his Lisbon Lions became the first British team to win the European Cup (at least that was the oft-quoted verdict of Liverpool manager Bill Shankly), gave his services to the festival. And so too did writer Cliff Hanley and disc jockey Tiger Tim Stevens. The festival included a celebrity football match, a talent contest, a street play involving local children and a parade through the streets – it was all a far cry from blood, guns and no-go areas. It was certainly a brave attempt at trying to change things and perhaps it did have some far-reaching effects.

A few years later, the silent majority in the gang-ridden area were praised in the papers for standing up for themselves. A court report said that 'for years families in Barrowfield have kept a frightened silence about the vicious thugs on their doorstep'. A wild night of terror did something to change that, at least on this occasion. The police were called to the scheme when cars were wrecked, house windows and doors smashed and members of the Spur ended up in dock. The sheriff who dealt with the case, Norman McLeod, was forthright. 'This uncivilised savagery is the sort of misfortune the decent folk of Barrowfield have had to suffer for too long and too often.' He praised locals for speaking out. The youths before him had admitted to being part of 'a riotous mob which conducted itself in violent and tumultuous manner to the great terror and alarm of the lieges and that they brandished swords and other weapons'. Apart from the swords, other weapons brandished included pickaxe handles and sickles. An invalid car was among those wrecked. The mob had marched along the streets hammering at the doors of houses with their weapons. Although this was in Barrowfield, the law noted that similar things happened in other areas in the city – such was life thirty years ago. Today, there are at least some new houses and front gardens with flowers but there are still some areas that offer a visual memory of the bad old days.

BARROWS, The

Clichés can become clichés because they are simply the best way of expressing something and there is no more accurate description of The Barrows – or The Barras, as the more gallus prefer – than to say this world-famous market is a Glasgow institution. The stalls are packed together under the Barrowland Ballroom, where Bible John once hunted his prey and which is now a regular venue for the biggest stars in pop. A visit to the market is still a weekend must for Glaswegians in search of a bargain or a spot of fun, mixing with the rich collection of characters who have set up stalls to sell everything from the latest carpet cleaner to an antique commode. The patter of the salesmen and -women is legendary and it is worth a visit just to hear this, even if you buy nothing.

What was started as a few market stalls by old Maggie McIvor has grown into a large covered market under the ballroom and spread into many of the buildings and spaces between the **GALLOWGATE** and **LONDON ROAD**. It is mostly innocent fun with the punters mobbing the place at weekends, especially at Christmas time and holidays. The traders are legitimate and now, in a concession to modern worries, even wear identification badges. But, Glasgow being Glasgow, any gathering of folk in the mood to spend hard-earned cash, hunting for stuff not available in regular shops, attracts the attention of the scam merchants.

In 2004, The Barras area, if not the barrows themselves, has become a major outlet for pirated CDs and DVDs and electronic porn. The most disturbing aspect of the growth of this trade is that it is being carried out largely by schoolchildren and youngsters. They mingle with the crowds, offering their wares, and disappear into the shadows when a sale is made. It's a long way from the old fun of The Barras when folk hunted for dolls as Christmas presents, sought out brightly coloured towels for their new high-rise council flats that came complete with inside toilets or watched a remarkable collection of street entertainers. One much-remembered act was that of the muscled and bare-chested Ivan Orloff who attracted huge crowns. He had originally been an officer in the Tsar's army but found his métier in entertaining at The Barras.

On the new crime wave, Robert O'Neill, the city's environmental protection director, said:

> Our trading standards officers are continuing to have success in confiscating illegal goods and stopping illegal trading at The Barras. We have made it clear, through our well-publicised zero tolerance policy, that we will not condone that kind of activity.

For their part, the police issued a statement in July saying, 'We are working closely with the council and other agencies to combat illegal trading and criminality associated with intellectual property theft.' The size of the problem is illustrated by the fact that, in one weekend, undercover operators seized more than 6,700 counterfeit DVDs and CDs, some of them of films that had not even been released in the cinemas, and clothing carrying fake designer logos.

Those involved in the war against this illegal trading, including the Federation Against Copyright Theft, worry that a knock-on of all this will be that such scams will set hundreds of youngsters on the road to lives of crime. Everyone wants this mess cleaned up so that the institution that is The Barras can carry on as it has over the years – providing a fun outing for punters on the hunt for legitimate bargains and maintaining plenty of the entertaining old patter.

BAR-STICK

This is a specially designed implement that is superior to the ordinary crowbar and which was frequently used for break-ins. Burglaries and raids on shops with cash or large quantities of cigarettes, drink or other easily resalable products were rampant in many areas. In the days before hi-tech electronic security arrived on the scene, the prudent shopkeeper invested in iron bars to cover the windows of his premises and keep out the thieves. In the schemes and many areas plagued with crime, the bars, for all the world ironically like those on a prison cell, were a highly visible and common part of the scenery. The bar-stick – made of extremely strong iron and shaped like an elongated letter U with ends that could be grasped – could be forced in behind such bars and a couple of strong hoods could lever the protection off noiselessly in seconds and get in through the window.

BEATTIE, COLIN

He was one of the old-time street-fighting men of **PARTICK**. Known as 'Collie' or 'The Big Man', in his heyday, he was not to be tangled with.

BELL, BAILIE

Mrs Bell added a gruesome footnote to the history of the emancipation of women in 1925 when she became the first female Glasgow magistrate to witness a hanging. In 1918, the right for women over thirty to vote was won but it was to take eleven more years before women joined men in being able to vote on reaching eighteen. During the intervening years, women had begun to take a more important role in public life. One of the onerous duties of magistrates in the city was to make a dark early morning journey to witness the despatch of some murderous villain or other. In 1925, Mrs Bell travelled to **DUKE STREET** Prison to see the execution of one John Keen who had killed an Indian pedlar in a house in

PORT DUNDAS. Keen, it was said, met his fate with courage, walking with steady step and erect posture to the gallows. Pierpoint, that legendary expert with the rope, was the hangman and Keen was dead forty-five seconds after leaving his cell. Apart from Mrs Bell, the official party watching this horrific scene at the traditional hour of 8 a.m. included a magistrate colleague, Dr James Dunlop, the prison governor, the chief constable and the town clerk depute.

Executions attracted large crowds outside the prison gates and the newspapers of the day milked the ritual for all it was worth. They reported that Mrs Bell went through the ordeal 'unflinchingly and retained full possession throughout this trying experience'. There was much debate about the fitness of asking a woman to undertake such a duty. Mrs Bell had no doubt that she had to do the full range of duties that fell to a magistrate and, later that day, when interviewed at her home, she opined that she had not been the least upset or nervous about the ordeal. She was said to be pale and composed even a few moments after Keen had taken the drop. Mrs Bell was obviously a strong-minded person who felt that, when a woman offered herself for election, she had to be prepared to do the full range of work that the job entailed. She remarked that, in her opinion, any of the women members of Glasgow Corporation could have undertaken the duty equally well.

BELTRAMI, JOE

This defence lawyer and author is one of the major figures in the criminal history of the city. Tall, powerful and impressive in court, he demands and gets attention. He is one of the great pleaders to have prowled the corridors of the courthouses of the city. Nicknames are not solely the prerogative of the criminals, though they are inordinately fond of them. Joe Beltrami, too, has a couple of nicknames – The Great Defender and The Sage of West Nile Street (home to his offices and a magnet for criminals in trouble). Take your pick.

Glasgow has always seemed to have a rich crop of charismatic legal figures who make headlines – men like Len Murray (who also turned author late in his career), Ross Harper and Bill Dunlop. Beltrami walked in the footsteps of the legendary Laurence Dowdall and, indeed, saw him in action as a young man. Joe himself became a household name in the city. Renowned for his brilliant and inventive defences, Joe was involved in Walter Norval's early court appearances and he had a more lasting relationship with Arthur Thompson. Thompson was to take over from Norval as Godfather after Walter was removed from the scene to do a long stretch in Peterhead.

Thompson always posed as a successful businessman and denied he was a Godfather. Indeed, Joe Beltrami and Thompson sued a local Sunday newspaper for giving him that tag. They won and gave half of the substantial out-of-court settlement to Radio Clyde's Cash for Kids appeal. Beltrami, incidentally, also always denied that the city had Godfathers and would wax eloquently on the subject to any passing reporter or feature writer who asked him his opinion. He had, however, he said an 'excellent business relationship' with Thompson for more than thirty years. But the term Godfather rankled as his comments that follow show:

I represented Arthur for many years. People always claimed he was in charge of organised crime in Glasgow, but I never accepted that. Arthur used to scoff at the term Godfather and made a point of making me take action when the media used it. He was nothing like an organised-crime boss in Chicago with a team of lieutenants and henchmen in structured form around him. That was never the case with Arthur and it is not the case with any other person in Glasgow. There is no 'el Supremo' or big city boss controlling things. I am not saying we do not have crime because we have plenty of that. What you find is that Glasgow has people who grow up and surround themselves with like-minded people who get involved in crime. These people then carry out criminal acts. Is that organised? Well, one man has to organise holding up a bank with a gun before he does it, but I don't think anyone would call that organised crime.

Organised crime as defined by the National Criminal Defence Service does not apply to what we have here [in Glasgow]. We have major problems with drugs but it is all small groups of people. There is no kingpin directing operations from an office in the city. In London and other major world cities, organised crime is the domain of Mafia types. In Glasgow, we have tiny strands of this but it amounts to nothing. People always talk about Triad wars in the city but how often do you read about Chinese people being attacked or going through the courts? It is not a major issue. I keep my eyes open about what is going on in this city all the time and I can say the whole thing is a fallacy.

His position is well argued and I suppose it all depends what your definition of a Godfather is. However, of one thing there is no dispute – Glasgow Godfathers, gang bosses or whatever you choose to call them tend to have territory in a single part of a city rather than being in control of the whole area – as can happen in Chicago, New York or St Paul. Even at the height of their infamy, Norval and Thompson – and they both fit my definition of a Godfather – only controlled limited areas.

Joe is of Swiss extraction and his parents owned a famous fish-and-chip shop near **GLASGOW CROSS**. He and his younger brother Ray – a well-remembered award-winning Herald-group photographer who died tragically young – were brought up in a flat in the **BRIDGEGATE**. Some of Joe's success must be put down to his upbringing. Being raised in the Bridgegate helped him to communicate easily with people of all backgrounds and on both sides of the law. He himself says, 'I spoke the language of the people I was representing. I was brought up in the same places. I was not an outsider coming in from some place like Bearsden.'

Initially, he intended to matriculate for a Master of Arts degree but bizarrely, while on a tram journey, he made a sudden decision to go for law instead! It turned out to be a wise move both for him and the folk he was to defend so successfully down the years.

As they did with Dowdall, newspaper readers followed the career of big Joe with interest. This wasn't hard to do as, in his heyday, barely a day passed without the papers reporting on cases involving him. Joe favoured braces over belt in the trouser-retaining department and the coloured straps running over his ample chest provided ideal resting places for his thumbs when he declaimed on some point or other on behalf of his client. His style was described by one colleague as having all the subtlety of a Sherman tank going over a tray of crystal. An amusing example of this ability to pile it on comes in the story of a Beltrami client who was arrested at 10 p.m. but not charged till 4 a.m. The Great Defender claimed that this smacked of Russia were people could be detained for years without charge. At full volume, he addressed the jury, saying, 'Your choice is between my client and the Rutherglen police who practise the Russian system.' The verdict? Not guilty, of course!

There is a legal axiom that a good lawyer does not ask a question of a prosecution witness unless he knows, or has a good idea, what the answer is likely to be. Joe illustrates the point with a funny story about himself. In the 1950s, he was defending a client charged with wilful fire-raising. The crime took place on a dark evening in a street where the lighting was not great. Identification of a fleeing figure was an issue in the case and a young CID officer was insisting he had recognised Joe's client escaping from the premises. Joe pounced on this, pointing out how difficult it would be to make such an identification. The detective agreed that it was diffi-cult. Joe thought he had him and continued asking what sort of eyesight he had to be able to be so accurate. The witness replied calmly that he had 20/20 vision and had been a night pilot with bomber command during the war. The result was the collapse of the case with the wisdom of that old axiom underlined.

One of Joe's many claims to fame is that he played a major role in the freeing of Paddy Meehan, wrongly convicted for the killing, in 1969, of a seventy-two-year-old pensioner, Rachel Ross, in her bungalow in Ayr. In the end, Meehan was granted a royal pardon but his story, and that of Joe Beltrami's involvement in it, covered many years. It all ended with Joe and his one-time client being at odds with each other. The tale of the trial and Meehan's early life of crime is told in detail elsewhere in this book. It is a great credit to Beltrami that, despite his client's ultimate animosity towards him, he persevered in his efforts to overturn one of the greatest injustices in Scottish criminal history. The story is well told in one of Joe Beltrami's books, *A Deadly Innocence* (Edinburgh: Mainstream, 1989).

In Peterhead, Meehan joined the awkward squad, refusing to cooperate with the authorities and ending up doing seven years in solitary. Beltrami understood Meehan's difficultness – after all, he was behind bars in one of the country's toughest jails for a crime he had not committed. After three years in the grim penal fortress, on the cold and wind-swept north-east coast, Meehan moved his battle to prove his innocence into the national conscience by writing to author and broadcaster Ludovic Kennedy, a man with an interest in miscarriages of justice.

By this time, Beltrami's extensive range of contacts with the Glasgow underworld had convinced him that the word on the street was correct – Meehan was innocent of the murder of old Mrs Ross. Meehan also wrote to such Glasgow legal figures as Len Murray and Ross Harper. Beltrami was magnanimous about all this, acknowledging that, if many legal heads were put together in a campaign, they could be more effective than one lone repre-sentative. A committee, that also included lawyers David Burnside and Bert Kerrigan, was formed. Onboard, too, was that effective communicator on the Scottish scene, David Scott of Scottish Television and later of the ill-fated *Sunday Standard*.

After many legal stramashes, victory was won and Meehan was freed. However, his compensation was less than Joe Beltrami would have wished – £50,000 rather than £100,000. Then came the unedifying sight of Beltrami and Meehan in a war of words over their books. Meehan had penned a volume packed with bizarre theories and accusations called *Framed by MI5* which Joe took exception to and his legal advisors threatened to sue the bookseller John Smith if they sold it. Meehan took to hawking his volume on the streets of Glasgow, becoming a somewhat sad figure.

But all this was something of a diversion in the career of The Great Defender – a man who, in the spring of 2004, was still a forceful figure in major cases, pleading with wit and ingenuity and using a knowledge of the law that he has honed over years, in courts throughout the land.

BIBLE JOHN

Books on Bible John continue to be trundled out. And there are still occasional newspaper series purporting to shine new light or produce a nugget of new evidence on what is perhaps the most enduring mystery in the story of crime in Glasgow. But, in the torrent of words that surrounds this case, there are no definitive answers. Who was Bible John? Did he even exist? There is no dispute that, in 1968 and 1969, the city held its breath in fear as, one after another, three young women met their deaths after what should have been a fun night out at the dancing at the famous Barrowland Ballroom near **GLASGOW CROSS**. For months on end, the killings took the lustre off that favourite Glasgow pastime – a visit to one of the many dance halls that peppered the city and a trip or two round the polished floor, following the beat of a live band, preferably as big a band as possible.

For many of the participants in this harmless hobby – a pursuit that has now largely gone, to be replaced with discos, bars and lap-dancing establishments – a successful end to the evening was for the man or woman to get a 'lumber'. In Glasgow parlance of that time, a lumber was a companion to take home for a bit of a snogging session in a close mouth or, if you got really lucky, a bedroom. But, during the time when the main concern for city's young women was just getting home safely, the chances of it happening in either location had diminished considerably.

There can be no dispute about the statistics relating to the hunt for Bible John. More than a hundred detectives worked on the case and over 50,000 statements were taken. There were extensive and unparalleled door-to-door enquiries. In the popular halls, detectives mingled with the dancers, night after night, for months, in case the killer returned to the scene. A Dutch psychic was even consulted and enquiries were made as far afield as Hong Kong and Zambia. A thousand suspects were interviewed. Dental patients, who had had work done on their front teeth, similar to the work Bible John was thought to have had done, were traced and interviewed.

One clue that was followed up was the length of the suspect's hair. In the late 1960s, it was the fashion for men to wear it long. But evidence pointed to the suspect having short sandy hair that was cropped regularly, so around five hundred barbers were interviewed. The killer was said to favour smart suits and tailors galore were interviewed. Such was the high profile of the unsolved murders that no amount of effort was spared, no clue too insignificant not to be followed up. Bible John, some said, had an interest in golf, so local clubs were checked out. Mental hospitals, too, were investigated in case they unknowingly sheltered the feared killer.

Any straw, however flimsy, was clutched at and the investigation made criminal history with its innovative use of photo-fit posters. Bible John's nickname was derived from evidence given to the police that he talked a lot about the Bible and seemed to have had a strict upbringing. The photo-fit poster became a very familiar sight to thousands of Glaswegians. It glared down on them from the newspapers day after day and it was pasted on any likely space the killer might have visited. It was a strong image that is unforgettable, to this day, to anyone who lived in the city during the time of the search.

Bible John's three victims were: twenty-five-year-old Patricia

Docker, killed in February 1968; thirty-two-year-old Jemima McDonald, killed in August 1969; and twenty-nine-year-old Helen Puttock, killed in October 1969. At the time, photo-fit was in its infancy as an aid to detection and it was only after the killing of Jemima McDonald that Lennox Patterson of the Glasgow School of Art was approached. He was asked to draw a likeness from statements made by witnesses who were believed to have seen the killer, mostly in action dancing across the polished floor at the Barrowland Ballroom. Patterson's image was lifelike and haunting. Indeed, Helen Puttock's sister, on first seeing it, said:

> My whole inside just churned. To me the resemblance was there. When I looked at it, it's a funny feeling – it's like something just turns in your guts, you know, like a wee shiver or something. When I saw that, I thought, 'God, a terrific likeness.'

The general approval of the likeness and the many distinctive features – short hair, auburn or sandy in colour, dark eyes, crooked teeth – were all commented on by people thought to have seen the killer.

Yet, despite all this and the unprecedented exposure the image was given by the media, Bible John has never been found. The suspect was something of a Glasgow 'type' and so many people seemed to have known someone who looked like the poster that an astonishing three hundred identity parades were held to eliminate suspects. Helen's sister, who was thought to have been the best person to make an accurate identification, had to endure a great ordeal. She was whisked around by the police to look at workers streaming from factories or to watch cinema crowds leaving the theatre so that she could eliminate even more people who had been mentioned to the police as looking like the man in the poster. I had a colleague in the newspaper business who looked so much like the poster he had to be given a note from the police explaining he was not Bible John.

The police must have been sick and tired of dance halls and dance music by the time the enquiry was coming to a close. The city's dance halls attracted thousands of men and women a week. Many had regular partners and were just intent on enjoying a night out. Others were on the hunt for a new companion. In the climate of the Bible John killings, almost everyone with sandy hair and a suit was a suspect. The dance hall provided the only solid link and clues to the killings, for this was where Bible John stalked his prey.

At the time, the nature of the killings seemed to point to the work of one crazed pervert. All three girls had been strangled. All had been raped. All were dumped dead near their homes. All had been at Barrowland on the night of their deaths and all were seen to have left in the company of a personable young man who looked so like the photo-fit. But delve deeper into this complex case and there are discordant notes in each of the killings that might lead a detective to suspect copycat killings rather than the work of one man.

The fate of the victims points out yet again how chance plays a role in our lives. If the first of the girls killed, Patricia Docker, had stuck to her original notion, she would not have died. On a cold winter night, she left the cosy flat she shared with her mother and young son. The flat was in **LANGSIDE**, not too far away from the old Mearnskirk Hospital, now an up-market housing estate, where she worked as an auxiliary nurse. That night, the attractive young woman intended to visit the Majestic Ballroom, known on the streets as the Magic Stick, but, for no known reason, she decided to change course and give Barrowland her custom. In these days, Barrowland had, perhaps, more than its share of dodgy patrons. However, visiting a dance hall was not normally something that put your life at risk. But, the next day, Pat Docker was found dead in a lane near her south-side flat. The detectives on the scene found a disturbing sight that was later to act as a link to the killing of the other two girls. Pat had been menstruating and police found a sanitary towel that had been placed on top of her body.

The crime shocked the city and very soon there was surprise that no one had been charged with the rape and killing. But it was some eighteen months later that the Bible John frenzy moved up a further notch. Mima McDonald was strangled after a night at Barrowland. The second victim was a single woman of thirty-two who lived in a room and kitchen in **MacKEITH STREET**, Bridgeton, not far from the ballroom. She enjoyed her nights out there and, on those occasions, her sister would babysit her three young children, the oldest of whom was aged eleven.

On the weekend of her death, Mima went to the jiggin' on Thursday, Friday and Saturday. It was reported that, on the night she was murdered, she was dolled up, as Glaswegians tend to say, in a frilly white blouse, a black kimono-style dress and sling-back, high-heel shoes. She was thought to have gone out with her hair curlers still in place and covered by a headscarf – another touch that was common in Glasgow at the time. She also carried a large leather-look handbag. From this level of detail, it is clear that a description of the man seen in her company would also be accurate.

Not long before midnight, she was said to have been seen with a tall man with auburn hair who was wearing a well-cut suit. It was said that, later that night, she was seen with a man who also seemed to answer to the description of Bible John. This was in **LONDON ROAD**. Even later, she was seen with a man near a derelict property near her home. This was the last time she was seen alive. Her sister found her in the morning, lying face down on the floor in a condemned first-floor flat near her home. Her coat was half pulled off and her shoes were off. Her stockings had been removed and were found at the scene, all torn. She had been punched in the face and strangled. Pat Docker had also had face and head injuries. And, like Pat, Mima had been menstruating. But there were differences in the two killings – although the first victim's clothes had been torn off, she still had her shoes on.

This time, there was no eighteen-month wait for the killer – if, indeed, the murders were the work of one person – to strike again. The final victim in this complex mystery was Helen Puttock, a

twenty-nine year old whose husband was in the forces and station-
ed in Germany. He was home on leave in October 1969 when his
wife suggested a night at Barrowland along with her sister, Jeannie.
In those days, that sort of outing was far from unusual but Helen's
husband didn't want to go and, after a little bit of an argument, the
two girls pitched off to the dance hall without him. The serviceman
opted for a night in and babysat the kids. Another night spent
under the bright lights was to end in death.

However, the differences between this murder and the other
two were a bit more clear-cut. And the police also had much more
to go on. Helen and Jeannie met a couple of men. Jeannie took to
the floor with one of them. He turned out to be an excellent dancer
and they spent most of the rest of the evening together. Helen, in
black dress and shoes, seems to have caught the eye of a rather
different man that night. He was neatly dressed with well-styled
short hair and there was a feeling that he was a cut above the rest
of the male 'talent' in Barrowland that night. But, unlike Jeannie's
partner, he was not a good dancer.

It was actually Jeannie who had introduced Helen to him and,
as it turned out, both he and the man Jeannie was dancing with
were called John. In the world of the dance hall, where men would
pocket their wedding rings on entering the hall, this was really no
surprise! The surviving sister had plenty of opportunity to eye up
her sister's new friend and she noticed he had a rather aggressive
attitude, as if the man was used to giving orders and being obeyed.
At the end of the evening, the foursome set off for a taxi rank but
Jeannie's friend decided to catch a late night bus from **GEORGE
SQUARE** for **CASTLEMILK** instead.

Unfortunately, this man, who became known as Castlemilk
John, was never traced which was an immense blow to the police
for he obviously had had a good insight into the life of the other
John, Bible of that ilk. His importance was underlined in an
interview given to the *Evening Times* in 1993 by Joe Beattie, one of
the detectives who worked tirelessly on the case (as did another
legendary Glasgow sleuth, Tom Goodall). Joe Beattie said:

One of my biggest regrets is that Castlemilk John never came forward. He would have been able to help. He was in Bible John's company that night and he may have known something about the killer that would identify him.

Back at the time of the murder, extensive enquiries were made in Castlemilk but it would seem that Castlemilk John had himself something to hide – perhaps his Barrowland nights out had to be kept secret from an unsuspecting wife who stayed at home. Whatever the reason, on the fateful night, he hied off home on his own and Helen and Jeannie took a taxi ride with Bible John from **GLASGOW CROSS** to **SCOTSTOUN**.

Bible John, if that's who the man in the taxi was, was said to be around 5ft 10in. tall and aged around twenty-five to thirty-five. In the dance hall, he had been cool and polite but, in the taxi, he began to show signs of irritation. He had been the one who had suggested that he should accompany the sisters home – drawing their attention to the fact that two girls had recently been killed after just such a night out. Despite his irritation, he could still turn on the charm and Jeannie reported that the sisters felt safe in his company. Interestingly, he made a couple of Biblical references during the journey. As can be the way with these friendships, when the taxi arrived at **EARL STREET**, John arranged for Jeannie to get out while he spent a little more time with his new friend Helen. Helen was never seen alive again. But a dishevelled man, with a red mark under one eye and bearing a striking similarity to the Bible John poster, was seen on a late night bus heading back to the city from the Earl Street direction.

A man taking his dog on an early morning walk found Helen's body. She was lying face down and clothing torn off her had been used to strangle her. There were the same kind of head and facial injuries of the two previous victims, making it a scene that the CID were becoming familiar with. A few coins that were known to have been in Helen's bag were missing and her gold chain was broken. The killer had left a few clues this time but not enough to trap him. A broken cheap cufflink was found at the scene and this matched the story of witnesses on the late night bus who told the police that the dishevelled man had one shirt cuff tucked up his jacket sleeve.

The public furore over the killings reached new heights. The pressure on the police was enormous. Joe Beattie was the man in charge and he was on the case till his retirement in 1976. He died in 2000 and, right up to the end, he thought endlessly about the case. All the work of the cream of the CID – including Beattie, Chief Inspector George Lloyd, Superintendent Tom Valentine, Detective Chief Superintendent Elphinstone Dalgleish and Superintendent Jimmy Bird – and the back-up of hundreds of cops who pounded the schemes, knocked the doors and followed up the hundreds of leads supplied by the public came to nought.

Although the public's fascination with the case never ended, gradually, life in the dance halls of the city returned to normal. Going out to the dancin' no longer meant risking your life. Couples who loved a turn or two round the floor and the guys and the gals on the look out for a pick-up began to flood back without a worry.

Despite this, the mystery was always in the background and everyone had a theory, some wild and impossible. Were the girls victims of the Yorkshire Ripper who'd come on a visit north to indulge his hate for prostitutes and good-time girls? Was the killer a seaman? That would account for the gaps between the murders – not the norm for serial killers. Could he be a serviceman, maybe an Englishman? The alleged sightings of that unforgettable face, gazing out from the posters with a enigmatic, half-smile, continued for years. The speculation was endless. But, as the case receded into history and the facts could be examined in a less frenetic and less emotional manner, doubts about one man being the killer began to emerge.

It is, perhaps, significant that the newspapers covered the story in almost unprecedented detail. In the absence of an arrest, the press were able to work unhindered by the need for caution on the legal front. And, maybe, one or two of the hundreds of police involved could have let slip aspects not known to the general public at the time, thereby increasing the chances of copycat killings. The suspicion that this might have happened was growing among some students of the case. But there was still one dramatic twist left in the tale.

Bible John was back in the headlines in 1996 when, nearly thirty years after the murders had horrified a dancin'-daft city, old accusations resurfaced. One of the earliest suspects in the case was a man called John McInnes who superficially fitted the description given by Helen Puttock's sister. A sometime furniture salesman, he had a military background, which some of the investigating officers found significant, and he had definitely been to Barrowland the night before Helen died. He had been quickly picked up and eliminated from the inquiry. This was not surprising since Helen's sister – the only person other than Castlemilk John known to have had a really good look at Bible John – was adamant that McInnes was not the wanted man. She did not pick him out at an identity parade and, for years afterwards, she continued to insist he was not the killer. It must be remembered that she did spend a considerable amount of time in Bible John's company at the dance hall, at the taxi stop and during the twenty-minute taxi journey to Scotstoun. If anyone would have been able to pick him out at an identity parade, it was Jeannie.

Joe Beattie was not impressed with McInnes as a suspect either. Ten other so-called witnesses all failed to finger him as the man. What's more, his clothes did not match those of the description of the murderer and he lived nowhere near the bus stop where the dishevelled man had left the late night bus taking him back from Scotsoun.

McInnes took his own life, aged forty-one, in 1980. It was so many years after the killings that his suicide did not suggest it might be linked with the deaths. But his name had stayed on the police files. By the 1990s, DNA testing had become a new weapon in the armoury of the detective and the police now had a growing database that stored DNA for matching purposes. A small semen stain, found on the stockings worn by Helen Puttock, had been kept in case of a fresh investigation. Detectives of the modern era got the notion that the new technology could perhaps be used to finally solve the mystery of Bible John. It was an interesting theory and it was worked up into something of a frenzy by the interest of newspapers and television.

Permission was given to open up McInnes's grave. There were grim scenes on that cold February day when the frozen ground was broken into to expose the body of McInnes. His mother's body had been laid to rest on top of his and it had to be removed first. That done, the suspect's remains were taken away for laboratory examination. The semen failed to match McInnes's DNA in the first tests, which were conducted in Scotland. Samples were then sent to specialists in Cambridge and, after five months, back came the answer – no match. McInnes was officially cleared by the Crown. This was a great relief for his relatives who had not only endured that five months' wait – for years, they had suffered as rumours circulated that he was the killer.

Is it all over or will a new theory still emerge? Who knows? But it might be wise to listen to the views of the man who led the hunt, the late Joe Beattie. Before he died, he told *The Herald* that he was never convinced that the same man had killed the three women. Did Bible John exist? I tend to go with the veteran cop and his theory of copycat killings. But one chilling thought nags me. One of my underworld contacts, who was active at the time of the killings, tells me that not only does he believe the murders were the work of one man but he knows who he is. And this informant is usually right. He won't name names in this case but he does provide some comfort for a Glasgow that is still dancin' daft, even if, these days, it's clubs rather then the dance halls that are the big attractions. According to him, Bible John is dead – killed in a crime feud. The only certainty in this case is that the arguments about it will go on.

BLOODHOUND FLYING CORPS

This gang of the 1930s is surely one of the most unusually named gangs anywhere. The group was familiar to the newspaper readers of the time who followed, from the safety of their armchairs, the doings of this particular bunch of thugs. Staying at home was the wisest move when they were on the prowl. One court appearance of three of the members of the gang emphasised that. Albert Gallagher, Patrick McGrory and John Dunn were charged with breach of the peace in **GREENDYKE STREET**. The trial heard that their weapons included 'a hammer, a piece of stick loaded with lead, a heavy bolt attached to waxed thread and an iron bolt attached to string'. The accused claimed that the weapons were for protection. And, in the time-honoured manner of the Glasgow court scene, their mothers kept their faces straight as they claimed the boys were hard-working lads who supported their families. In equally time-honoured fashion, the sheriff, having listened carefully to the mothers, found all three thugs guilty as charged.

BODDAM COO, THE

This is the nickname for the red-and-white striped lighthouse built on Buchan Ness, in 1827, by Robert Stevenson of the lighthouse dynasty. It perches on the far north-east coast near the village of Boddam – not far from Peterhead and its infamous prison. The inside of P-Head, as many call this jail, was as familiar as Barlinnie to the thousands of Glasgow neds and gangsters who ended up doing time in this forbidding place. The flashes from the light, once every five seconds, in the dark hours of summer and winter alike, can be seen up to twenty-eight miles away. But, for the men locked up in the frugal cells, the impact of the lighthouse came not from its flashing light but from the deep mournful sound of the fog signal. That noise seemed to underscore their misery and disturb their sleep with its regular warning to seafarers, a mighty sound that drifted inland just as it did over the troubled waters offshore.

Because of the tendency of swirling fogs and North Sea haars to gather in the area, it was heard with regularity and old lags would have to endure listening to it for years. One old Glasgow gangster told me, 'I heard the Boddam Coo howl, night after night, for many a year.' Despite its nickname, he did not look back on the lighthouse, one of the most distinctive sights of the Buchan coast, with any degree of affection.

BORSTAL

For Glasgow's legions of youths who found themselves on the wrong side of the law, evil enough but a tad too young for the Bar-L or Peterhead, the punishment was to be sent to borstal. The best remembered borstal in Scotland was at Polmont near Falkirk. Anyone unlucky to be sent to this establishment usually ended up with bitter memories of a regime that was often cruel and violent. There were undeniably officers who had the well-being of their charges at heart but there were others who were all too ready to pull hair off heads and kick and punch inmates who stepped even marginally out of line. Shamefully, the regime didn't even have the virtue of preventing its young inmates from carrying on with a life of crime. Instead, many who endured a spell there returned to the Glasgow streets they'd come from, wearing their badge of borstal survival as a sort of medal to be proud of – proof of their fledgling hard-man status. Far too many of the inmates ended up in a sort of evil old boys' club, meeting up later in the Bar-L, Saughton and Peterhead after both growing older and graduating to more serious crime.

One of the most feared parts of Polmont Borstal was 'the digger'. This was a sort of underground cell where the worst offenders against the cruel regime and discipline of the institution were dumped. They spent their time there on bread and water in solitary confinement.

The culture of violence, in both staff and inmates, had one safety valve. If a couple of the young prisoners had a dispute they were encouraged to ask the officers for the chance of a 'square go' – a fist fight supervised by the warders. Often bloody affairs, they served a purpose in both allowing inmates to let off steam and keeping such disputes from taking up too much staff time. The only other organised sport was football and the inmates often took on, and beat, local teams. When games were played outside the institution, officers had to keep a watchful eye on their charges and be ready to spot a young 'athlete' who might do a runner to the local station and take the train back to Glasgow.

There was little other organised training or education – just un-remitting hard work on the prison farm or on a factory bench. One training they did receive, however, was how to slop out. This was the disgusting morning ritual that involved the inmates, who were kept overnight in cells with no toilets, emptying their chamber pots. It was training, in fact, for one aspect of what many of them would go on to experience – life in an adult prison.

Standing at attention for hours at a time was part of a discipline that was intended to break the spirits of the prisoners. Many ex-borstal boys will tell of lying abed at night listening to the screams of miscreants getting a beating at the hands of a sadistic officer. But, as always, in even the most shameful of places, there were some moments of humanity from the kindly officer or the civilian worker – like the cook who would try to pass on some of his skills to the inmates.

And the spirits of the inmates were not completely broken. Earlier in this book, the song 'Barlinnie Hotel' appears. Borstal, too, had a poignant little ditty that would be sung by inmates. Like the Bar-L song, who wrote it and when is a mystery but it has some resonance to this day, as the debate about how we run the prison service and the redemption or punishment of lawbreakers goes on.

THE BORSTAL SONG

I'm a lad who done wrong,
Very wrong, in his time.
It was company that led me astray.
And, like many a youth,
I was led into crime,
And to borstal they sent me away.
I once got a job in a dockyard,
Beside some old pals that I know.
But, while working one day,
My foreman did say,
'My lad, you must pack up and go.
You're a jailbird, I know,
So pack up and go,
For jailbirds we do not employ.'
I said, 'Give me a chance to be honest –
Give me a chance, won't you, please?
For, if luck's in my way,
I may find it some day,
'Cause I am out on my Ticket of Leave!'

BOWMAN, BULL

In the 1930s, Bowman was the leader of the Norman Conks. The gang took the first part of their name from **NORMAN STREET**, where they were based, and the second part is generally believed to be derived from 'conquerors'. Another gang, this time from **NUNEATON STREET**, were less well known but they also adopted the sobriquet 'Conks'. The members of the Norman Conks were mainly Catholic and their chief rivals were the Protestant Bridgeton Billy Boys whose leader was Billy Fullerton. Bowman is less well remembered than Fullerton but, in his day, he was a fearsome leader with a dangerous mini army. The Norman Conks and the

Billy Boys fought many bloody running battles, with bottles and bicycle chains flying.

BOYD, STEWART 'SPECKY'

Many who operate in the world of drugs and gangs spend as much time as they can in the sunshine of Spain. Boyd, a feared figure in the Glasgow/Paisley area was one such. He died, aged forty, in a car smash near Malaga in July 2003. The ex-pats in these foreign parts tend to drive expensive motors and Boyd was no exception. His Audi TT was in a head-on collision with a BMW. Five other people died in this Costa del Sol crash, including his daughter. His burial back home was a remarkable gangland affair. Friends and family had a list of bizarre items which were buried with him in Neilston Cemetery – a machete, a magnum of champagne and a gram of cocaine were all said to have been in his coffin. The funeral itself was a tense affair with the cops, wary that the committal might spark attacks between the rival gangsters who were there in force.

The gang lord did not lie in peace long. In February 2004, his black and gold headstone was split in half and then smashed into dozens of pieces. Underworld sources told the tabloids that such an attack on the grave had been on the cards for some time. Gang feuds fester long. Not long before the grave was desecrated, two of Boyd's associates had been shot in a **NITSHILL** bar as they chatted to crime boss Tam 'The Licensee' McGraw.

BOYLE, JIMMY

Along with Hugh Collins, Boyle is one of the major success stories of the controversial Barlinnie Special Unit. As a result of his time in this innovative penal experiment, Boyle's previously untapped talents as a writer and sculptor were nurtured and developed. His is an interesting case history that exposes the old conflict between redemption and retribution. Before going in to the Special Unit,

Boyle was incarcerated in the harsh confines of Peterhead for murder and, at that time, the chances of him creating the sort of life he now lives were zilch. No matter what kind of man he is now, there is no doubt that, in his early days, he was seriously flawed. The press labelled him one of the most fearsome gangsters in Glasgow's history.

He was jailed for life in 1967 for a particularly brutal killing. The red-top tabloids have a favourite word that is regularly wheeled out from their voluminous collections of clichés when a Glasgow ned is imprisoned. On such occasions, the headlines usually scream the word 'caged'. In the case of Boyle, it was no lurid exaggeration. This one-time hard man was no pussy cat when he was removed from the streets. The inner anger that drove him to violence on the outside swelled dangerously in prison. Serious violence against prison staff resulted in long spells in solitude and, for a time, he was locked away in the cells within cells that were the infamous cages of Porterfield Prison, Inverness.

The cages were the prison service's answer to the banes of their lives in Scotland's hardcore prisons where violent attacks on warders, dirty protests with excrement smeared on walls, attempted breakouts, warders held hostage, rooftop protests and the like were alarmingly frequent occurrences. Some violent men, when faced with long sentences, just put their heads down, attend the prison library and opt for the quiet life. Others try their hardest to continue with the mayhem that had led to their sentence in the first place. For such prisoners, the logic behind this behaviour is that, if you are facing long sentences, you have nothing to lose. Being a prison officer entails facing daily danger in the form of unprovoked attacks from frustrated men whose very violent tendencies are what put them behind bars. The idea of the cages was to break the spirit of the toughest. The cages, a brutal reminder of the failure of the prison regime, were finally dismantled in 1994 as more enlightened penal theories began to have an effect.

The cages had been temporarily abandoned in 1972 after one of the most violent disturbances in Scottish criminal history in which five prison officers and four inmates, including Boyle, were injured. The cages were, however, reopened in 1978 and used for a further sixteen years as a brutal weapon for controlling troublesome long-term prisoners. If you were a lifer in those difficult days, there was no incentive whatsoever to mend your ways and this was a major factor of the attacks within prisons – some against officers, others a result of feuds that had started on the streets but were not forgotten over the years. And it should be remembered that, although the majority of prison officers got on with their job and had an interest in the rehabilitation of offenders, there was a minority who were always ready to join a 'batter squad' or take it out on the prisoners they disliked.

Life in Peterhead, the old Barlinnie, Porterfield and Craiginches in Aberdeen was a million miles away from that prisoners experienced in the Special Unit. There, the regime was designed to replace that feeling of hopelessness with a degree of freedom, despite the fact they were held in a penal establishment, and to give the prisoners some sense of responsibility and personal choice. At the time this regime was first introduced, it was pretty controversial and, although the Special Unit experiment foundered in the end (as is chronicled elsewhere in this book), amid tales of drug use and prisoners having sex with visitors, some of the theories behind it went on to become commonplace in mainstream prisons. It was, therefore, a victory of sorts for the believers in redemption over retribution.

The Boyle story and how the Special Unit really did turn around his life have fascinated the Scottish media for years. However, many of the reading and viewing public find it hard to be as forgiving of the likes of Boyle as some of the writers who have tackled his life story have been. There is still real anger around that, these days, a man with such a record should slurp fine wines, live some of the time in the lush pastures of France and enjoy the trappings of the modest wealth that his artistic talents as sculptor and writer have provided.

His transition from violent gangster with a bloody record to artistic favourite of the chattering classes even spawned a film. In *A Sense of Freedom* (John Mackenzie, 1979), respected Glasgow actor and director David Hayman plays Boyle. Jeremy Isaacs, an independent producer, was commissioned to make the film and, even before any footage was shot, the flak started. In a tribute to the late Bill Brown, a well-respected and well-remembered Scottish Television chairman, Isaacs said, '*A Sense of Freedom* was a big film on a difficult subject, but Bill Brown bravely stood by me and the film-makers against a hostile press and public opinion.' The film, however, went on to garner some critical success – as did Boyle's book on his life, *The Pain of Confinement* (Edinburgh: Canongate, 1984). It is recommended reading for a picture of what it was like in Peterhead at that time and it also offers an extraordinary insight into what goes on inside the brain of an intelligent man during his punishment for a cruel crime.

All Boyle's new life has been as a direct result of the turnaround brought about by his time in the Special Unit. He had spent twenty-five years in institutions before the regime in the new unit resulted in a life change so profound that he was deemed fit for release and free to take up a legal and productive way of life – something he did achieve despite the doubters.

Boyle married psychiatrist Sarah Trevelyan but, in 2001, they separated after twenty years of marriage. The announcement of the separation came from the Gateway Exchange Trust, a charity they ran for problem youngsters in Edinburgh.

Life out of prison may have been eased by the ability to indulge his love of fine wines and beautiful homes – and the money to provide them – but it wasn't without personal tragedy. James, Boyle's son from his first marriage, got involved in drugs and died in a stabbing. And the years of freedom often found Boyle in conflict with that other Special Unit success Hugh Collins, who also went on to become a writer and sculptor. They just didn't get on. This was perhaps because, amid all his success in the arts world, Collins, who had married artist Caroline McNairn, was ready to publicly condemn the life he led in his youth and speak with genuine concern for the feelings of his victim's family. Boyle does not seem, publicly at least, to share such thinking to the same extent. In one interview, Boyle dealt with the position of his critics in a way that showed there was still some real anger simmering just below the surface of the artist. He attacked those who publicly grudged him his material success head-on, saying:

> The only thing I can say about people like that is that they have allowed themselves to become prisoners of my past. I have moved on but they have allowed themselves to become stuck. My life has moved on beyond my wildest dreams. There is a thrawn jealous aspect to some people's attitude.

BREAD RIOTS

Some of the bloodiest violence ever seen on the city streets occurred as long ago as 1848. And, once again, **GLASGOW GREEN**, so prominent in the gang wars of the 1920s and 1930s, was its locus. Many of those involved were displaced Highlanders or immigrants from Ireland – and most were out of work and starved of cash and food.

In the years after the Reform Act of 1832, which gave the vote to almost all members of the middle classes, great social unrest had festered throughout Britain. The spirit of the times helped spawn the Chartists, a largely working-class radical movement that had universal male suffrage and other parliamentary reforms as its main aims. Over the years since the Chartist Movement was founded in 1838, they had built up considerable support and, in 1848, the revolutionary activity in France encouraged the Chartists to hold a rally at the Green.

More than 3,000 people turned up. However, after the speech-ifying was over, the passions of the disenfranchised spun completely out of control and the crowd rioted. Looking for weapons, they tore up iron railings in **MONTIETH ROW**, at the edge of the Green, and went on the rampage. They then marched into the city centre, looting shops, including a gunsmith's in **ROYAL EXCHANGE SQUARE**, as they went. Now armed, the rioters streamed into nearby **BUCHANAN STREET**, firing their guns in the air.

One brave doctor, believing that such behaviour was simply 'not on' in douce Buchanan Street, took matters into his own hands and disarmed some of the mob. But curbing the violence was beyond the power of one man – or, indeed, the town guard, which had been called into action when the scale of the violence became evident. Eventually, special constables forced the mob back in the direction of the east end – an area that always seems to be a place of tension. Shots had been fired into the crowd, killing several people, and it took the army, who, by then, had been called in, a further twenty-four hours to finally bring this bloody riot to an end.

The early law enforcers found the usual difficulties in ascertaining who in the mob had actually done what and the number of arrests – around thirty – was surprisingly low, considering how many must have been involved and the length of time of the unrest. Some of the culprits – who, no doubt, had social justice on their side – were sentenced to transportation to Australia.

This outbreak of political violence on the streets was not unique. Something similar had been seen before, in 1727, when the government irritated the lieges no end with a plan to put a tax of sixpence on every barrel of beer produced. At the time, the amount of revenue coming from Scotland was seen as inadequate and this was to be the solution. Of course, the tax plan meant horrendous price rises for the consumer. The government was forced into an early example of a spectacular political U-turn and the increase on the barrel was halved to threepence, though the establishment still clearly saw the Scots' liking for a pint as a means of cashing in.

There was a continuing public outcry and the Jacobites, supporters of the Stuart claim to the throne, who were described at the time as being in a state of 'thinly veiled rebellion', saw this unrest as an opportunity. They had been taking every chance they were offered to annoy an unpopular government 'by tumults and petty raids'. It took six troops of Dragoons and Highlanders to calm what became known as the 'beer riots'. Citizens today still show a certain sensitivity towards the price of a pint – something even a modern chancellor has to take into account when preparing budgets.

BROWN, LESLIE

In 1972, after spells as a detective in Partick and with the Flying Squad, this former beat cop in the **GORBALS** ended up as a detective inspector in the Serious Crime Squad. Deeply involved in the police efforts to control Arthur Thompson Snr's east-end mob, Brown also played a leading role in the investigation of many Glasgow murders and drug crimes. He helped to set up London's anti-terrorist squad and, on leaving the police, he worked for the Federation Against Copyright Theft. Brown still does voluntary detective work and is involved in the fight against wrongful arrests and convictions with an organisation whose web site is called www.asearchforjustice.co.uk

C

CARMONT, LORD JOHN

There are those who thirst for the return of the death penalty. And there are plenty whose solution to any crime wave is a 'lock 'em up and throw away the key' attitude. One man who proved that long sentences can work, at least for a time, is Lord Carmont who presided over a remarkable decrease in knifings and slashings during the 1950s. His time on the bench happened to coincide with one of the regularly occurring peaks of crime – one of the clichéd crime waves that the lurid red-top tabloids love to report on. He firmly believed that convicted slashers and knife men should be locked away for long periods. And he applied this belief consistently – any guilty villain appearing before Carmont knew what was coming at the end of a trial. His name still has resonance in criminal circles, where getting a particularly long stretch in prison is know as 'doing a Carmont'.

In private, he was a kindly and gentle man but, on the bench, he was committed to the iron fist rather than the velvet glove. In one circuit, this hard-man judge imposed sentences of up to ten years and a total of fifty-two years imprisonment on eight people for their crimes of violence. It is interesting that, while this policy did work at the time – and that is borne out by a lowering of crime rates – it did little in the long-term to prevent street and pub violence continuing to blight the city right into the twenty-first century. However, it did earn him much praise at the time. *The Herald* said of him:

> His salutary sentences on razor-slashers, knife-wielders and thugs in Glasgow High Court in the years following the Second World War had a marked effect on the criminal classes

and earned him the respect and approval of law-abiding citizens.

My book *Glasgow's Godfather*, a biography of the gangster Walter Norval, tells of an interesting judgement made by the noble lord. It was well known in the city, where such matters are the cause of much pub discussion, that Lord Carmont was a practising Catholic. There was much speculation on the streets and in the tabloids about how this hard man in a wig and robes would deal with the first Catholic slasher to appear before him. It happened that the first villain to fit the categories of both slasher and Catholic was one Willie Collins. He operated around Norval's patch – the 'High Road', as the gangsters then called the **GARSCUBE ROAD** area.

It was Collins's bad luck that, just before he appeared before him, Lord Carmont had recently dealt with two slashers. One was a man called John Totten. His Lordship had given Totten five years for using two razors in a fight that had resulted in the victim having to get some serious stitching done in the emergency department of a Glasgow hospital. The other slasher had been given seven years for cutting a man right across his face, again an injury that tested the skill of the emergency surgeons and required many, many stitches.

So, how would Carmont deal with the Catholic Willie Collins whose crime was to cut an enemy on the cheek? This was a comparatively modest wound that required only two stitches. Collins got ten years. The sentence equated to five years per stitch and the underworld gave Carmont even more respect from then on. The message was understood loud and clear. Although it was perceived as a stern warning, it was seen as not being very fair. 'After all,' Norval reflected, 'if you jailed some of the old timers on that basis, they would still be behind bars to this day.'

Carmont continued in his profession into old age and was working almost till the day he died, at the age of eighty-five, while on holiday in Kirkcudbright in 1965. He was held in extremely high regard by his fellow lawyers and was said to have such a remarkable legal mind and retentive memory that he was able to quote, without reference to text books, a formidable number of decisions and authorities in both Scottish and English courts. The public knew him best as the scourge of the gangs but he was also an outstanding authority on commercial and maritime law. But the staid old *Herald* perhaps got it just right with the remarkable lapse into tabloidese that allowed them to run the following headline for his obituary: 'The Judge who Rocked the Glasgow Underworld'.

CARRACHER, PATRICK

A man seemingly destined to dangle at the end of a rope from an early age, this infamous Glasgow killer was one of many who took his final walk, the dreaded eight steps from the condemned cell to the scaffold, in the Barlinnie hanging shed. He had killed John Gordon of **AITKEN STREET** by stabbing him in the neck. It was said that Carracher was dragged screaming to meet his death at the hands of the hangman in 1945.

The Gordon case was the third time he had been before the High Court on charges of murder. On the first occasion, he was eventually convicted on the lesser charge of culpable homicide and jailed for three years. Later, a further prison term was given to him for using a lethal weapon in an assault but, clearly, jail had not taught this razor slasher and knife man to mend his ways. It was, perhaps, not surprising, given his background, that an appeal against the death sentence failed.

Carracher did not run with a gang. Like many razor slashers, he was a lone wolf. A monstrous and dangerous individual, he was described as a 'human time bomb'. He was clearly a psychopath with a long history of assaults with knife and razor – a man with no conception of right or wrong. His defence in the Gordon murder trial was a fairly new one for that time. His team claimed that he was a 'medical psychopath' and that the verdict of the court should be that he was of diminished responsibility at the time of the murder. These were harder times and his undoubtedly defective psychological state was not taken into account. The black flag was to fly above the prison gates regardless of the state of his mental health.

CHEEKY FORTY

The antics of this large 1930s' gang illustrate the size of the pre-Second-World-War gang problem. The actual numbers involved are, on occasion, staggering. With no television cameramen around and little chance of the street battles being photographed, contemporary newspaper reports are the prime source. One famous battle involving the Cheeky Forty took place on a Saturday night at 10.30 p.m. in **CASTLE STREET, MONKLAND STREET** and **PARLIAMENTARY ROAD**. Around three hundred people were involved and they were described as a 'riotous mob'. A police constable from the Northern Division gave the following dramatic account: 'The crowd, which was composed fairly equally of men and women, was swaying from one side of the street to another. Bottles and stones were thrown freely in the fight.'

Of this lot, only four appeared in court. There was no doubt about their identity and they were all described as prominent members of the Cheeky Forty. But, back in those days, as is the case now, witnesses in and around the crowd were reluctant to come forward, fearful that, if they did, the outcome would either be a 'doing' from the gangsters or they'd have their businesses or families threatened.

Another constable who gave evidence said that local people were terrified of the gangs – a blow to the oft-held belief that the old-time gangs only fought with each other and ordinary folk were left in peace. Complete rubbish. The constable told the court that 'you get shopkeepers complaining about the Cheeky Forty gang coming to their shops to get money to pay fines'. This gang was partial to premeditated violence and took steps to thwart the police.

Another massive rumble, this time in **CATHEDRAL STREET**, where the Cheeky Forty took on members of the Row Amateur Social Club over some dispute or other, is interesting. Those were not the days of mobile phones, squad cars or instant radio communication. It wasn't even the era when cops in trouble and needing the cavalry just barked 'Code 21 Red' into their radios and some extra muscle would arrive. In the heyday of the Cheeky Forty, it was rather different and, when the police realised the size of the Cathedral Street battle, they went to the nearest telephone kiosk to phone for help but the telephone lines had been cut. The 'cavalry' did eventually arrive and, somewhat belatedly, put an end to the fighting.

The weapons found after such battles point to the level of violence involved. In this case, they included beer bottles, pieces of wood, parts of billiard cues (this was a time before snooker became king), an iron bar, a baton, a bamboo stick, part of a barber's pole and a large piece of metal roughly shaped into a dagger.

CHRISTMAN, BILL

Bill Christman was a Church of Scotland minister who, in the 1970s, became the first full-time chaplain in Barlinnie. He arrived in the job via a route more tortuous than that of the prisoners he worked among. He came from Joplin, Missouri, and started his working life behind the counter of a record store specialising in rhythm and blues. A serious illness gave him some valuable thinking time and a holiday break he had taken in a dirt-poor area of West Virginia helped turn his mind to the church. A friend suggested studying for the ministry in Edinburgh and the idea appealed to him.

After his studies, he found himself ministering in the tough area of **NIDDRIE**. Later came a call to move to **EASTERHOUSE**, ironically almost in the shadow of Barlinnie, where he worked amongst the usual mixture to be found in a Glasgow scheme – many hard-working, decent folk, trying to make the best of things for themselves and their families, and gangs and violence. He spent some years in the scheme and, at one time, was running five football teams in an attempt to give the youngsters some focus in their lives. This is the same sort of work that the Easterhouse Project got involved in and which goes on to this day in the Easterhouse Festival.

The next move was to Lansdowne Church in the more plush acres of the **WEST END**. It was a different challenge here and Christman said he was 'trying to build multi-faith bridges with a community of many religions and with the support of the congregation'. It was no easy task and, after Lansdowne, he sought a new challenge in an Ayrshire church created by the amalgamation of three congregations. He had been there five years when he saw the advert for the Bar-L job.

When visiting any prison and dealing with its inmates, this American-born Church of Scotland minister had a golden rule: 'Regardless of what the crime involved is, I don't want to know the details of why any man or woman was sent to prison before I meet them. I am human like anyone else and I could be prejudiced.' He saw his role as continuing the valuable work of a series of part-time chaplains and this can involve home visits to relatives. One nightmarish scenario for a prisoner is when letters and contact with the outside world stop. He or she is left alone, behind bars, with their imagination. There could be some family crisis going on and they feel helpless to do anything about it. Or it might be that a wife, husband or partner has decided to cut the cord permanently but cannot bring themselves to let the person in jail know their decision. Once contact has been broken, the inmate is left totally unaware of what's happening to loved ones on the outside and often they begin to think the worst. When this happens, the chaplain can help.

Bill Christman was a real man of the people. He once ran a soup kitchen in **GEORGE SQUARE** and liked to talk to the late-night denizens of the darkened streets. Indeed, he was so often on the scene when trouble flared that one chief constable gave him a card to let the guys on the beat know who he was and what he was about! It was all in a day's work for a man who had been nicknamed Godfather during his spell in Easterhouse. If only Glasgow's other Godfathers had had the same peaceable instincts and the faith of . Bill Christman . . .

CITY OF GLASGOW POLICE

The onerous task of being responsible for law and order in a place where, according to historian John Prebble, 'brawling is in the blood' now falls to the Strathclyde Police. The force came into existence after the amalgamation of several local forces, brought about by changes in local government and the demise of the City of Glasgow police as an entity, the force employs around 7,000 people all of whom are kept fully occupied by the city's denizens who so often find themselves on the wrong side of the law. The cops have all the accoutrements of modern policing – squad cars, radios and helicopters – and they are controlled from hi-tech headquarters in **PITT STREET** just a few yards from the buzz of the pubs and restaurants in **SAUCHIEHALL STREET**.

It is all a far cry from the beginnings of the force. The start of what could be called organised policing in the modern way began in the city in 1788. Glasgow's magistrates at the time were far-sighted enough to realise that something better than the old system of watchmen and a 'city guard' was required. At the time, the city had about 40,000 inhabitants and it was unwise to go around the town after dark because of the danger of theft or assault or, more probably, both. Alastair Dinsmore, an inspector who became a knowledgeable and respected deputy curator of the city's famed police 'black' museum, has been quoted as saying that:

> People tended to stay in after dark, and with good reason. The only ones who ventured out were ladies of the night and such like. There was a lot of poverty in the city and, of course, where you get poverty you get crime.

A cynic might remark that little has changed.

Of some interest to those who, today, clamour for the return of the death penalty and stringent 'lock 'em up and throw away the key' sentencing is the fact that the almost barbarous penalties that faced the lawbreaker back in the late eighteenth century appear to have been of limited deterrent value. Offences like theft or forgery could result in you taking your final few steps to the gallows or being transported to Australia via a six-month sea journey in the harsh confines of a prison vessel.

So the 1788 attempt to build a police force was both necessary and pace-setting for Britain in that time. It is thought that this initiative, an attempt to set up a force to prevent crime before it happened, had not been tried anywhere in Britain up to that time. Initially, it was a small-scale operation with just an inspector and a handful of officers. This was an early example of a municipal police force controlled by commissioners elected from trades' people and merchants. Alastair Dinsmore, also chairman of the Glasgow Police Heritage Society (Honorary President Sir David McNee), says of the aims of the fledgling organisation:

> The list of ideas they came up with would easily fit into today's police function. The police would have a uniform and swear an oath. They would patrol the streets in shifts for twenty-four hours. They would deter thieves by concentrating on the receivers of stolen property – without the people to buy stolen goods, the market for the thief would be diminished, the same as it is today. They would keep an eye on taverns, where criminals hung out and create a book containing information on all the criminals they had dealt with – an early form of intelligence.

This brave start to the building of a modern police force was swiftly blighted by the same curse of modern policing – the cash to fund it ran out! Handwritten minutes in the Mitchell Library tell of another attempt a year later in 1789 when a Master of Police was appointed with eight constables under his control. But, after a year, lack of money again ended the experiment.

Most historians give Sir Robert Peel the credit for founding policing as we know it today. But, in July 2000, the lively Glasgow paper, the *Evening Times*, reported that the roots of Glasgow policing go even further back. In an article, Mr Dinsmore pointed out:

> Most history books credit Peel with the founding of modern policing in 1829. But, for some reason, historians in England have ignored the fact that Glasgow's police was established under the Glasgow Police Act of 1800 – fully twenty-nine years before hand . . . It would be nice to see the credit going where it belongs. All we want to do is set the record straight.

Considering the failed efforts of 1788 – the year before the French Revolution – Glasgow's place in police history is well merited.

The Napoleonic Wars got in the way of further attempts to finance police forces. The obvious answer was an Act of Parliament to allow the levying of rates to cover the cost of law enforcement. There was some resistance to Glasgow's efforts to get a financially sound force. The city seemed too far away from the seat of government in London. As Alastair Dinsmore points out, 'Most of the people in power weren't too worried about what was happening in Glasgow. Plus the rich merchants in London didn't want mere commoners having power over them and did everything to prevent policing in the capital.'

Glasgow's rich merchant class seems to have been made of sterner stuff. The tobacco barons who had such influence on the city had a hand in the founding of the police. Patrick Colquhoun, who had been Lord Provost and in charge of the local Chamber of Commerce, played an important role. In 1789, he moved to England and saw what a bad effect the lack of proper law enforcement was having on the community down there. He was so influenced by what he saw that, in 1795, he wrote a book outlining how effective policing could help the capital. In it, he drew on what he had seen of the Glasgow experiments of 1788 and 1789 and used these ideas in a plan for a London force. This was the inspiration for the setting-up of the Thames River Police and the Metropolitan force in 1829. All this proves Glasgow's claim to be a world leader in policing.

Down the years, as well as having to deal with the regular and constant battle against big-time gangs and Godfathers, Glasgow's boys in blue have had some difficult murder cases – Bible John and Manuel, to name but two – to contend with. The splendid Police Museum in Pitt Street has reminders galore of this on-going fight against crime. One of the most chilling is the blood-stained footprint that featured in the Jessie McLachlan trial.

Strathclyde's current Chief Constable is Willie Rae. He walks in the footsteps of a series of strong men who made their names fighting the assortment of head-bangers, neds, gangsters, drug dealers and loan sharks who defile the city – as well as nipping minor crime in the bud. Mr Rae came to work in Glasgow and its surroundings from Dunbartonshire Constabulary when it merged with the city force in 1975. A diligent copper, he worked his way up from constable to assistant chief constable and, in September 1996, he left to take the job of chief in Dumfries and Galloway.

This move was to catapult him into the high-flying world of international crime. During his time there, he led the organisation of the Lockerbie bombing trial in the Netherlands. It was rather bizarre that the smallest force in the UK was called on to police the largest mass murder trial in the history of Scottish judicial procedure. The Pan Am clipper that was blasted from the skies over lowland Scotland, killing 270 people on the plane and on the ground, still makes news. The Libyan who was controversially convicted of responsibility for placing the bomb on the airliner languishes in Barlinnie in a special area away from the normal run of Glasgow thugs who people the grim Big House in the east end.

One of Willie Rae's strengths in the job is his all-round policing experience. You don't get to the top in a blue uniform in Glasgow without running up against the nasty side of human nature. Only a few weeks on the beat is enough to provide the aspirant lawman with insight into how some people can defy the conventions of a normal well-ordered life. A lifetime in uniform moulds men and women into people who know their fellow human beings better than most.

On taking up the job, Willie Rae gave some newspapers some pertinent interviews on how policing had changed since his early days. The biggest change he saw was in the area of drugs and drug dealing. Mr Rae remembered his time as a cadet straight from school and his early days as a constable and sergeant. During that time, he never ran into drugs other than alcohol whose effects, it has to be said, then as now, took up much valuable police time. It is no surprise that, these days, drugs, their distribution and the control of 'patches' are major factors in gangland crime in cities.

But, sadly, it's not just urban areas where this is a menace. Not so long ago, there was an upsurge of drug usage in the picture-postcard Argyll fishing village of Tarbert and Willie Rae found it to be a problem, too, in rural Dumfries and Galloway. It is impossible to overestimate the damage caused by addicts. They will thieve, assault and even kill to maintain their habits. The violence of the gangsters importing the 'goods' and fighting over their distribution also takes up many policing hours. Beating the dealers is one of Willie Rae's main priorities.

He also has strong views on domestic violence, something he had to deal with in his early days at the coalface of crime fighting. Strathclyde Police inherited a rich heritage from the old City of Glasgow Police, which, as we have seen, is a force with a longer history than that of any other in Britain. The one certainty of the future is that the fight against crime will go on. The police can win battles. The history of Glasgow and crime is littered with tales of the 'gangbusters'. But the gangs are never truly busted. After each defeat or setback, new gangs and crooks emerge to test the mettle of the current police force. But, thanks to men like Willie Rae, it is not one-way traffic.

COLLINS, HUGH

Like Jimmy Boyle, Collins is a murderer whose life was turned around by the Barlinnie Special Unit. However, he was critical of some of the happenings in the legendary penal experiment which was eventually closed down in great controversy. Collins made a remarkable impact after he had been freed. His abilities with a sculptor's chisel and as a writer are both of the highest order. Maybe his artistic talent relates to his painful honesty about his past life. Hugh Collins is an extremely complex character and he does not dodge responsibility for what he has done – like many a hard man, he is a realist. In one perceptive newspaper interview, he told the reporter, 'I was never a gangster – only a bampot.' He went on, 'The only person I can apologise to is dead. The only man who can forgive me is dead.' His victim was one Willie Mooney and, in the 1970s, Collins stabbed him to death. The murder put Collins behind bars for life and he served sixteen years of that sentence.

In prison, be it Peterhead or the Bar-L Special Unit, there is plenty of time to think. Collins used it well. 'I was afraid of death. I was afraid of rejection. I see now that my violence was a product of fear.' The Special Unit was much more than the cushy cells, with curtains and paintings on the walls, that so angered its critics. One of the guiding principles was to capitalise on any talents each prisoner had. While there, Collins learned the basics of sculpture and remarked, 'I was fortunate. I was no' bad at it.' In this assessment, he was correct – many important art critics have praised his work in stone. And, as a wordsmith, he has found favour with the literary critics too. Two of his books, *Autobiography of a Murderer* (London: Macmillan, 1997) and *Walking Away* (Edinburgh: Rebel Inc, 2000), touch raw nerves.

However, it was sculpture that came first. 'When I got the idea to carve the statue of Christ, I took it like a sign. This makes me sound like a maniac. It took me two years. But this is the bizarre thing – it was the best time of my life.' He saw the project as 'a punishment – a penance'. His life-saving move to the Special Unit came after years in a normal jail, years where life behind bars was a dark mixture of attacks on warders, drugs, hunger strikes and solitary. He was exactly the kind of troublemaking, long-term prisoner the Special Unit was set up to try to help. His take on life in the Nutcracker Suite, as the cons called the unit, is interesting:

> The Special Unit saved me but it also tortured me. I was made into a pet lion for the social workers, psychologists and lawyers who came there. Some of it was disgusting. These people were like groupies. They patronised you, got a thrill from being near you. Some of the women who visited the unit would even sleep with you.

The unit may have saved him and turned him into an artist but his writing has a streak of self-loathing in it, as well as plenty of scrupulous honesty. He resents any accusations that his books produce blood money. He says, 'I don't want to be a hero of the underworld. The books make me look horrible. I want to show how horrible violence is.'

He married fellow artist Caroline McNairn and went on to live a settled life, working hard at his writing, including fiction. With his wife, he runs a studio in Gorebridge. But a reminder that the crime of murder – no matter how far in the past it was committed and no matter how the killer has changed – is hard to forgive came in June 2004. The erection of a sculpture in Harvieston Cemetery in Gorebridge to commemorate the life of a local schoolgirl who had been murdered had been planned. But, when word got out that Collins had been approached to produce the memorial, the girl's mother was outraged. She took exception to a man with Collins' past being associated with her daughter and the plans for the memorial were dropped.

70

CRONIN, DAN

This legendary gunman and all-round hard man of the 1940s was said to rule 'the town' – as the city centre was known to gangsters operating in the schemes and peripheral areas. He was a fighting man whose fists, as well as his weapons, brought him respect from the criminal fraternity.

CURRAN, AGNES

Ms Curran became the first female governor of a male prison in Britain. She was a fifty-eight-year-old grandmother when, in 1979, she took the top position at Dungavel, in the Lanarkshire hills, just south of Glasgow (where the majority of her inmates came from, naturally!). She had previously been deputy governor of the women's prison at Cornton Vale, near Stirling. Dungavel now swirls in controversy as it is used as a temporary home for asylum seekers. But, when Ms Curran took over, it was a medium-security prison with 106 prisoners, 60 per cent of whom were serving sentences for rape or murder. It was a sort of halfway-house prison whose function was to prepare long-term prisoners for transfer to open prisons or for release into the community. The prison had a good success rate and only a few prisoners had to be returned to the stricter regimes at the likes of Barlinnie and Peterhead.

Agnes Curran was a remarkable woman but this was no easy posting for her and she was determined to make a success of it. An example of her down-to-earth, realistic attitude is shown when, on her retirement, after five years in the post, she said:

> I never forgot that some of these prisoners had been sent to prison for doing terrible things. It was natural that, being a woman, some of them thought they could pull the wool over my eyes or manipulate me but I had been in the service long enough to know when that was happening.

Her years of control over this domain, filled with hard cases, did prove successful. Talking of the innovative thinking that had led to her being given the post, she said:

> I am not a bra-burning, flag-waving feminist, but I believe I have done the job as well as any man. In fact, I feel that, because I was a woman, I was treated with far more respect, in certain situations, by the prisoners.

That this was, indeed, the case was confirmed by an old lag who told me many a tale of his time in Dungavel.

She went on to say, 'I received a few compliments about my perfume and was often called "madam" but, apart from that, I imagine I was treated the same as anyone else.'

She could apply a firm hand when one was needed but she also had an excellent sense of humour. On finding out that her successor was to be a man, she said, 'Men require equal opportunities, too.' The Scottish Prison Service is not without its critics but its decision to appoint 'Aggie', as the prisoners called her, was a notable piece of pace-setting.

D

DALZIEL, JAMES

This infamous gang leader of the 1930s went by the nickname of 'Razzle Dazzle'. He was the leader of the Parlour Boys, a gang who considered the Bedford Parlour Dance Hall to be their HQ. Ironically, he died in a brawl with San Toy gang members in that very dance hall. His throat was cut and he was taken, on the back of a commandeered lorry, to the nearby Victoria Infirmary where he was declared dead on arrival. No fewer than sixteen men appeared in court in connection with his death from 'a stab wound or razor slash'.

The trouble had started after a bunch of youths had forced their way into the hall. The violence between the two clashing gangs was such that young girls huddled together, screaming, as they desperately tried to avoid the fighting men. Other dancers fainted at the sight of the blood, bottles, knives and razors. The death started one of the biggest murder hunts in the city with almost the entire CID force involved. But the crime threw up again one of the biggest bugbears in investigating gang fights. With dozens of desperate men, all with weapons, on both sides, and general mayhem happening, it was almost impossible to prove who had delivered any particular blow. It was a problem that constantly faced, and still faces, the police. In this case, the villain who killed 'Razzle Dazzle' escaped the hangman.

An interesting insight into the social mores of the time is that, on his frequent trips to the dance hall, Dalziel, a married man with children, considered it effeminate to dance with women and tripped the light fantastic with his fellow male gangsters.

DENIERS, THE

This is my term for those who fail to recognise the historical and current level of crime in the city. From the 1920s to this day, in the letter columns of newspapers, more recently, in TV and radio interviews, such folk have regularly been aggressive about those who chronicle crime in the city. But it seems they fail to understand what is going on in the crime pages of the city's newspapers, past or present. And nor do they appreciate how much blood is actually spilled on the streets. They find it impossible to concede that, although the city is turning away from the deprivation and social unrest of its industrial past towards a more cultured lifestyle, with a growth in pavement café society, the regeneration of the riverside and the burgeoning interest in the theatre, music and visual arts, it does not mean that crime in Glasgow no longer exists – or, if it does still exist, it does so in some kind of diluted form.

To address a problem, you first have to assess the size of it. But, down the years, in Glasgow, there have been those, particularly in local politics, who have preferred to sweep problems under the carpet. Such myopic thinking fails even to concede that the historical problems in Glasgow are little worse than those in any similar cities that have a record of immigration, industrial poverty and housing deprivation. The difference is that the citizens of other cities, such as London, Manchester, New York, Naples, Marseilles, St Paul and Chicago, seem to be able to discuss the problems and take measures to ameliorate them without the chips on both shoulders that make some Glaswegians attack those who point out an unpalatable history or the dangers in the future.

Such head-in-the-sand attitudes, so evident in the history of politics in the city, were particularly prevalent in the early days of the Easterhouse Project and the involvement of Frankie Vaughan in it. The well-meaning showman was vilified by some local politicians. He was trying to join the locals in their attempts to sort out the problems of gangs and violence with hard work and involvement but, by highlighting what was going on, he was accused of driving investment away from the area. Such an accusation was mistaken then.

Now, with the aid of the internet, a would-be tourist or an industrialist wondering about where to site a new factory can, at the click of a mouse, read the local newspapers and make an informed decision on where to go or not to go, in the full knowledge of the upsides and any potential downsides that might be encountered in a particular place. Indeed, no one seems to have recognised the tourist potential that the city's long-standing reputation for crime and hard men might offer. This is surprising especially considering the popularity worldwide of police museums (Glasgow has two). Black museums of all kinds devoted to crime and criminals and even waxworks are known to attract crowds in their droves. The peculiar fascination for true crime is undeniable – just look at the proliferation of books, TV documentaries and films which chronicle the doings of folk who get on the wrong side of the law.

Unlike Glasgow, cities like Chicago do capitalise on this somewhat morbid curiosity. There, you can go on crime tours to view the warehouse walls that were left bullet-pitted by the machine guns of the St Valentine's Day Massacre. Or you can wonder at the lift (elevator to the Americans!) that was built as a security measure to hoist Al Capone, still in his limo, to the top of the city-centre skyscraper from where he ruled his fiefdom.

Such tours in Glasgow may not be as absurd as some might think. In question-and-answer sessions that I've done in bookshops, I am often asked why the city doesn't have them. Maybe one answer is that, even today, if the itinerary wasn't very carefully planned, the guide and the tourists might be at some risk! But it could be done.

With their belief that history can be rewritten and the black spots in the story of Glasgow painted out, in the fashion of Russia when in the grip of hard-line communists, the deniers don't grant outsiders with even a modicum of intelligence. Thankfully, at the beginning of the new century, a new breed of politicians is showing signs of taking a more balanced view, as well as initiating new measures to combat gangsterism, drug dealing and street assaults. By all means beat the drum for tourists and accentuate the positives in what some are calling the renaissance in the city. But, when there is a problem, acknowledge it, investigate it, expose it and take action against it.

DOWDALL, LAURENCE

One of the best-remembered lawyers in Glasgow legal history, he died in 1996. It was said that, for many years, the first words on the lips of any villain who had had his collar felt were 'Get me Dowdall!' Indeed, after the Second World War, there was a joke doing the rounds concerning Rudolph Hess, Hitler's aide. Hess had parachuted on to an **EAGLESHAM** field. He was on an ill-considered scheme to end the war and his mission was to find the Duke of Hamilton. When the British Army found him and put him under arrest, according to the joke, Hess was said to have uttered the immortal words, 'Get me Dowdall!' It might not have been such a bad idea!

Dowdall, a smart dresser who would have looked the part in any Hollywood epic on legal eagles, was the defence lawyer supreme. His knowledge of the law was encyclopaedic, his wit was finely honed and his understanding of how juries, sheriffs and judges thought was unsurpassed. It is little wonder that his profession admired and treasured him. That famous chronicler of Glasgow, Jack House, referred to him as Glasgow's answer to Perry Mason. Others would opine that Mason (as played on TV by Raymond Burr) was Los Angeles' answer to Laurence Dowdall.

He really was an amazing legal character. After some years of retirement, he returned, at the age of eighty-six, to work as a consultant with his old firm which had been founded with his friend Joe Hughes almost fifty years before. Still spry and active, he confined himself to backroom work, remarking, 'I couldn't go into a courtroom now because the judges are so much younger than I am and the sheriffs are just boys.'

There was no legal background in his family and it was the cut and thrust of the courtroom that attracted him to the law. Even at eighty-six, his memory was razor sharp and he could vividly recall one of the first cases he was ever involved in where the fiscal, the defence (Dowdall) and the accused all had degrees in law. In the public perception, the law is a profession not always noted for humour. But those who practise it in the courts, those who frequent the witness box and even those who stand accused can tell tales of real laughter in court. And Dowdall was an expert in using humour when pleading for a client. He took one procurator fiscal to task for calling a production in a trial 'a pair of knickers'. The Glasgow Perry Mason waved the garment in dispute in the air and insisted that such a diaphanously gossamer confection should properly be described as 'panties or scanties'!

Curiously, underwear seems to have featured frequently in his defence submissions. In another case, he produced a flimsy garment but this time the angry young woman involved described her panties as 'mothproof, fireproof and tear-proof'. On another occasion, he blew up a condom in court (heaven knows what point this was making) but the gesture backfired when he let it go and it dive-bombed the jury.

One of his most amusing tales from a lifetime in court, during which he attained a remarkable success rate in defending the villains of the city, concerned an identification parade. And, for once, it was the men on the parade who rigged the result and not, as did happen in the bad old days, the cops. The client was a taxi driver with a limp. When the parade was arranged, the people in the parade were all very similar in height and appearance. The witness and a lawyer looked through a peephole at the parade. The witness could not pick out the taxi driver so he asked for the parade people to go for a walk to see if that would jog his memory. At this moment, the lawyer's heart fell – the limp would surely give the game away. But, no – in an ingenious ploy to obscure the taxi driver's guilt, everyone in the parade had a similar limp!

But life in the courtroom was only occasionally lightened by such amusing incidents. For the most part, it was painstaking work, defending men and women whose freedom was at stake. Dowdall took his work and reputation seriously. His high success rate could be put down to natural caution and expert reasoning in how the prosecution works. One much respected retired sheriff's officer told me that Laurence Dowdall was extremely careful to choose winnable cases. If it looked as if the evidence against a client was going to be too strong, he would advise a guilty plea and then work on mitigation. And, if a client insisted on a not guilty plea in the face of solid evidence, he often walked away. This realism is confirmed by the recollection of one of his successors, Joe Beltrami. Beltrami, aka The Great Defender, learned a lot from Dowdall in court. Beltrami says:

> He was a wonderful tactician and I tried to model myself tactically on him. What really impressed me, even from those early days, was his complete knowledge of every case. He knew his cases backwards. He had a goal in view from the outset – knew exactly where he was going – and, as often as not, reached that goal.

This respected man of the law had another attribute that was much commented on by his peers. On Dowdall's death, his long-time friend Robert Cassidy said:

> Laurence defended his clients with great skill, humour and humanity but his reputation went further. The bench respected him for his integrity, his great knowledge and also, importantly, for his brevity. He was listened to by judges with an interest in pursuing justice. One of his chief virtues as a lawyer was never to be long-winded or boring to the jury.

Amen to that.

DUKE STREET PRISON

These days the words 'prison' and 'Glasgow' usually mean only one place – the infamous fortress that is Barlinnie, aka the Bar-L. But, in Duke Street, Glasgow had another feared place of incarceration.

Hangings were carried out in Duke Street Prison until 1928 when the executioner took to plying his trade at Barlinnie, not far away. The last inmates left the prison in July 1953 and it was later demolished. It had an interesting history and it was commented on by no less a literary figure than Charles Dickens who, on visiting it in December 1847, called it 'a truly damnable jail', in a letter to friend. Dickens also noted at the time that the city was in a state 'of tremendous distress' and, indeed, there were to be riots on the streets the next year.

Duke Street was also notable as the place where Elizabeth Dorothea Lyness, an early female medical pioneer, was imprisoned for her part in the suffragette movement. Lyness, who died in 1944, ended up as a GP in **DENNISTOUN**, just a short distance east of the jail. She led an adventurous early life and got involved in many campaigns on behalf of women's rights, the most remarkable of which took place in 1914 and was known as the 'Park Mansion Affair'. Along with another suffragette, Ethel Moorhead, Lyness was caught in the act of setting fire to an empty mansion and taken to Duke Street Prison. There, they went on hunger strike and created all sorts of bother. They were released before their trial but didn't turn up for it and became fugitives from the police. When they were eventually caught, they were tried and jailed for eight months. At the trial their supporters pelted the judge with apples.

But the bloodiest episode in this jail's history involved the IRA. In 192I, the prison walls were peppered with bullet holes during a break-out involving a Republican commander, Frank Carty. And the prison was peripherally involved in another IRA incident that year when a captured Irishman, Frank Somers, was being taken to the jail by a police inspector, Robert Johnston. The van they were travelling in was ambushed near Rottenrow by thirteen armed IRA men who had sworn to free Somers. Johnston was killed and one of his fellow officers stood astride his body, firing at the ambushers, until he, too, was hit.

Johnston's watch and baton are on view at a new police museum, run by the Glasgow Police Heritage Society, in **TURNBULL STREET** in the **SALTMARKET**. The society's chairman is Alastair Dinsmore, the respected retired policeman turned historian. It is rather different from the better known police museum, in the **PITT STREET HQ**, which concentrates on famous cases. The new museum is more concerned with the men and women who made the force.

E

EAGLESHAM

This most attractive and desirable conservation village lies on the edge of the Fenwick Moor. The locals do not like to think of themselves and their leafy enclave, with its village green and pubs, as part of the Glasgow scene – that might not help to maintain the high house prices! But the fact is that this picture-postcard village has views over the city centre and east end and its postal address is G76. It is within sight of Castlemilk, a scheme that is now being improved but, in the past, was no stranger to crime. And, perhaps surprisingly, Eaglesham has also featured in the murderous history of Glasgow.

The centre of the village looks today much as it did in the eighteenth century when it was built as a 'model village' by the Earls of Eglinton, whose family base was at Irvine. A cotton-spinning mill that burned down in 1876 was powered by the Linn Burn – known locally as the 'Orry' – that still runs through the village green. The mill provided work in congenial and healthy countryside for mill girls from the city. Indeed, the elevation of the village, almost 500 feet, and its nearness to the unadulterated sea air sweeping in off the Atlantic once gave it a good reputation as a place for a healthy holiday. There was also a special school so that the mill girls could improve their minds as well as their health.

But, in a long forgotten murder case, the health of one young mill worker was not in the least improved by a stay in Eaglesham. The date of the murder most foul in this rural paradise is significant – 1857. This was the year when the papers in Glasgow were dominated by the Madeleine Smith case. Much is made these days of the copycat murders and, while not a classic case, the Eaglesham murder was, in some respects, a copycat crime.

The perpetrator was John Thomson, a twenty-six-year-old tailor, who lived in lodgings in the village. Like thousands a few miles away in the inner city, he read the voluminous newspaper reports of the Madeleine Smith case in great detail. Something caught his eye in the spicy tales from the court – a mention of prussic acid. Madeleine was accused of lacing the cocoa she gave her boyfriend, Pierre Emile L'Angelier, with arsenic as they indulged in some hanky-panky behind the back of her douce father. Indeed, where the arsenic came from was one of the key issues in her trial. But prussic acid was also mentioned and that was enough to get Thomson thinking.

His victim, Agnes Montgomery – an apt name as one of the two main streets of the village abutting on to the green is **MONT-GOMERY STREET** – worked in the local mill and Thomson lodged with Agnes's sister and her sister's husband, James Watson. Thomson seems to have been a bit of a suspect character. He had accusations of theft floating around him and had used different names at different times. He also had 'form', as the police would say, having been sentenced for theft at Inveraray in 1853. But Agnes and the Watsons knew nought of this. Thomson also seemed to be a bit of a ladies' man, flirting and telling tall stories to impress them. Agnes became a tad too friendly with this villain. They were seen in each other's company in a local pub, Dollar's. Thomson was a man who was quick to take offence and he was unhappy that Agnes would not come to Glasgow with him as he had planned. In another local, the Cross Keys, a weaver who was in his company said that Thomson had made an odd remark to him, which he took to be possibly in reference to the Watsons. The weaver reported that Thomson had said, 'There is a lot of them has me at ill will but I am determined to do for the buggers yet.' When Agnes took ill and died with symptoms akin to poisoning, his background and such remarks were remembered. And Thomson had been the last person to see her alive.

Agnes was buried in the local churchyard and, for a few weeks, the matter seemed closed. But suspicion grew that the itinerant tailor with a suspect record was involved in the death. He, therefore, decided to get out of the village and headed along the road a few miles and into the city centre. There, he intended to disappear into the dark tenement canyons and forget the rural life with its suspicions and threat to his liberty. But, once in the city, he continued thieving and came to the attention of the police on another matter.

His ex-landlord in Eaglesham, James Watson, had also contacted the police about Thomson, a theft and his suspicions about the poisoning of Agnes Montgomery. More evidence against him began to emerge, including that of the three-year-old daughter of Agnes's sister. The little girl said she saw Thomson give Agnes a drink on the fateful day. As to prussic acid, he denied sending a boy to buy some but, in a further nod in the direction of the Madeleine Smith case, he admitted he did use the chemical as a hair dye. It was enough to get him arrested and Agnes's body was exhumed from the Eaglesham Kirk's graveyard. Medical evidence proved that there was prussic acid present and that the chemical had no effect as a hair dye.

There was no clear motive for the murder but Thomson was found guilty and hanged in public outside the County Buildings in Paisley. The full stories of this, the black secret of Eaglesham, and other murders are well told in great and gory detail in *Bloody Valentine: Scotland's Crimes of Passion* (Edinburgh: Black & White Publishing, 2004) by the accomplished crime writer Douglas Skelton.

ELECTRIC CHAIR

Glasgow never had its own 'old sparky', the execution method so beloved of Hollywood B-movies. Instead, the rope was good enough to despatch the city's villains into eternity. But, in the 1950s, there was a rather gloomy little pub just off the **CANDLE-RIGGS** which was called the Hangman's Rest and here, reputedly, the hangman steadied his nerves before taking the short walk to

HIGH STREET and then on to the gallows at **GLASGOW GREEN**. No doubt, after the grim deed was over, he stopped off on the way back for few more quickies. Before it was swept into the dust of history, this little howff had something of a makeover with chrome and Formica replacing dusty smoke-stained wood. This led to it being given the nickname the Electric Chair by drouthy hacks from the Express building in nearby **ALBION STREET**. Ironically, had it been left standing in what is now the **MERCHANT CITY**, some imaginative entrepreneur would probably have turned it into a trendy theme bar with old photographs of its death-delivering customers and their victims! It would have been quite an attraction in an area much frequented by tourists and local trendies – a welcome change from sushi and tempura.

ELLIS, WALTER SCOTT

This bank robber's trial on a charge of murdering a taxi driver had a lasting effect on the way Scottish newspapers report crime. When Scott Ellis was cleared of the murder charge in the 1950s, there was a street battle of an unusual kind outside the High Court. Rival factions of newspaper men fought each other to whisk the accused man off to a hideaway where a large cheque – and perhaps some nice malts – would ensure his story was splashed over *their* brand of breakfast reading matter for Scotland the next morning. The Scott Ellis story was said to have been 'bought up' in advance by one of the morning papers but, in the event, after that distasteful mini riot, he was bundled into an *Evening Citizen* car. It was nasty stuff, although there was a moment of humour when it was reported that, at the height of the action, a man with a broken leg was flaying out at all and sundry with his crutch.

The event became notorious in newspaper history and led to a judgement by Lord Clyde on how cases in Scotland should be handled by the press. Modified over the years, Lord Clyde's strictures still affect press coverage to this day. The modern Press Complaints Commission also has something to say about such unseemly cheque-book journalism and criminals profiting from their actions, though it should be remembered that Scott Ellis was innocent – at least in this case.

Later, he ended up in Peterhead in the 1960s for a bank robbery he committed along with John 'Bat' Neeson and James McIntyre. (Neeson's nickname was not a reference to his skill with that weapon of choice for the Glasgow hard man, the baseball bat, – rather it was an acknowledgement of his poor eyesight!) In the Big House up in the north east, Walter Scott Ellis spent many hours in gentler pastimes than had been his wont when out on the streets – he took up marquetry and became an accomplished exponent of the art.

F

FERRIS, PAUL

Probably the most visible of the modern era gangsters, Ferris was born in Blackhill – a housing scheme described in one *Herald* report as a 'foul crime nursery in the north east of the city'. In a TV documentary of 1995, Ferris said, 'If anyone was born into crime it was me. Crime is in my blood.' Chilling. He now claims to have turned against life as a law breaker and is, instead, penning fiction.

At one time, he acted as an enforcer for the Thompson clan and was an erstwhile friend of the family. Ferris liked to present a well-dressed image, mostly appearing in sharp suits and collar and tie. If the sun decided to take a peak through the usual dark clouds that hang over this city, designer shades would be his accessory of choice. The image is vastly different from the sweatshirt and base-ball cap of some of his dangerous contemporaries. The fashionable approach to his line of business is a trait he seems to have acquired from his old mentor, The Godfather, Arthur Thompson Snr. Thompson liked to mix pinstripes and the demeanour of a business-man with complete and violent control of what was perhaps the biggest criminal enterprise the city has seen.

Ferris had a classic career in big city crime and became a godsend to the tabloids. For years, they built up their circulation figures on the back of his escapades and controversies. But, in 2004, this undoubtedly quick-witted and intelligent man adamantly told any reporter who would listen that he was now on the right side of the law. He had sufficient gall – a gall that complements his self-confidence and ability to express himself – to suggest that, now he was back in the security business, one of his prime motivations in life was to help other ex-offenders into the business. He said, 'I am, at present, looking into the provisions of the Rehabilitation Act for the employment of ex-offenders as consultants within the security sector.' Of himself, he said, 'I can see no reason why I can't be a director [of a security firm]. Nor can I see any reason, legal or otherwise, that can prevent me earning a living, albeit in a controversial industry.' He had the humour to add, 'But then I have always been a controversial sort of guy.' The aforementioned gall extended to an intention to tender for security contracts on offer from the city council!

He could, at least, claim to have a long connection with the sometimes murky world of security. His first foray into the industry ended dramatically in 1998. In July of that year, he was jailed for ten years at the Old Bailey after being found guilty of a number of charges involving the supply of weapons such as submachine guns, shotguns, handguns, ammunition and explosives. The sentence was later reduced to seven years on appeal and he was freed in January 2002 after serving almost five years.

But the drama of the Old Bailey in London had been preceded by even more spectacular courtroom happenings back home in Scotland. In March 1992, when only twenty-eight years old, but still showing his passion for the business suit rather than the tracksuit, he stood in the dock for what was the longest running murder trial in Scottish criminal history at that time. Unofficial estimates put the cost of this High Court extravaganza, which lasted for fifty-four days, at £750,000. The trial was a headline-grabbing mixture of sex, drugs, humour, violence and tragedy, with three hundred witnesses cited to appear.

The charges Paul Ferris faced were:

1. The supply of heroin, cocaine and ecstasy
2. Attempting to murder Arthur Thompson Snr by repeatedly driving a car at him in May 1990
3. Conspiring to assault John 'Jonah' McKenzie on 26 May 1991
4. Shooting William Gillen in the legs and threatening to murder him

5. Murdering Arthur Thompson Jnr in 1991 while acting with Robert Glover and Joseph Hanlon
6. Illegal possession of a firearm
7. Breach of the Bail Act

Paul Ferris was found not guilty on all charges and emerged from the High Court to make a famous 'walk' to freedom.

The weeks of the trial had provided a fascinating glimpse into the underworld. Hundreds of thousands of words were spoken in the search for justice – it is said that one *Herald* reporter filled forty notebooks! The productions in the trial formed a demonstration of the deadly world that the victims and perpetrators of crime inhabited. They included a bullet-proof vest, several firearms, ammunition and cartridge cases.

The successful defence and clearing of Ferris on all charges was a mighty victory for his legal team which was led by the redoubtable Donald Findlay QC. In his final address, Findlay eloquently touched on the length of the case, observing to the jury that, during Ferris's trial, 'the seasons have come and gone, a general election has been won and lost, royal marriages have waxed and waned'. The trial judge, Lord McCluskey, had listened to much rhetoric during the long days of evidence, claim and counter-claim. He described the case as 'an extraordinary catalogue of lies, deceit, cruelty and death'.

The stories from the court gave newspaper readers an inside view of the criminal depravity involved in the struggle for the control of the drugs scene. One witness described a package of heroin as 'many happy days'. Another blamed drink and drugs for his unhelpful amnesia concerning certain matters. And, in a link with the Ice-Cream Wars, there was talk of vans being firebombed and used to sell drugs to children on street corners.

To the man in the street, it was also notable how well turned out many of the witnesses were and their ability to finance mobile phones and fancy foreign holidays on what appeared to be meagre handouts from the taxpayer was not appreciated.

But there was humour on display as well as drama and tragedy – laughter in court, as they say. One hardened criminal described a fellow lowlifer as 'not a very nice person' and, when asked to clarify this comment, he blurted out, 'He's a fucking toerag!' Another witness claimed that a woman who gave a statement was an alcoholic and 'at the time she spoke to the polis she wasn't compos mental'.

Even the bench got involved in some light-hearted banter about, of all things, chess strategy. Apparently, in the Bar-L, it was the habit of some inmates to enjoy this age-old test of intellect, shouting the moves to each other's cells. Paul Ferris showed his mental agility here, too, winning, it is said, £500 in one game. Lord McCluskey gave a moment or so of his time to discuss castling with the accused. The judge's wry humour as well as his humanity showed in an exchange with another witness who, it was said, left in some haste for a holiday 'doon the watter' at Irvine and, in his rush, he had neglected to take any luggage. Lord McCluskey inquired incredulously, 'Didn't he bring a beach towel?'

But there was deadly drama in the various interrogations of witnesses. One of the most remarkable figures in the witness box was Dennis David Woodman, who was once a police informer in England. In acknowledgement of his services and to ensure him some measure of safety in case anyone might take exception to the fact that he had helped the cops in criminal matters, he had had a new identity created for him in Scotland. However, Woodman was soon in trouble north of the border and tasting life in the Bar-L. There, he met Ferris and claimed that Ferris had admitted to him that he had shot The Fat Boy, as Arthur Thompson Snr's elder son was commonly called. The exchange was said to have taken place in snatched conversations between an exercise area and the cells. Some witnesses said that such conversations were possible but others said it would have never have happened. Woodman was a difficult witness. His evidence lasted nineteen hours and fifty minutes and, during this extensive grilling, he showed flashes of temper – even, on one occasion, trying to rile Donald Findlay over the QC's well-documented support of Rangers Football Club.

Ferris denied having the conversations and described Woodman as 'no competition'. Lord McCluskey gave Woodman a lot of rope and, for a spell, tolerated his bad behaviour though, in the end, he warned him about it, saying he had allowed him to act as he did in the box in order to show the court what kind of person he was. This subdued Woodman and his credibility as a believable witness was further eroded when his claim that his two children had been killed in a car crash proved to be false. The truth that they were alive came out by accident in a question to his half brother.

On Thursday 11 June 1992, the jury retired to consider its verdict. They spent the night in hotels and returned to deliver their verdict at 3.30 p.m. on the Friday afternoon. Ferris, smartly dressed as usual, listened as the clerk asked the jury if they had agreed on the verdict. The quiet unemotional reply was, 'Yes.' When the jury spokesman was asked the verdict on the first four charges, he added, 'Not guilty by a majority.' The next charge was the crunch one – the accusation that Ferris, with Glover and Hanlon, had killed Arthur Thompson Jnr. A cry of delight and some muffled applause spread through the court as the spokesman announced a unanimous verdict of not guilty. Ferris was also acquitted on the charges relating to the illegal possession of a firearm and breaching the Bail Act too.

The court reports the next day spoke of Donald Findlay turning round to congratulate a visibly drained Ferris. Lord McCluskey told Ferris he was free to go and thanked the jury for their service. He went on to say it was not the practice in Scotland for the judge to comment in any way on the judgement of the jury but he told them that it was plain to see that, on the murder charge, they had 'wholly rejected the evidence of Woodman'.

Clearly the dismissal of the Woodman tales played a major role in freeing Ferris but Donald Findlay had had other good cards to play – especially where the charge of shooting William 'Gillie' Gillen was concerned. He made much of what he called the Crown's 'failure to call a key witness'. This was one Tam McGraw whose story is told elsewhere in this book. McGraw was alleged to be the instigator of Gillen being shot in the legs in a lay-by on the Glasgow–Kilmarnock Road. He was not called to the witness box. Donald Findlay told the court that Gillen had claimed that McGraw was there on the night of the shooting and that he had ordered it. He went on to say, 'McGraw was supposed to be a participant and he is Crown witness number 214 – and yet the Crown never called him. If you leave a gap like that, it is too much to ask you to ignore it.'

The trial also saw Arthur Thompson Snr get some headlines and grab a final spot in the limelight. He took it with some panache. Asked if he was a criminal overlord in Glasgow, he seemed almost hurt. He said that it was all nonsense. He joked he would have to stuff his mouth with cotton wool and talk like Don Corleone. He said his son's conviction on drug charges was a police fit-up. Was The Fat Boy's murder anything to do with a drugs war? Nothing at all! Thompson told the court that he received £93 a week invalidity benefit as a result of one of several attempts to assassinate him years before. It is interesting that he was far from unique among the gang leaders and members in extracting as much as possible from social services no matter how prosperous their criminal enterprises were. Even when the criminal proceeds were rolling in, it seems that no state benefit was too small to collect.

If, on this occasion, 'Wee Paul Ferris', as some in the underworld are bold enough to call him, escaped a spell behind bars, it was only a temporary respite. As mentioned earlier, he was jailed in England and sentenced to ten years which was then reduced to seven on appeal. It is a measure of Ferris's reputation as a dangerous hard man – a reputation he earned during his rise from being Thompson's foot soldier to becoming a major criminal – that, at the end of the Old Bailey trial, *The Herald* could editorialise thus: 'The vast majority of those to whom the name Paul Ferris means anything will be, frankly, disappointed that Judge Henry Blacksell was unable to send him down for fifteen years. But tariffs are tariffs.' The leader continued in the same vein saying, 'We are well pleased that and relieved that Ferris, a ruthless professional criminal, in Judge Blacksell's phrase, will be off the streets of Glasgow for six and a half years.' The leader writer then made elegant reference to that famous earlier 'walk' to freedom down the steps of the High Court in Glasgow. 'Cleared of the charge of murdering Arthur "Fat Boy" Thompson, the gangster, given the sobriquet "Houdini", is now in figurative chains but behind real bars where he belongs.'

But, before all this, with the Glasgow High Court accusations behind him, Paul Ferris continued to make headlines in England as well as Scotland. When Thompson Snr succumbed to a heart attack – ironically, natural causes claimed his life, something Arthur's many enemies had tried to do many times and failed – Ferris was in demand by reporters in search of a meaty quote or two. Paul Ferris, aka 'Baby Face', another of his nicknames, did not disappoint. Shifting into Mafia Don mode in true B-movie style, he said:

> My only regret is not having spoken to him. I did try to do so after the trial but a meeting could not be set up. I really did not get the opportunity to clear things up – and I will not now.

It might have been an interesting meeting if it had happened. There would have been much for the two big-time criminals to discuss and remember. At one time, Ferris, making his bloody and violent way in the criminal world, was said to have been treated like a member of the family by old Arthur. And he was, for a spell, close to the doomed young Arthur. Ferris had been brought up in Blackhill, near the Thompsons' home, and, for a time, worked in the old man's garage. The 'day jobs' of the aspiring young gangster were as a second-hand car salesman and dabbling in double-glazing. And, before he fell out with The Fat Boy, Ferris made the odd prison visit to console young Arthur. The Fat Boy was unhappy that, despite his connections, his reputation as a hard man was under threat from his more successful criminal pals on the outside who were making big money as enforcers or drug dealers.

Ferris was growing in underworld stature and, by 1993, he was making headlines in England. His name cropped up in a trial about a failed bank robbery in Devon. There was talk that the volatile Scot was the mastermind behind the raid but he never stood trial for it. Although he never appeared, the jury in this trial heard a selection of lurid tales of the merciless methods used by Glasgow gangsters. These included executions in which the victim would be shot in the buttocks and the head. All this gave credence to the existence of the 'Glasgow goodbye'. In the late 1990s, there was said to be 'signature' killings in the city in which the victim was shot in the head and this was followed by a bullet up the anus – just in case or as warning and message to those in the know. Leggy blondes were also said to be used to seduce victims who were later informed that the tauntresses had, allegedly, been infected with the Aids virus. Elderly relatives of participants in gang wars were also said to have been threatened.

For Ferris, however, there was to be an English courtroom appearance on minor charges of drugs offences and he was fined £250 for possession of cocaine and cannabis. His lawyer claimed that the drugs were taken to help with a skin problem. The condition, said the bold Glaswegian, who was described as a second-hand car dealer in court, was brought on by stress. 'The drugs help me to relax but I am not a habitual user of the stuff,' he claimed. As he piled into a friend's Jaguar for the journey north from Manchester, he told the English hacks outside the court, 'I am no gangster. The last gangster in Scotland was Arthur Thompson.'

Hs ability to talk well made Ferris an attractive TV proposition. In 1995, he had a spectacular interview with John McVicar, once Britain's most wanted man but, by that time, a journalist and broadcaster. McVicar was told with a straight face that Ferris was a 'reformed criminal' who was being demonised in the eyes of the public. Ferris said then that he believed that he would die a violent death. In a preview of the programme, he had been asked if he believed he would end up on a mortuary slab. He took the chance to put the knife into his old enemy – the law. 'I think everyone ends up there some day but my biggest fear is that I will be put there by the police.' He has long claimed that he has been set up by certain sections in the police.

In the programme, Ferris claimed not to be a bully or a gangster but said that that doesn't mean you have got to let people stand on your toes. He added, 'If they do that, you have got to jump on their neck and break it.' He went on to give a chilling description of a way of life not unfamiliar to many youngsters in the east end. 'I've always used a weapon of sorts – whether it be a baseball bat or a knife.' The early days as a collector of 'dues' for old Arthur were also discussed.

But the cells doors that were to eventually shut in the face of Paul Ferris were not those of the two most likely destinations for most of Glasgow's hard men – Barlinnie or Peterhead. He was soon to taste the English penal system in London's top security jail Belmarsh, known as 'Helmarsh' to the English crims. It was the place that had played host to such characters as Ronnie Biggs and Jeffrey Archer, as well as the cream of the London and Manchester gangs.

As noted, in July 1998, Ferris was found guilty of masterminding a shipment of guns and explosives. He was posing as a security expert when he was caught red-handed after a massive two-year operation by detectives working for what was known at the time as the National Crime Squad. This was a major success for inter-force cooperation by the police – something that is, in 2004, a matter of much concern for the authorities. After a series of recent high-profile mix-ups concerning English forces, there are now plans afoot to create a sort of British FBI.

But the cooperation of the 1990s worked well enough to catch Paul Ferris. For the dapper gangster from the east end of Glasgow, it meant a day in the metaphorical footlights of England's most famous criminal stage, the Old Bailey. Ferris was convicted of trafficking in submachine guns and explosives. Judge Henry Blacksell said Ferris had 'arranged, paid for and taken delivery of a lethal parcel of weapons'. And he hardly dared speculate on the potential for death and destruction they might have caused had they reached their criminal destination. 'I have no doubt you are a dangerous and ruthless professional criminal. Those who choose to deal in such arms can only expect prison sentences of great length.'

Glasgow police officers were present when armed surveillance teams swooped on Ferris and his associates. The police had followed as the gang's Nissan Prairie headed north through London's west end. The destination of the guns was not known for sure although a senior police source told newspapermen that the weapons – three 9-mm Mac 10 submachine guns, capable of firing 1100 rounds a minute – 'had limited application to the Scottish drug scene'. This seemed to indicate a northern English city, such as Manchester, as the destination. Manchester was, at the time, in the middle of some bloody drug wars.

All this was a long way from the baseball bat of Ferris's youth. Chief Inspector Peter Splinder underlined the seriousness of the case when he said, 'If these military weapons had found their way into the hands of the criminal underworld, the consequences could have been devastating.' Ferris claimed that he had been duped and that he thought that the boxes that had been found by the police had contained counterfeit bank notes and plates, not weapons which, he said, must have been put there by someone else. It was a sort of a 'a big boy did it and ran away' plea and it just didn't wash. He was on his way to jail.

On his release, he claimed on TV and in newspapers that he had gone straight. But there were a couple of minor interludes that resulted in a further short spell in the nick. Again, on release, he claimed to have turned over a new leaf. He still does.

FINDLAY, DONALD, QC

This lawyer and author is one of Scotland's most celebrated modern-day pleaders with a remarkable string of successes in defending those accused of the ultimate crime – murder. He's the man who walks in the footsteps of, and creates similar headlines to, Laurence Dowdall and Joe Beltrami. But he has a very different background from his legendary predecessors. He is the grandson of a miner from Cowdenbeath and proud of it.

His interest in the law started not by reading the accounts of the great trials or thick leather-bound biographies of the famous defenders of the past. The road that was to end with Donald Findlay treading the boards of Scotland's highest criminal courts began when, as a small boy in Fife, he watched a snowy black-and-white TV series called *Boyd QC*. Findlay says, 'He was a bewigged defender of the underdog and I thought, away back then, "That'll do for me." – or sentiments to that effect.'

The desire to be centre stage in the great trials was further stimulated by the trial of Peter Manuel in 1958. The newspapers of the day devoted thousands of pages and millions of words to this epic trial and Donald Findlay read most of them. He has written that his much-loved father was a bit dubious about the youngster's interest in all the lurid details of crimes of violence. But, in his own defence, the young Donald convinced his father that, if anyone was to profit from human misery, it might as well be him. It was a pragmatic argument that convinced Findlay Snr that the boy was on the right lines career-wise.

Another influence was Jack House's book, *Square Mile of Murder* (Edinburgh: Chambers, 1961). When Donald Findlay came upon it by chance in a bookshop many years go, House's reputation as an expert in Scottish trivia – a reputation burnished by umpteen appearances on the amateurish television programmes of that era – made him hesitate to spend his then meagre resources on the book. But he found it fascinating, a deep read. Starting it in the afternoon of the day he bought it, he continued straight through to the end at five the next morning. 'By the end of the week I had read it again,' he says.

His take on the four Glasgow crimes that make up the book, which is still a great read today, is interesting. He is slightly ambivalent on Madeleine Smith's guilt or innocence but quotes a remark reputedly attributed to Ms Smith's defence counsel, after she had been acquitted of poisoning her lover – 'She's a bonny lass but I wouldn't take supper with her.'

On Jessie McLachlan, he is more direct, believing she was incorrectly convicted of murder. This is largely because, in those days, there was an assumption that, if there was a choice between a lower-class person and an upper-class person as the perpetrator of a crime, the lower-class person was more likely to be the guilty one. In Jessie's case, she was the lower-class person and she was convicted of murder while the probable killer of servant Jess McPherson, Old Fleming, was upper class.

The conviction of Dr Edward Pritchard for poisoning his wife gave Findlay no cause for doubt. 'The Human Crocodile', as Pritchard came to be known, due to the false tears he wept over the body of his dead wife – deserved to die on the gallows.

As far as the verdict in the Oscar Slater trial is concerned, Findlay says, 'His conviction for a crime he did not commit still stands as a permanent stain on the legal system, the police and the fraudulent morality of Victorian Glasgow.'

Over the years, Donald Findlay's career as a defence lawyer has created many headlines and sold many newspapers. His success rate is remarkable and anyone charged with murder could at least take some satisfaction that, if Findlay was in his or her corner, the prosecution case would be fought with skill and great knowledge – knowledge of the law, human nature and, most importantly perhaps, the way juries think. The Sherlock Holmes pipe, the glistening cufflinks, the teddy bear ties and mutton chop whiskers that make Donald Findlay instantly recognisable also disguise a brilliant legal mind.

One of the most spectacular defences was that of Paul Ferris who stood trial in 1992. Along with Bobby Glover and Joe 'Bananas'

Hanlon – who were both killed before the trial took place – he was accused of the murder of Arthur Thompson Jnr. This was, at the time, the longest running trial in Scottish criminal history and it lasted fifty-four days. This remarkable trial, dealt with in depth elsewhere in this book, ended in a legal victory that will long be remembered in the city. It resulted in Paul Ferris, then a baby-faced twenty-eight-year-old with the demeanour of a well-dressed businessman, being found not guilty on all charges – just one of many successful defences for Donald Findlay.

Findlay is a complex man with interests other than the law. He learned how to pilot planes and likes to spend weekend afternoons at Ibrox Park, watching the Rangers play football. Maybe this explains some of his successes with accused and jurors alike. He is, like Joe Beltrami, a man who understands ordinary folk and who is not overly impressed by the robes, the wigs, the intricacies and the semantics of the law – he is a man with the common touch.

However, this man-of-the-people approach did get him into a major spat when, some years ago, he was unknowingly secretly filmed joining other Rangers fans in singing 'The Sash' and 'Follow, Follow', both considered sectarian songs, at a supporters' function to celebrate the team's winning of the Scottish Cup. A fuzzy picture ended up on the front page of a tabloid and the outcry lasted for weeks – at one stage threatening Findlay's very career. The furore it created temporarily knocked this mentally strong man for six. In defence of his part in the singsong, he said he felt he had not done anything terribly wrong. 'I have always been pro the fans – just a bluenose – and I joined in.' He had to resign as vice-chairman of Rangers FC and there were calls – every lawyer accumulates some enemies – for him to be expelled from the Faculty of Advocates. But the majority of his legal colleagues rallied round and he found support from the man in the street. In interviews and letters to the press, it was pointed out that those who knew him considered him to be a completely non-sectarian person. Joe Beltrami, that wise old Sage of West Nile Street, put it succinctly, 'He made a mistake but has learned from it over the past few months. This whole matter must now be brought to an end in the interests of fairness.'

Glasgow has a big heart and proof of this was evidenced in the letters of support Donald Findlay got from Celtic supporters and Catholic organisations. Findlay rode out the storm and resumed his legal career a wiser man. He was soon back striding the city streets with his head held high and ready to exchange banter with the Glaswegians to whom he was such an instantly recognisable and high-profile figure.

The whole episode demonstrated the down-to-earth approach of this remarkable lawyer. He takes his cases exceptionally seriously, admitting that he seldom sleeps the night before a final address to the jury. He says, 'The day I stand up and address a jury and my stomach isn't churning, then I will just turn on my heel and walk out of court and never come back.' Such commitment must surely be of great comfort and support to those anguished folk facing the might of the law and trial by jury.

FOY, JOHN

In the 1940s and 1950s, Foy was a street fighter, bouncer and general hard man. His partner in crime was Joe O'Hara and together they became known as the Kings of the **GARSCUBE ROAD**. A fearsome duo, they commanded great respect from the gangs and criminals of the area, which was often referred to by its denizens as the **HIGH ROAD**. Foy came from **CAITHNESS STREET** and O'Hara from **LYON STREET**, a stone's throw from the old **ROUND TOLL**. Both these characters had learned to fight in bare-knuckle battles on the banks of the Forth and Clyde canal and in a place called the 'Piggy'. The Piggy was an area not far from the Round Toll where, in the early 1930s, the remnants of farming near the city centre were to be found. It consisted of a few scruffy acres of open land where the odd pig or two could root around in the mud and a cow could do its best to graze on any surviving grass. When this 'agriculture' finally ended, the old name hung on.

The illegal fights that Foy and O'Hara engaged in drew large crowds and much fame was attached to the winners of such battles – which were bloody and dangerous affairs outwith the Queensberry Rules and without the benefit of doctors or ambulance men. The fights, termed 'square jigs', were often arranged to settle disputes that had been spawned during drunken nights in the proliferation of pubs round about. The police generally let the hard men get on with the business of resolving their own quarrels. The combatants were often very skilful and it is said that many went on to defeat big-name fighters in the more sanitised arena of professional boxing.

In their heyday, as they strutted the streets of Maryhill, Foy and O'Hara were given much respect, by all they met, for their prowess with their fists. And the fame of their criminal exploits made them undesirable role models for the youngsters of the area. They regularly acted as bouncers at the old Tower Ballroom, at the Round Toll, where the patrons would usually have been well refreshed in the local pubs before arriving for a spot of dancin'. Often the men would be tooled up with knives, or sometimes worse, ready to fight over the favours of some particularly glamorous female, and it would fall to the likes of Foy and O'Hara to ensure that the 'best of order' was kept amongst the dancers.

FULLERTON, WILLIAM

Although he was the leader of the Bridgeton Billy Boys in the 1930s, the infamous gang were not named after him. The gang took their name from William of Orange. It was born out of a dispute during a football match on Glasgow Green in 1924 when a handful of Bridgeton tearaways got together to take on their enemies. In its heyday, the gang had around 800 members, many of them recruited from the tenements of **MAIN STREET**. But their infamy and the attraction of their sectarian warfare was such that they also recruited from areas like Coatbridge, Airdrie and Cambuslang.

A dangerous, violent man, Fullerton led what was virtually a private army. They drilled and marched and their flute band was a sound feared by Catholics on the streets. At the end of meetings, the band would take themselves off to **BRIDGETON CROSS** for a final playing of 'God Save the King' as a reminder to those who didn't know (not many, it must be admitted) what their Protestant affiliations were all about. They battled with their enemies, mostly the Norman Conks and the Calton Entry, on **GLASGOW GREEN** and **RUTHERGLEN BRIDGE**.

The open razor was just one of many fearsome weapons. Hammers, hatchets, bayonets from the First World War, bottles, lead-filled sticks, bolts on the end of ropes and bicycle chains, often filed sharper to maim and scar even more effectively, were all popular weapons of choice. The fist and the boot were also put to regular use.

The chief constable of the time, Sir Percy Sillitoe, had a grudging regard for Fullerton as a general and organiser and felt that, had he chosen a path other than that of gang leader, he would have made his mark on society a much more positive one than it was.

Fullerton thought about what was driving his men – apart from their sectarian beliefs – and concluded that the massive levels of unemployment of the day had much to do with his successful recruitment rate – fighting on the streets was one antidote to the boredom of unemployment. Gangs on both sides would turn up at the 'buroo' – a Glaswegian corruption of Unemployment Bureau – waiting for the opposition to arrive to claim the government's shilling. Pitched battles occurred, with men having to fight their way in and out of the offices.

But he didn't believe that unemployment was the sole cause. He reflected that the young enjoyed the excitement of fighting for its own sake. And he theorised that they liked discipline. The Billy Boys met regularly in a hall in **LONDON ROAD** and Billy Fullerton was their parade-ground sergeant major. He told a reporter, 'I drilled them like a battalion of soldiers. Many of them had already experienced discipline in borstal and I took advantage of that fact.'

Money was not a problem. The organisation had secret bank accounts that were accessible only to Fullerton and two of his lieutenants. Some of the considerable amounts of cash involved came from thieving and protection money but the members themselves had membership cards and paid a weekly sum into the coffers. Some of this stash was used to buy instruments for the band which was a very popular way of keeping the troops amused between street battles. The Billy Boys took every opportunity to play their inflammatory music in those streets that were known to be where Catholic homes were predominant.

They even went as far as organising a trip to Belfast. There the taunting of people of a different faith had reached a high point of development and the Billy Boys thought they could learn a thing or two in the home of bigotry. It is no surprise that, although the visit was deemed to be a success musically, two members of the gang were involved in shooting incidents. The band was important to the ethos of the gang and even Sir Percy acknowledged that they were 'genuine musicians in a rough sort of way'.

In later life, Fullerton tended to wear rose-coloured spectacles when he examined his memory of the battling days. He opined that, if you didn't wear 'party colours' or show too obviously on which side of the religious divide you stood, then you were safe. This was true up to a point but bigotry doesn't mix well with hammers and razors and often the merest hint of a green affiliation was enough to trigger violence. And, of course, it wasn't just down to the Billy boys – the Conks were gang men of a similar stripe when it came to initiating street rumbles.

One newspaper tale of the time illustrates the savage climate of hate in the east end. At a church wedding, the groom stood before the minister with a sword concealed in his formal dress. The best man had a gun in his pocket. Fullerton himself attended with his head swathed in blood-stained bandages covering fifteen stitches, a souvenir of a battle a few days previously. Outside the church, the Calton Entry Mob waited for the ceremony to end and, as the guests spilled out, there was a running battle till the Billy Boys reached the sanctuary of the Masonic hall in **STRUTHERS STREET**. Here, the reception then proceeded as if nothing had happened.

This little episode involving the Calton Entry is illuminating. They were primarily a Catholic gang – hence the desire to wreck a Billy-Boy wedding. But they also had Protestant members. Indeed, at one time, one of their best-known fighters was not a Catholic.

In the late 1930s, the grip of the Billy Boys as a gang weakened – although their sectarian philosophy remained as strong as ever. This was a direct result of Sir Percy Sillitoe's hard-men cops – known as 'The Untouchables' – and his mounted police squads – known as 'Sillitoe's Cossacks' – having aggressively attacked the Billy Boys' marches and diluted their power base. But there was a dark footnote to the history of this gang.

Fullerton, known as King Billy, went on to join the British Union of Fascists and became a section commander with 200 men and women under his command. This episode in his life later became another victim of the rose-coloured-spectacles routine and some strictly selective memory. In the 1950s, he was telling the papers that, despite his affiliation with his sinister black-shirted friends in Oswald Mosley's party, he 'couldn't give you a definition of a fascist to this day. It just seemed a good thing to be in at the time.' It would appear that the movement's anti-Semitism and their open support for Hitler had passed him by.

The erosion of Fullerton's authority, which had started with the defeats at the hands of the police in street battles, was exacerbated with his arrest in remarkable circumstances. A copper spotted him on his own patch surrounded by men and carrying a baby (whose it was or why he was cradling it in his arms are not recorded). A singularly brave PC asked him to put it down and, when he refused, the officer accused him of being drunk in charge of a baby. A riot ensued but the outnumbered police won through. The era of King Billy Fullerton was ending.

This keynote figure in the history of crime in Glasgow spawned something of a lawless dynasty. Fullerton's son died in a stabbing in **JAMES STREET**, Bridgeton, in 1994 and a grandson was involved in a shooting in the **CANDLERIGGS**.

Fullerton himself died in 1962, aged seventy-five, and was given a real gangland send-off. The police were out in force and they must have been glad to see the back of a man who had caused them so much trouble down the years. Around a thousand gathered to watch to the funeral party leave a Bridgeton tenement for Riddrie Park Cemetery. In a symbolic touch, the cortege stopped the traffic at Bridgeton Cross, the scene of so many bloody battles between the Conks and the Billy Boys. For part of the way, a flute band led the procession.

G

GANG NAMES

It is extremely doubtful whether a complete list of gang names in Glasgow can be found. The police keep a note of names – not least those that feature on the ugly graffiti that defaces so many walls in public spaces. Sadly they add new names to the list almost on a daily basis. Some gangs are large and dangerous and some consist of just a few wild youths out for trouble. The names listed here are simply those mentioned in the books, documents and newspapers that I consulted, over many years, doing research for this book and my previous books on crime in the city. Some gangs would be in existence for just a few weeks. At the other end of the spectrum were gangs with membership that ran into hundreds and whose malign influence could haunt an area for years or even decades. There are gangs not mentioned in the list at all – gangs can exist without being chronicled in the papers or meeting a social worker! Or even a policeman!

A
Aggro
Anderston
Antique Mob – Shettleston
Apaches
Argyle Billy Boys – Bridgeton
      (Hosier Street)

B
Baltic Fleet – Bridgeton
Bal Toi – Easterhouse
Bar G – Bargeddie
Bar L – Barlanark
Barlanark Team

Bath – Anderston
Beehive – Gorbals
Bell On Boys
Big Doe Hill
Billy Boys – Bridgeton Cross
Bingo Boys – Govan
Biro Minors – Bridgeton
Bishopbriggs Toi
Bison – Bishopbriggs
Black Diamond Boys – south side
Black Hand
Blackhill Toi
Black Muffler – Clydebank
Black Star – Calton

Blade – Eastfield
Bloodhound Flying Corps
Blue Angels
Border – Tollcross/Parkhead
Bowrie – Whiteinch
Brig Ahoy
Brigade – Bridgegate
Brigton Derry – Bridgeton
Buck – Drumchapel
Bundy – Priesthill
Butny Boys – Maryhill
BYC (Busby Young Cumbie)

C
Cadder Young Team
Calton Emmet – Stevenson Street/Abercrombie Street
Calton Entry Mob – Tollcross
Castlemilk Cumbie
Castlemilk Fleet
Castlemilk Toi
Castlemilk Young Team
Cheeky Forty – Roystonhill
Choirboys – Scotsoun
Coburg Erin
Coby Heind Team – Ruchazie
Cody – Queenslie
Corner Boys – Blackhill
Cowboys – Dennistoun
Cow Toi – Cowcaddens
Craigton Goucho
Crossy Posse – Govan
Cumbie – Gorbals

D
Dally Boys – Dalmarnock Road
Death Valley Boys
Dempsey Boys – Govan
Den Toi – Easterhouse
Derry Boys – Bridgeton
Dickie – Bridgeton

Diehards – Govan
Dirty Dozen – south side
Drummie – Easterhouse
Drygate Youths
Dumbarton Riot Squad

E
Easterhouse Derry

F
Fenian Drummy – Drumchapel

G
Gaucho
Gestapo – Dennistoun
Ging Gong
Gold Dust Gang – Gorbals
Goucho – Carntyne
Govan Team
Gray Street Billy Boys
Gringo – Barmulloch
Gyto - Garthamlock

H
Haghill Toi
Hall Boys – Bridgeton
Hammer Boys – south side
Haugh Boys - Partick
Hazel Boys – Bridgeton
Hi-Hi's – Mile End
Himshie – Cambuslang
Hole-in-the-head
Hutchie – Gorbals/Polmadie

I
ICF (Inter City Firm)

J
Joytown – George Street/Shuttle Street
Jungo Boys – Possilpark

K
Kelly Boys
Kelly Boys – Govan
Kelly Bow – Govan
Kent Star – Calton
Kill Me Deads
Kinning Park Rebels (KPR)
Kinning Park Stud
Ku Klux Klan – Bridgeton

L
Lady Buck – Drumchapel
Liberty Boys – Gorbals
Lollipops – George Street/Shuttle
    Street.

M
McGlyn Push – south side
McGrory Boys – Bridgegate
Maryhill Fleet
Maryhill Young Team
Mealy Boys – south side
Milligan Boys – Anderston
Milton Tongs
Monks – Dennistoun
Monty Boys – Mongomery Street,
    Dalmarnock
Mummies

N
Naburn Billies
Norman Conks – Bridgeton
Nudies – Errol Street
Nuneaton Conks – Nuneaton
    Street/Parkhead
Nunnie Boys – Bridgeton

P
Pak – Easterhouse
Parlour Boys
Peachy Boys – London Road

Peg – Springburn
Pen – Bridgeton
Penny Mob – Townhead
Port Toi – Port Dundas
Possil
Powrie – Dennistoun

Q
Queenslie Fleet
Queenslie Rebels
Queen Street Posse – city centre

R
Rebels – Easterhouse
Rebels – Rutherglen
Redskins – south side
Romeos – Garngard
Royston Shamrock
Rutherglen Fleet

S
Sally Boys – East End
San Toi – Calton
Scurvy
Shamrock – Germiston
Shanly Boys
Sheiks – Drygate
Sheilds
Sighthill Mafia
Silver Bell
Skinheads
Skull – Bridgeton and Cathcart
South Side Stickers
Spur
Spur 78 – Barrowfield
Star – Garthamlock
Stick-it

T
Tay – Castlemilk
Temple

Thistle – Queen Mary street.
Thrush – Townhead
Tigers – Shettleston
Tim Malloys
Tiny Glen – Rutherglen
Toi – Easterhouse
Tongs – Calton
Toon Tongs – Townhead/
    Garngad
Torch – Calton
Torran Toi – Easterhouse
Tradeston Rebels

U
Uncle – Ruchill

V
Valley – Maryhill
Village – Baillieston
Village Boys – south side
Vordo – Govan

W
Waverley Boys
Wee Doe Hill
Wee Men – Tollcross
Wee Mob – Garscube Road
Wild Team – Rutherglen
Wimpey – Dalmuir
Wine Alley – Govan

X
XYY – Govan/Garscube
    Road

Y
Yoker Toi
Young 41
Young Fernhill Team
Young Glen – Rutherglen
Young Rolland Boys (YRB)
    – Ruchill
YY Mods – Easterhouse

GILVEAR, BILL

A one-time gang member, he was converted to Christianity by a famous preacher called Seth Sykes in the unglamorous sur-roundings of the Tent Hall. This hall was so called because it was built in the days after the American revivalists, Moody and Sankey, who was also a composer and known as the 'singing pilgrim', had a highly successful late-nineteenth-century mission in a tent on the nearby Glasgow Green. Following his conversion, he devoted much of his life to evangelical work. He was a counsellor during Billy Graham's famous 1955 crusade in the city. Bill Gilvear was anxious to steer youngsters away from the early path he had taken and gave newspaper interviews that offered a distinctive insight into the old gangs. He had been a member of the Stick-it gang at fourteen and remembered, in those days, hiding up closes in the **GALLOWGATE** to dodge 'Holy Joes' who were intent on converting him.

But the conversion did come. His father had been a convert of the Tabernacle Church in **MARYHILL** but had died in an accident when Bill was ten. Following his father's death, the family had turned away from religion, living a hard life in the Gallowgate with 'feet sticking out of our soles, not two ha'pennies to rub together'. But, somehow, the lingering memory of his father's beliefs one day drew him to that famous old evangelical hall, near **GLASGOW CROSS**, and the preacher worked his magic to bring another soul back into the fold.

Bill's memories of life as a fourteen-year-old in the Stick-it recalled that the gang's main objective was to do its worst to its greatest rival gang, the San Toi. It was a training ground for lives that would lead to periodic stays in the Bar-L or worse – one member ended his life on the gallows there. In a 1991 interview, Bill was described as a gentle figure in a sports jacket and wearing pebble glasses. But his memories were vivid. He reached into his inside pocket and told an interviewer:

> This is where you kept your bicycle chain hidden. You pulled it out and a member of a rival gang got it against his face. And you took a safety razor blade and split it in two and that gave you a long thin blade. You hid it in the edge of your cap and, if someone said good evening to you, you could slit their throat from ear to ear. We were the terror of the east side of Glasgow.

They were appallingly bloody days and this account of them is all the more remarkable as it comes from such a man as Bill Gilvear. When he told his pals of his conversion, he was met with derision. 'You stupid, daft Holy Joe – you'll be back in a week.' His fellow gang members called that one wrong. Bill Gilvear went to Bible College and spent years in Africa as a missionary.

GLOVER, BOBBY AND HANLON, JOE 'BANANAS'

Along with Paul Ferris, these two gangland characters were alleged to have taken part in the killing of Arthur Thompson Jnr. Ferris appeared in the High Court on that and other charges and, after a lengthy trial, was declared innocent of the killing – and all the other charges thrown at him. Glover and Hanlon never made it as far as court – they were found dead in a blue Ford Orion car on the morning of Arthur Thompson Jnr's funeral. These were true Mafia-style killings – both in their timing and manner. It made a statement to the underworld, underlining the dangers facing those trying to muscle in on the current rackets and it was a precursor to the mayhem that was to follow on the death of old Arthur himself.

Who killed Glover and Hanlon is a mystery, according to the police who call the murders 'unsolved'. However, there were theories as to why they were killed. The first, and most simplistic, is that they were taken out in revenge for the death of young Arthur. The second theory is subtler – it suggests they were killed by their own associates in an effort to patch up relationships with the Thompson firm. Crime writer Reg McKay's biography of Thompson, *The Last Godfather* (Edinburgh: Black & White Publishing, 2004) claims Thompson personally executed the two gangsters in an act of revenge.

Both Glover and Hanlon were well known to the police – indeed, they had been warned that they were in the middle of a gangland dispute that could see them killed. They gave the cops' warning no attention and paid the price instead.

Shortly before the double murder, after an incident in which a man had been knee-capped, Glover, who was under suspicion for this crime, had been given bail. Hanlon was reputed to be an enforcer for the Barlanark Team. No matter what their connections were, no one in the east end was prepared to talk to the police or the press about their murders. Despite the spectacular nature of their demise and the huge tabloid headlines the double murder was generating, the cops ran into a wall of complete silence from relatives, neighbours and associates.

Their funerals were delayed, as is normal in such cases, while the police struggled to solve the mystery of their deaths. And, when Bobby Glover was eventually laid to rest in Old Monklands Cemetery in Coatbridge, there were ugly scenes as the relatives chased press photographers away. This was a time when many young men were dying in drug wars – it wasn't just users whose lives were at stake – and such scenes at funerals were not infrequent. The snappers were getting used to it. Earlier, at Bobby Glover's funeral service at Old Shettleston Church, the minister had told the congregation:

> Much has been written and said. We don't know what happened or the motive and I won't concern myself with them today. What we do know today is that the events have led to lots of pain, suffering and misery. A wife is without a husband, a little boy without a father, a mother without a son and a family without a brother.

Gangland funerals are a challenge to any preacher. But this was a look at the reality of the lives of those close to gang combatants.

There was a curious little sidebar to the story of Glover and Hanlon some five years later. Glover's mother saw fit to verbally attack no less than Paul Ferris. Ferris had placed an in memoriam announcement in the *Evening Times* to mark the fifth anniversary of Bobby Glover's death in that Ford Orion outside the Cottage Bar. Kathy Glover, clearly a forceful woman, was not impressed. She told reporters this was the kind of tribute folk can do without. She continued:

> Robert would be alive today if it wasn't for people like Paul Ferris. Why has he never stood on my floor if he is such a friend of my son? I knew nothing of my son's life but I knew he was up to no good. I always let him know I loved him as a son but didn't like what he did.

In reply to this emotional and honest outburst, Paul Ferris told reporters:

> I think I am speaking on behalf of both families. It is a time when both want to get on with their lives. I think the female members of the family want to put this behind them. The memorial was placed as a public recognition that it was a bad time of year for his friends as well. Every year the number of tributes gets less and less.

It would be hard to make it up!

H

HANLON, JOE 'BANANAS'
See under GLOVER, Bobby

HIGH RISK

Glasgow is famous for its splendid sandstone tenement flats. Both in the west end and the south side there are spectacular blocks of apartments. These are the survivors, the cream of the many thousands of such buildings that were at the heart of city life. From the turn of the nineteenth century, for seventy years or so, generations were raised 'up a close'. But the standard of comfort and the services in the tenements varied enormously. Many were crumbling and substandard with loos located on the stair landings. Typically, a close had four main landings and, on each landing, there could be eight single-end flats, sharing one landing toilet. Social workers called them 'castles of misery'.

By the late 1970s, most of such places had fallen victim to the bulldozers and the wrecker's ball. Their occupants were decanted to new homes on the fringe of the city where they lived in undeniably better housing but, for many years, they were denied access to pubs, libraries, swimming pools, cinemas etc. The move to the schemes was well intentioned but poorly thought out and, in the event, contributed to much of the crime generated in these areas.

The tenements that survived demolition were much better built and were designed with spacious rooms. The main room often has a huge bay window that allows maximum natural light in. With their high ceilings and inside toilets, they became highly desirable and began fetching huge prices. Often, particularly in the west end, the main front door is a beautiful affair, featuring stained glass, and the entry close mouth is attractively tiled. Refurbished with security doors and all mod cons, it is little wonder they are now in such demand.

But, as always in Glasgow, the lawbreaker even affects this market. The top-floor flats often have beautiful views over the rooftops and those facing west can look out on spectacular sunsets. But the top-floor flat also carries a higher risk of being broken in to. For more than a hundred years, burglars, and would-be burglars, have clocked that access to the flats in the middle of a tenement is difficult but, up top, the roof provides possible ways of entry and escape. However, the views from the top do compensate for the risk!

HILDREY, MIKE

Hildrey was a Commonwealth Games athlete, nicknamed the Balfron Bullet, who turned to journalism after his days on the running track ended. During the 1970s and 1980s, he became a long-serving and brave investigative *Evening Times* reporter, exposing many of the loan sharks and drug dealers who blighted the city and whose evil practices go on to this day. He also made exposing property scams and protection rackets one of his specialities. He flourished under the campaigning George McKechnie's reign as editor of the *Times*. It was McKechnie who encouraged Hildrey, and a succession of assistants assigned to him, to take on criminals and scam merchants of every stripe and he would allow the reporters time 'off diary' to give them the time and resources to do the job thoroughly.

Hildrey then left newspapers to concentrate on fiction and film-making, becoming an expert on the Scottish east-coast fishing scene. His novel, *Sharks* (Glendaruel: Argyll Publishing, 1996), based on his newspaper experiences, was praised for its gritty realism and accurate picture of the poverty and deprivation he had encountered in his years on the road as a reporter.

Loan sharking has been a dark Glasgow tradition since the

1920s and has always featured in the activities of the major gang leaders like Walter Norval and Arthur Thompson Snr. But, in the past, illegal moneylending was just part of the portfolio of crime for a gangster. Nowadays, many specialise in it and ignore all other criminal activities. This development led one respected news editor to bemoan to me that, these days, criminals are of much less intrinsic interest than those of the past. The current lot were dismissed by this observer as merely 'violent, greedy neds'. But they are still neds who are able to do considerable damage to society.

Even under the old gang leaders moneylending never descended to its current depths. Norval told me of his loan business and the horrendous rates of interest he extracted from those who turned to him for help. But, even at their height, those rates were miles away from what is now charged. One newspaper report recently said that trading standards investigators had found a case where a resident of a hostel for the homeless was charged 1,300,000 per cent. And the papers told of girls as young as fifteen being forced to work as prostitutes to pay off debts. At the end of 2003, it was estimated that there were more than sixty gangs of illegal lenders operating in the west of Scotland alone.

Once again, the leader writers were taking up that recurring newspaper cry of 'something must be done'. And a government initiative, in early 2004, targeted the loan sharks with undercover hit squads to stop the gangs who collect benefit books from those unfortunate enough to have had to turn to them for help. Once a week, the lenders hand out the books to enable their owners to collect cash. Large lumps of the cash are taken from them and the books collected to be held for the next week and the next pay-out day. It is a vicious circle that entraps the most vulnerable and, of course, any attempts to break out of it are met with violence. The old problem of life in an area ruled by force surfaces yet again.

Ian Wilson of the city's Consumer and Trading Standards Office has been quoted as saying, 'People are too scared to testify against the moneylenders. The loans are enforced through intimidation and that makes it difficult to get people to come forward.' Current investigators have found neds standing outside post offices, their pockets bulging with other people's benefit books, and taking as much as £100 from someone who had borrowed just a tenner.

The idea of the new scheme is to tackle it in a different way from that used by the police in the past. Up to a couple of million pounds is being poured into the scheme and the loan-shark hunters are expected to gather the evidence necessary under the Proceeds of Crime Act to strip lenders of illegal profits. And there are plans to tackle one of the main problems associated in the past with crackdowns on moneylenders. When a lender was arrested, it merely removed him or her from the streets, leaving the folk who had borrowed from them still in deep trouble. The only option they had was to turn helplessly to new illegal lenders who popped up to fill the gap in the market that had appeared. Now, the idea is that local authorities will have money and plans at the ready to plug the gaps legally. Money advisers and access to credit unions are also to be provided. Will it all work? Who knows?

The complexity and extent of the problem is shown by a report that found that the average debtor owed up to £10,000 to six different creditors. Whatever happens, much of the credit for the new moves has its roots in the activities of Mike Hildrey and others like him who risked their lives and the well-being of themselves and their families to highlight a major problem.

I

ICE-CREAM WARS

The city's name is inescapably linked to the horrific saga of the so-called Ice-Cream Wars of the 1980s and, in particular, the massacre of the Doyle family in **BANKEND STREET, RUCHAZIE**, in 1984, in a deadly fire-bombing. The complexities and the horror of the case have attracted the attention of countless newspaper writers since and have also spawned films, books and TV programmes.

On the face of it, an ice-cream van, selling its wares on the street corner in schemes, seems harmless. The sound of its tinkling bell or its pre-recorded musical chimes is an invitation to children and adults alike to enjoy treat – a little relief, particularly in the bleak surroundings of the schemes, is always welcome. But life in Glasgow is never that simple. Those white vans tended to stock more than ice cream, confectionery, crisps, lemonade and the like. They sometimes had stolen liquor and cigarettes available at cut prices and, on occasion, they had more dangerous and malignant products on sale – drugs.

In Glasgow, drugs always mean bloody battles over their importation, price, delivery and on whose patch they end up. The ability of the humble ice-cream van to deliver drugs and launder the ill-gotten money that their sale accrued, while simultaneously running a legitimate business that attracted little attention from the police, was a massive lure for the city's hard men, always on the lookout for an easy touch.

For more than twenty years, the city has followed the saga of the Ice-Cream Wars. From the news of the fire that killed six people, including a baby of a year old, to the wrongful convictions of T C Campbell and Joe Steele for that dreadful act of murderous fire-raising, through their years of appeals and constant pleas of innocence, to the dramatic happenings of 2004, its citizens have been fascinated.

The case reached its penultimate climax on Wednesday 17 March that year when the Court of Appeal, sitting in Edinburgh, quashed the convictions and life sentences of Campbell and Steele – but only after they had spent sixteen years behind bars for a crime they did not commit. It was a remarkable finale to their ceaseless quest to prove their innocence. Back in 1984, Campbell and Steele had been no choirboys but the decision of Lords Gill, MacLean and Macfadyen to clear them implied that they had been victims of a police fit-up. It also posed the ultimate question – if it hadn't been Campbell and Steele, who did do it?

Because the fire had started in the wee, small hours, it was too early for the morning papers to report it. And few who did read the first sketchy newspaper stories, in the early editions of the *Evening Times*, realised what lay behind a seemingly not all that unusual fire on a sink estate. Such fires often involved fatalities and they were meat and drink to the *Times* reporters on the hunt for a front-page lead. But the full scale of this particular tragedy – the death toll and its implications for the reputation of both the city and the name of justice in Scotland – came later, as it leached out over the years in ugly stories, with accusations and counter-accusations.

Bankend Street had long been a source of headlines of the wrong type for the residents. There were sixty-four houses in the street which could be glimpsed as an uninviting place by motorists speeding past on the nearby M8. If it was unappealing to the passer-by, it was a horrendous place for anyone unlucky enough to have to spend their days there. In the late 1970s, it was a blot on an already unattractive landscape – an unpleasant place with boarded-up windows, littered streets, graffiti and an aura of neglect and decay. It would not have looked out of place as part of some eastern European slum of the day. The council earmarked it as a priority for change. Each house had £11,000 spent on it and, for this, they got new roofs, new paint jobs and little balconies. The well-intentioned politicians hoped that all this would make life more pleasant and cut down on the crime around the area. Dream on. It takes more than a lick of paint to change the way of life for certain denizens of this city – as the council soon learned.

The improved housing stock lasted only a few years before the whole of the street was swept away by bulldozers. By this time, occupancy had dropped to fifty per cent and one section was completely burnt out. Antisocial tenants and destructive youngsters never gave the new Bankend Street a chance and the decision to demolish it was inevitable. Fear – one of Glasgow's oldest problems – played a role in its demise. Those tenants who watched as the neds speedily returned their refurbished homes to slums were too scared of retaliation to try to bring the culprits to the attention of the police.

Such was the place that was home to the Doyles. The family members who died were: James Doyle Snr, fifty-three, James Doyle Jnr, twenty-three, Tony Doyle, fourteen, Andrew Doyle, eighteen, their sister Christine Halleron, twenty-five, and her baby, Mark Halleron, aged one. It took some time to sort out the death toll. The first reports told of the deaths of Christine and Tony in the blaze and said that doctors had not been able to save Baby Mark. The intensity of the fire had left James Doyle Snr on a life-support machine in hospital and young James Doyle was critical in the Burns Unit of the Royal Infirmary. His brothers Daniel, twenty-eight, and Andrew were also seriously injured in the Burns Unit. Another brother, Stephen, twenty-one, who fled the flames by jumping forty feet from a window, had an operation on a shattered leg. He also had back injuries. Mrs Lillian Doyle, fifty-two, received treatment for smoke inhalation but was able to leave hospital for the home of one of her daughters in **MEADOWPARK STREET**, **DENNISTOUN**.

It was obvious that the fire had been started deliberately and, as the true toll of the horrendous act became clear, one of the detectives involved, Norman Walker, told the papers, 'The fire could have been lit anytime between midnight and one o'clock. We are waiting to interview members of this hard-working, decent family to try to find a motive for the murder.' The head of the CID at the time, Detective Chief Superintendent Charles Craig, declared it to be a murder inquiry and Norrie Walker called it a 'bloody murderous act'. This was the first involvement in the case of Detective Superintendent Walker but he was to become a pivotal figure who featured much later in the saga. He died in a fume-filled car in 1998 and, down the years, there were allegations that he had been involved in planting evidence in other cases. Charles Craig died in 1991, aged fifty-seven.

The Doyle's three-bedroom flat was brimming over with folk celebrating the birth, a few days before, of a granddaughter. The fire had been started in a storage cupboard which had been used for keeping tyres and timber, a dangerous combination in the event, and, once the flames had exploded out of it, they quickly flashed through an L-shaped corridor in the flat and into the family's bedrooms. Nine people were trapped behind a wall of flames that night, as the family home became an inferno.

The police were as outraged as the public at the atrocity and threw manpower at it – forty officers were involved. With hindsight, now that it has emerged that the prosecution was flawed in the resolution of the case, it is easy to see that, yet again, public clamour for arrests may have contributed to the mistakes that were made. This is a common factor in miscarriages of justice in the city going right back to the cases involving Jessie McLachlan and Oscar Slater. This city's inhabitants grow up reading the crime pages of the tabloids as keenly as they follow the exploits of Rangers and Celtic. Because of this, whenever a major crime dominates the headlines, day after day, the police are constantly under pressure to do 'something about it', to 'arrest someone'. A reading frenzy builds up. Often the pressure becomes too strong to resist and the usual suspects are rounded up in an effort to show that 'something is happening'. And, occasionally, one of them is fitted up.

As the gravity of these particular killings began to emerge, the police set up a murder HQ at Easterhouse Police Station. Appeals were made for anyone with information to come forward. And public concern over the case was heightened even further as the story unfolded.

The Doyles had lived in the flat for twenty years and newspaper reports said they were liked and respected. Their downstairs neighbour was Mrs Elizabeth McKenzie, who said, 'I don't know who could have done such a thing. They had no enemies as far as I know.' Mrs McKenzie's husband Albert had seen the full horror close up as he was wakened by banging and attempted a rescue. Mr McKenzie said:

I tried to get into the flat but smoke and flames were shooting out of the door. There was no way anyone could get in. I ran to the back of the flat and found Stephen shouting for help. He was lying in a pool of blood after cutting his arm, jumping through the window.

By that time, the fire brigade was on the scene and, in a dramatic rescue, firefighters, wearing breathing apparatus, managed to stretcher some of the desperately injured to safety. Twenty-four hours after the initial deaths were announced, the toll rose as young James Doyle succumbed to his injuries in hospital. At this stage, Daniel and Andrew were still critically ill. Andrew rallied for a time but, in the end, lost his fight for life, as did James Snr.

All this emergency-room drama meant that the family were mostly unable to talk to the detectives searching for a motive. But possible reasons for the fire attack slowly began to emerge. Andrew made his living as an ice-cream salesman, touring the Garthamlock area in a van, after taking out a franchise from the Marchetti Brothers of Maryhill, a well-known firm in the ice-cream trade.

All the appeals to the public for help were slow to provide information. Presumably the reason for this was that those in the know, or those who were just suspicious, knew that their lives would be endangered if they pointed fingers. Nonetheless, the picture of a dangerous feud began to emerge. Prior to the fire, Andrew Doyle, who, like young Arthur Thompson, was sometimes called The Fat Boy, had been attacked at least twice in his ice-cream van. In one incident, he had been fired on with a shotgun and in another he was savagely beaten up outside his home just after parking the van.

Feeling they might be on to something but that they were still needing more information, the police turned to the *Evening Times*. A poster was produced, appealing for help in what was, by now, a case of mass murder. It seemed to do the trick and stirred citizens' consciences. As a result, the controversial detective Norrie Walker announced that a few interesting lines of inquiry had been thrown up and that he was confident the murderer – singular – would be caught.

In Glasgow, there are always those who are eager to take advantage of public concern in such situations. In this instance, Ruchazie police had to investigate bogus collectors who were going round the doors ostensibly trying to raise cash for the stricken family but were actually trousering the proceeds.

Eleven days after the fire, the six victims were laid to rest at Old Monklands Cemetery in Shettleston. A ceremony was held at St Phillips Church, Ruchazie, beforehand. Hundreds of mourners squeezed themselves inside the church and hundreds more gathered outside. Big crowds also attended the cemetery and detectives mingled with the grieving masses hoping for clues. Among the mourners was the legendary soccer star Danny McGrain of Celtic, a friend of the family. Local politicians also attended with representation from both the regional and district councils.

By this time, the investigative reporters were in full flight, having been alerted to something really nasty going on in the seemingly harmless ice-cream business. One *Evening Times* feature writer found that weekly ice-cream van sales could be as high as £2000 – major money in the 1980s. The feature writers and investigative reporters found it hard to get people with knowledge to speak on the record. There were too many violent men about with vested interests in hiding the facts and with no conscience about using muscle or weapons on those they thought were talking too much.

The legitimate traders were fearful for their lives and their businesses but, by talking anonymously, they spelled out what was going on. One told of being attacked by an axe-wielding thug at his garage. His was a lucrative run in a tough scheme and the advice of the heavies nosing him up was that it would be wise to leave the business if he wanted to stay healthy. No prizes for figuring out who would take over!

One man who was up front with the reporters was Lorenzo Boni of Bathgate who was a representative of the Ice Cream Alliance whose members had vans operating in most parts of Britain. Lorenzo himself had a fleet of vans and knew the business inside out. Of the Doyle murders, he told the police that he would not be surprised if there was a vendetta involved. He spelled out what was happening to legitimate traders as the thugs moved in on the business. He and his drivers had suffered bricks through their van windows, beatings, nails in their van tyres and sugar in their petrol tanks. He sold up.

The police had, by now, built up a case that was to trigger the start of a succession of court appearances, releases, convictions and appeals that was to go on for twenty years. Two men were accused of murdering the Doyles by setting fire to their home. Thomas Campbell, thirty-one, and Thomas Lafferty, eighteen, were remanded in custody at Glasgow Sheriff Court. The murder charges had followed on from Campbell, of **BARLANARK**, and Lafferty, of **GARTHAMLOCK**, appearing in the same court, accused of attempting to murder Andrew Doyle and fifteen-year-old Anne Wilson by firing a shot at them through the windscreen of their ice-cream van. They also faced charges of plotting to build up an ice-cream business by means of threats and intimidation. A few days later, three other men faced charges. They were Joseph Steele, twenty-two, Gary Moore, twenty-one, from Garthamlock, and thirty-one-year-old Thomas Gray, from **CARNTYNE**. The charge against the three men was that, while acting with two others, they wilfully set fire to a cupboard door and the entrance to a house. The fire took effect and the family residing there died as a result and that they murdered them.

The murder charge against Lafferty was later abandoned and, in September 1984, Thomas Campbell, Thomas Gray, Gary Moore and Joseph Steele went on trial in the High Court, accused of killing the Doyles. From day one, Campbell and Steele screamed their innocence. It was a cry that was to echo on and on and spark hunger strikes, rooftop protests, escapes and a constant war with the prison authorities about the conditions the two men, innocent as it turned out, were held in.

The trial had echoes of that of Peter Manuel in that it attracted huge local and international attention. The gang wars in the east end of Glasgow were big news on television and radio down south and abroad, as well as at home, where page after page of court reports and background investigations thickened the papers of the day. The accused denied the charges and lodged special defences of alibi and incrimination, naming other persons.

But perhaps the most significant fact to emerge is that, right from the outset, Thomas Campbell claimed the police knew he was not responsible for the massacre. He told the court he had only been charged to force him into naming the real culprit. He said he was at home in bed with his wife on the night of the fire. His claims against the police were originally made in a judicial examination that had been held before a sheriff some months before the actual trial. His defence counsel, Donald Macaulay QC, asked the clerk of the court to read the judicial examination to the jury. It merits careful study, bearing in mind what was to happen in the Court of Appeal in early 2004. Before the examining sheriff, Campbell had denied saying to the police that 'the fire at The Fat Boy's was only a frightener that went too far'. The court heard that he had been asked if he had anything to say on the allegations that, along with Thomas Lafferty, he had been in Bankend Street on the night of the fire. He replied, 'We weren't there. No way was I there anyway.' Later in the judicial examination, Campbell had

124

been asked if he wished to incriminate anyone in the setting of the fire. He replied that, if he knew who was responsible, he would say so but he didn't. He again denied being the killer and said that the police said they would drop the charges against him if he named the murderer.

The trial went on for almost a month and, in the end, T C Campbell and Joseph Steele were convicted of the murders of the Doyles. The judge, Lord Kincraig, had instructed the jury to return a not guilty verdict on the murder charge against Gray and the crown dropped the case against Moore because of lack of evidence. The jury of five men and ten women returned a total of thirteen guilty verdicts against the accused in the case, on a variety of other charges. It had taken them eight hours to produce a verdict. Steele and Campbell were described as vicious and dangerous and jailed for life. In the case of Campbell, this was to be a minimum of twenty years. Campbell was also jailed for assault with intent to endanger the lives of Andrew Doyle and Anne Wilson during an armed attack on their ice-cream van. Lord Kincraig delivered a forceful address to the jury, warning them to put aside feelings of horror and disgust and to concentrate on the evidence. He said:

Persons involved directly or indirectly in blasting off a shotgun at an ice-cream van in a public place are villains of the first degree. And those who set fire to the top flat in a tenement at a time when it is occupied and the occupants are liable to be asleep, and there is no means of escape except through the very place where the fire has started – causing the deaths of six persons, mostly young – are wicked and depraved persons.

The jury had listened to much evidence in a long trial and, perhaps mainly on the assumption that the police case put before them was sound, found Steele and Campbell guilty. They should have believed the defendants as the final appeal showed. The long years of appeals and the constant reinvestigation of the case proved that, ultimately, two innocent men had been convicted. It is a case for grave concern that Steele and Campbell had to spend sixteen years behind bars before they were cleared.

Looking back at the court events all these years ago, it is obvious that much of the evidence was circumstantial. And, right from the day of the convictions, doubts began to emerge about the police case. One of the planks of the prosecution was the evidence of a Thomas Love who claimed to have been in a pub when he heard the two accused planning the attack. Later, he claimed that he was lying and that his evidence had been forced out of him by the police. This was to feature prominently in the pair's later appeals. An ironic fact about the convictions, which were later to be overturned because of police flaws and accusations of fit-ups, is that this was an incredibly expensive trial. The costs had reached £300,000 and a further £62,000 had gone on police overtime – a considerable sum in the 1980s.

With the legal shackles of a trial removed, the press took a long look at Campbell. He was a classic Glasgow hard man who grew up in **RIGBY STREET** in **CARNTYNE**. He was a member of the infamous Gaucho gang and would lead from the front in fights against other nearby outfits like the Powrie. Violence was second nature to him. In 1972, he had led the Gaucho in a night of terror when they had raided a street in **HAGHILL** armed with knives, meat cleavers and bottles. Windows were smashed and people locked themselves in their houses as the gang rampaged through the streets shouting, 'Gaucho rule!' and 'Kill!' He ran on the darkened streets with the three Steele brothers, James, John and Joseph, and all of them had had spells behind bars.

In 1980, Campbell stood trial charged with helping in an escape from Barlinnie but he was acquitted. Freed with him on this occasion was Thomas Lafferty known as 'The Shadow' because he was never far from Campbell's shoulder, in trouble and out of it. A self-confessed alcoholic and T C's brother-in-law, he played up his unreliable reputation in court to foster the notion that his alcoholism meant that he could not be trusted on criminal escapades.

Released from jail after the Gaucho episode, Campbell, the self-styled Emperor of Carntyne, began to build up a criminal empire. Moving in on the lucrative ice-cream van business seemed like a good way to thicken his wallet. Many other Glasgow scam merchants had the same idea and there is no doubt that, as well as offering a way of moving drugs around the schemes, the vans were useful for laundering dirty money and selling on stolen goods like cigarettes and drink. Getting control of the vans was a war on two fronts – legitimate traders had to be driven off and other crims had to be fought for the lucrative pieces of turf. This was the background behind the events in Bankend Street and the factors involved also accounted for some of the difficulties the police encountered.

The wars were compounded by the fact that, at the time, the heavy mobs thought that changes in the law were coming that would mean that ice-cream vans would have to be licensed just as taxis are. It wasn't an imminent problem but the thought that it was added an element of urgency to the wars on the street.

The battling still went on in the schemes but Campbell and Steele, now caged, could only follow the action in the newspapers. They still protested their innocence and no doubt their strong belief that they had been fitted up added extra fuel to Campbell's many confrontations with the authorities. An early incident in his long prison career underlined his fear of wrongful accusation. In 1986, he was cleared of punching a chief officer at Peterhead. The sheriff who heard the case said he entertained a doubt about the prosecution case and found him not guilty of assault. But, at the same time, he threw out Campbell's claim to have been beaten up and kicked by a squad of eight officers in retribution for a prison riot.

The next year, T C was into hunger strikes – something that was to become a bit of a habit for him in prison. This time, his protest was about being moved from Barlinnie to Peterhead. All this activity kept his case to the forefront and publicised his claims of innocence. The public found it hard to forget him, especially when his activities resulted in victories over the authorities. One example of this was when he won a payment of £250 in compensation for prison practices that caused him to suffer an attack of bedbugs. And his not guilty verdict on the charge of assaulting the prison officer and the allegation of being injured by a 'batter squad' was not the end of that episode. In October 1989, he was awarded damages against the then Scottish Secretary, Malcolm Rifkind, and this time he was awarded £4,000. He had claimed £40,000 but a civil jury made the lower award although they did say they were satisfied that Campbell's stomach injuries had been caused by the 'wrongful actions of prison officers'.

In the same year, Campbell's fight for freedom took a startling new turn. Lawyer, John Carroll, who had fought long and hard for his client, said he believed he had unearthed fresh evidence and lodged a petition at Edinburgh's High Court of Justiciary. This happened as Campbell entered the ninth day of what he said was an attempt to starve himself to death. A couple of days later, the Scottish Office took a less dramatic view. They released a statement saying, 'A prisoner at Shotts has been refusing food for eleven days. But he is buying food from the prison canteen. His condition is giving no concern to the medical staff.'

As far as the new evidence was concerned, Mr Carroll said, 'I have discovered that a witness in the trial of Campbell had three previous convictions for attempting to pervert the course of justice. This is important evidence.' That witness was Billy Love who was now living in London. He was said to have given a taped statement to an English barrister and Mr Carroll in which he claimed that CID officers in Glasgow had induced him to make the statements and, in return, they would arrange bail for the armed robbery charges he was facing. In this case, where so many police actions have been questioned, his new statement had a familiar ring to it. Love also claimed that he was threatened by a depute procurator fiscal who told him that, unless he confirmed the statements he had made to the police in court, he would end up on the same charge as Campbell. However, he later changed his story again, saying that what he had said in court was true.

The appeal plea was rejected by the Scottish Secretary who

ruled that no further appeal could be considered just because a key witness changed his story. In his tireless search for justice, Mr Carroll also tried to bring the European card into play. He told the European Commission for Human Rights that Campbell had been denied the right to a fair hearing at his appeal by being handcuffed throughout but this was dismissed on a technicality before a full hearing could take place. A petition to the Scottish Secretary, claiming failure of the appeal court to properly apply its mind to one of the appeal grounds, was also rejected.

By 1993, it was the turn of Joe Steele to make headlines and keep the case in the public's eye. On a visit home to see his sick mother in Garthamlock, he managed to slip his police escort and was whisked off to London by friends. It was not what could be described as a carefully planned high-tech escape. He pretended to go to the toilet and simply did a runner. His anguish and the strength of his belief that a great injustice had been done in this case surfaced in dramatic interviews with the English press. He said, 'I am not the beast that was portrayed in the media.' He went on to say that he had refused parole in order to pursue his innocence. 'If I admit my guilt to the parole board, I know I could be a free man a lot sooner. But I would rather serve fifteen to twenty years and finally prove my innocence than walk out a guilty man.'

Steele ended this brief escape in headline-catching fashion. He was dropped off outside the walls of Barlinnie in the late afternoon. He climbed halfway up a sixty-foot surveillance and lighting tower, yards from the main gate, and began shouting his innocence. He was now adept at stunts to draw attention to his case. He had earlier escaped from Saughton and had glued himself to the gates of Buckingham Palace.

Late in 1994, there was a further twist in the story of T C and Steele who, by then, were known as the 'Glasgow Two'. It emerged that evidence that could have been vital to their appeals had been destroyed by the police or the fiscal service. Each of them blamed the other for the destruction of material relating to William Love's retraction of his original evidence. John Carroll had asked the procurator fiscal for the original police notebooks, case notes, operational sheets, witness lists, laboratory papers and other court productions but he was told they had been destroyed. Indefensible and shocking as this admission was, it signalled another setback to Campbell and Steele. But, within a year, it looked as if freedom was a possibility for the Glasgow Two. But, it too was to end in yet more bitter disappointment.

The then Scottish Secretary, Michael Forsyth, decided to refer the twelve-year-old convictions to the Appeal Court. This effectively overruled the previous decision that 'there was insufficient reliable evidence' to justify proceedings against the key witness at the original trial, William Love, who had repeatedly admitted that he gave perjured evidence. Joe Steele was granted interim liberation until his appeal against the conviction was heard. He wept in the High Court in Edinburgh. A week later, T C was also back on the streets after being granted bail pending the appeal. *The Herald* reported that this was a first signal that the legal establishment's 'previously impregnable citadel of certainty over the convictions may be built on sand'. In the later course of this appeal that was shown to be a bit optimistic but things were beginning to move in the direction of the Glasgow Two's favour. That same *Herald* report made some valuable observations. It pointed out that Campbell and Steele had never had the support of well-organised campaigns like those that helped free Paddy Meehan and the Birmingham Six – this was an injustice that was being fought against the odds by John Carroll, a few journalists and family and friends. It also highlighted the ferocity with which the legal establishment strove to uphold convictions that the more you examined them, the more unsound they looked.

When the appeal initiated by Forsyth did start, Graham Bell QC said that William Love had been an essential witness for the Crown but that 'he has since made statements indicating his evidence at the trial was untrue'. This took things back to the nub of the matter – the claim that the overheard pub conversation, in which it was alleged that Campbell and Steele planned the fire bombing, never took place. Amazingly, the appeal was thrown out and the Glasgow Two were back behind bars again.

Three senior judges had decided, two to one, to refuse the appeal. Steele had married during his freedom and his wife was pregnant. Campbell's wife was also expecting a child. Steele's mother wept on the news and, in the public gallery, supporters of the Two were ordered to be silent as they roared their disapproval. The three judges had placed their decisions in sealed envelopes. Lord Cullen said he was minded to turn down the appeal as the Crown had produced compelling arguments to refute the appeal claims. Lord McCluskey disagreed and it was Lord Sutherland who gave the final decision that sent the Two back to jail after a year of freedom.

Apart from Love's evidence, his sister Agnes Carlton, who was cited as a witness all these years ago, back in 1984, signed an affidavit that she was giving evidence not heard earlier. She told the appeal hearing that, on the night an ice-cream van was blasted by a shotgun, she had seen her brother firing the shots. Lord Cullen said he was not satisfied that her evidence could be submitted for the appeal.

The *Evening Times*, in a leader the next day, brilliantly summed up this astonishing decision to rejail Campbell and Steele. The writer pointed out that similar cases in England had resulted in quashed convictions or retrials. And that a change in the law now allowed an appeal on the grounds of a witness changing evidence. That was what Love had done. But the new law required corroboration from a second source and a 'test of reasonable expectation' had to be passed. Here, the appeal foundered. The piece went on to say:

Lords Cullen and Sutherland sided against Lord McCluskey and decided that the appeal should be refused without hearing fresh evidence Both Campbell and Steele have steadfastly denied their guilt to the extent of refusing parole, staging hunger strikes and spectacular escapes. That in itself is no guarantee of innocence, but it has been consistent. The court's refusal to hear any new evidence might make legal sense. But it leaves a huge question mark over Scottish justice.

Few who have studied this fascinating case in any depth could disagree with that.

The wrong was on the way to be righted, as we shall see, but the stain on justice is permanent. Because of the length of time involved and the combination of the incompetence – and possibly maliciousness – of the original investigation by the police and the fierceness of the legal establishment in fighting the appeals, it is perhaps more disgraceful than any of the many other stories of injustice in the history of this city. It certainly seems so to this writer.

The next chapter in an astonishing saga came in February 2001 when it was revealed that the Scottish Criminal Commission was to issue a report on its investigation into the case. By the end of the year, the Glasgow Two were back out of jail on interim liberation as the authorities wrestled with the final conclusion to a troublesome case.

As they waited for the vindication of their long years pleading their innocence, the Two had different profiles. Steele largely disappeared from the headlines but the old Emperor of Carntyne, the hard man of the Gaucho, was still making news. In spring 2002, he was attacked in the street and whacked with a golf club. But he fought back and, after a trip to the hospital, he told reporters he was feeling 'brand new'. Clearly, at this time, some old feuds were being played out on the streets.

Paul Ferris and Tam McGraw were also in the headlines, following street attacks in broad daylight. The police are never too concerned with gangsters knocking lumps out of each other but this outbreak of violence so scared the populace that a senior officer had to point out that it didn't threaten the public. That was all very true but it did nothing to polish the image of a city coming to terms with a renaissance in music, theatre, architecture and the arts in general. But, gradually, the obvious violence of this new era died down though there were some notable exceptions.

All this had no effect on the destiny of the Glasgow Two. The slow march to justice continued to its climax on 17 March 2004. On that day, the long fight of T C Campbell and Joseph Steele resulted in their convictions finally being quashed. Campbell was in diplomatic mode. Delivering his comments outside the Court of Appeal, he said:

> There is no jubilation or happiness because I feel there are only losers in this case. The Doyles lost their family. We have lost our lives in prison and for twenty years justice has lost out and the people of Scotland have lost their justice system. There is a sense of relief my struggle is over. It has been a living nightmare for us. Only half the battle is over. There is still justice for the Doyle family to be got yet.

Asked what should happen to the police officers involved in the case, he played realist rather than diplomat, saying, 'I know what should happen but I know it won't. They should be done for perverting the course of justice.'

Steele, now apparently no close friend of Campbell, despite their shared fight over the years, was more low key. 'I am just glad to get it over with. I am just happy I am going home,' he said on his release.

What finally tipped the balance in the favour of the Glasgow Two? This was the third time the case had gone to appeal and there was crucial new evidence attacking the testimony of detectives at their trial who insisted that the pair made incriminating statements. The final vital expert witness was Professor Brian Clifford, a psychologist at the University of East London. He considered it 'very improbable' that the four police officers who detained Campbell back in 1984 would have identical recall of what he was alleged to have said. Professor Clifford had been called into action by the Scottish Criminal Cases Review Commission to look at statements allegedly made by Steele and Campbell and reported by the police. Campbell was supposed to have said, 'I only wanted the van windaes shot up. The fire at The Fat Boy's was only meant to be a frightener that went too far.' He denied saying it but it was in the notebooks of four of the policemen investigating the crime and the wording was extremely similar. People in England and in Scotland were tested by Professor Clifford on their ability to recall phrases immediately after hearing them. On average, people recalled between thirty to forty per cent of the actual words they hear. The highest score of anyone trying to recall the words Campbell was said to have used was seventeen out of twenty four. Given those statistics, it seemed distinctly unlikely that four officers would separately record what was said in such similar terms as they did.

The judge emphasised the importance of such psychological studies in the decision to overturn the 1984 conviction. His view was:

> Our conclusion is that any jury hearing Professor Clifford's evidence would have assessed the evidence of the arresting officers in an entirely different light. The evidence of Professor Clifford is of such significance that the verdicts of the jury, having been returned in ignorance of it, must be regarded as miscarriages of justice.

So, for the Glasgow Two, it was all over. In the end, some fairly esoteric psychological evidence about the police use of 'verbals', as they are called, closed one part of the saga. But haunting questions still remain. Who killed the Doyles? Will we ever know? Despite the rumours that still circulate in the underworld, I doubt it. Let John Carroll, who represented Steele in the final appeal and who played such a major role down the years in the case, have the final say:

> Suspicion is no good. It was suspicion and tittle-tattle that put

them in jail in the first place. From Steele's point of view it is a matter for the police to look into and the police have already said they are not looking for suspects.

J

JEFFREY, ROBERT

Described as a 'criminal officer', Jeffrey was a minor figure at the sensational Jessie McLachlan trial in September 1862. Jessie was convicted of killing her friend, a domestic servant called Jess McPherson, but was saved from the gallows and served a long sentence in Perth Prison instead. Many suspect that the real killer was a man known as Old Fleming who employed Jess at 17 **SANDYFORD PLACE**, not far from **SAUCHIEHALL STREET**. Suspected of sexually pestering her, Fleming was arrested but freed as the police, egged on by public feeling, in a manner reminiscent of the Oscar Slater case, put all their energies into proving Jessie's guilt.

Jeffrey assisted detectives in a four-day search of the murder scene in an effort to discover any clues that might implicate Fleming. He distinguished himself at the trial by coming up with a series of indecisive answers under cross-examination. In one instance, he could not remember on which of the four days of the search a particular object was found. Questioned on whether bloodstains were new or old, he was equally unsure. In the end, when asked if he was sure nothing, in the way of evidence that might have indicated Fleming's guilt, could have escaped his notice, he replied, 'I think so.' As the old saying about many a newspaper editor goes, his indecision was final.

K

KEMP, 'EVIL JIM'

The nickname of this post-war gang leader says it all. He was a 'chib merchant' – Glasgow patois for an expert with a knife and open razor. For a time, he controlled the rackets and scams in the **GALLOWGATE**, one of the toughest areas in a tough city.

Kemp was being held on suspicion of murder when he met Walter Norval in Barlinnie and became something of a mentor to the man who was to become one of the city's Godfathers. For a start, he taught Norval the prison skill of talking out the side of the mouth, the lips barely moving. This was no Hollywood affectation, but a vital skill for making sure prison officers did not hear what nastiness their charges were up to during exercise periods.

KOTARBA, JOE

Many Polish service men who came to Scotland during the Second World War stayed on after the conflict. Often they married Scottish women and made themselves worthwhile citizens of their new country – Poles were known to be a hard-working breed. But there is a rotten apple in every barrel and there was none more rotten than Kotarba or 'Joe the Pole'. A brothel keeper, he took up with the mother of Glasgow's first Godfather, Walter Norval – much to the gangster's annoyance – and made himself a thorn in the flesh of the vice squad. He ended up murdered but not before he had twice escaped charges of killing girls who worked for him. He had an associate, another Pole, Tony Kobuchiac who stayed in **THOMPSON STREET** in **DENNISTOUN**, although Joe's brothels were mostly in the west end rather than the east.

When call girl Janet Davidson died, a murder hunt, with Joe the

Pole as chief suspect, was sparked. It seemed the police had cracked the case when another prostitute, May Boyle, said that Kotarba had killed Janet in front of her and Kobuchiac. But Kobuchiac denied it and his friend was released.

Not many months later, another girl was found dead – this time in a flat in **WESTEND PARK STREET**. Again suspicion fell on the vice king. Kotarba was a violent man who was known to treat his girls badly, even to the extent of torturing them sexually with bottles for the entertainment of himself and his friends. This time, he escaped justice by claiming the girl, Irene, had been killed by a punter in the brothel. From then on, any of his girls who didn't work hard enough to provide him with cash would be threatened with the same fate as Irene and Janet.

But fate was to get its own back on Kotarba when he was found stabbed to death in a blood-splattered flat in **MARYHILL**. Suspicion fell on Norval who disliked his mother's association with Kotarba and had no time for the Pole or his methods of keeping his girls in line. But the Godfather had been out of the country when the killing occurred. He was in the clear.

One of Kotarba's call girls, thirty-four-year-old Agnes Delacorti, appeared in the dock at Glasgow High Court. She was accused of stabbing him more than twenty times with a kitchen knife. But, after pleading self-defence, she was found not guilty and was cheered from the court. Maryhill folk knew Kotarba and his methods well. The jury had heard how his operation, run from his home in **RAEBERRY STREET**, involved a string of six or seven prostitutes whom he would beat with iron bars or his fists. Agnes Delacorti said, 'It was him or me. There will be lots of happy people in Maryhill now he is dead. But none had the guts to do it.' A witness, Antone Angel, described him as 'a horrible man, a dangerous man, a man who could kill. He was cruel and liked to hurt women.' It is little wonder that the jury believed Agnes when she said she picked up the knife because she believed she was about to be killed by this evil man. 'I didn't know if the knife was going into the bed or him.'

So Kotarba was removed from the scene and with that the deaths of Irene and Janet were, to an extent, avenged.

KU KLUX KLAN

There were no white hoods or burning crosses on **MAIN STREET** in **BRIDGETON** during the 1930s. There were bigots about but they were not like the white rednecks who terrorised the black people of America's deep south. The Glasgow KKK was a sinister little offshoot, a sort of junior section, of Billy Fullerton's Brigton Billy Boys sectarian gang. These dangerous youngsters met in the Foundry Boys Hall in **LONDON ROAD**. Like the Billy Boys, they did some psuedo-soldiering and there was much bigotry and band music of the flute-playing kind. Members took an oath of allegiance and paid tuppence a week into the funds. There was a kind of uniform – black and white ties and 'K' badges that were specially made by a local tradesman. But, somehow or other, and this may be some sort of compliment to the moral sensibility of the youngsters of the time, the concept gradually failed and the Klan collapsed, its lifespan thankfully much shorter than that of the evil gangs of white bigots across the Atlantic. Maybe its collapse was speeded up by the fact that, although the Klan was supposedly a stepping stone to full membership of the Billy Boys, the youngsters began to miss out that stage and boys became members of the adult organisation at a younger age.

L

LYON, JOHN

At a mere twenty-one years old, Lyon was the first man to be hanged in the Barlinnie hanging shed when it opened for business in 1946. He paid with his life for the murder of John Brady, a navy man, in a brawl in **WASHINGTON STREET**. Lyon had appealed against the sentence at Edinburgh High Court but it was dismissed and he was led from the court on the way to the gallows shackled to Glasgow's first Godfather Walter Norval who was heading for borstal. Lyon told Norval, 'They are going to hang me in a fortnight.' The old gangster remembered him as being calm and resigned in the face of death. But Lyon's grisly fate did nothing to turn, the then young, Norval away from a life of crime.

M

MANUEL, PETER

Hanged, aged thirty-two, in Barlinnie Prison, at one minute after 8 a.m. on Friday 11 July 1958, he was one of Britain's most infamous serial killers. But his evil deeds, however, got less space in the national press and embedded themselves less firmly in the country's collective criminal memory than they actually deserved. He was charged at the High Court in Glasgow with eight murders and convicted of seven. But, he was thought to have been responsible for at least one other murder. Some have put the total number of his killings at as high as fifteen. An intelligent, if evil and perverted, man, he is said to have run the last few steps to the gallows, so eager was he for the end of his life to come. The story of what led him to his grim fate is a remarkable one.

Strangely, it began in Manhattan, New York, in 1927. But living in a city dominated by skyscrapers and concrete canyons and fighting battles with the FBI were not on the cards for Peter Manuel – his criminal tale was to be played out in the altogether less glamorous surroundings of Lanarkshire and Glasgow. Like many in the 1920s, Manuel's parents had moved to the New World, dreaming of a more affluent existence. They wanted a life that offered more hope, for children and parents alike, than was on offer in Scotland, where, for many, poverty, unemployment, poor housing and little in the way of medical care were normally all that could be expected.

When the Manuels first arrived Stateside, Peter's father, Samuel, had found work in the car factories of Detroit, Michigan. But the job was temporary and, before too long, they moved to New York State. But here, too, in Depression-hit America, the dream of a world of affluence and happiness failed to materialise and, by

1932, they were back in Lanarkshire, living amid the dark streets and the heavy industry and breathing the foul, smoky air in the heartland of industrial Scotland. The Manuels seemed a footloose crew and, after their return to Scotland, they again made a temporary move – this time to Coventry.

Down there, Peter, who was only twelve at the time, was put on probation for burglary. However, this was not going to control him and, during his period of probation, he committed a second housebreaking offence. This time, he was sent to an approved school for three years. Even at this early age, the man who was to lead the police such a dangerous dance for years, while on his killing sprees, showed his slipperiness. He escaped from the approved school no less than eleven times – a record that might say something about the abilities of his keepers as well as his ingenuity.

During his frequent spells on the run, he raised funds by housebreaking and, indeed, this was a crime at which he undoubtedly became expert. But he was no run-of-the-mill burglar who was ready to pop into an open window and creep away in the night undetected. Even as a youngster, he was ready to use extreme violence – a warning of the sort of nature that was to create what was virtually a reign of terror in the years to come. In the course of one break-in, he assaulted a homeowner who was unlucky enough to catch him in the act. Using a hammer, he inflicted horrendous injuries.

After the Coventry Blitz in 1940, the Manuels returned to Scotland – although, initially, they were without Peter who, to no one's surprise, was in a borstal. He had been placed there for robbing and indecently assaulting the wife of a school employee. This was the first hint that perverse sexual activities were to accompany the violence and love of firearms that were to become so evident in his later activities. But, with borstal behind him, he returned to the family in **VIEWPARK** near **UDDINGSTON**. This was bad news for the law enforcement in the area which, it has to be said, could be a pretty tough spot even without his presence.

142

Eventually, Peter Manuel, dark-haired and evil-looking, would find employment as a woodworker but his exploits on the wrong side of the law took up much of his time. The enormity of the effect he was to have began to drip its way into the minds of the local cops. Three years after his return to Scotland, in March 1946, a woman walking home with her daughter was attacked on a deserted footpath between **MOUNT VERNON AVENUE** and **CARRICK DRIVE** in North Mount Vernon. Soon after, there were to be two other similar attacks in the area. Just four days after the attack on the footpath, a nurse was attacked. And the following night, a woman was beaten and raped. This time, because of his record down south, Manuel was an obvious suspect and, indeed, the law took its course.

A couple of the women identified him in a parade and forensic evidence linked him with another of the attacks. There was a Sherlock Holmes touch to this as the scientists were able to match footprints at the scene to his shoe. He was sentenced to a year for the first two attacks, not much of a sentence since fourteen similar offences were taken into account. But the third attack merited a longer sentence – eight years, to be served in Peterhead.

Like all serial killers, Peter Manuel was a complex man with many psychological hang-ups. During this first long prison sentence, he showed nothing of the acceptance of reality that was to culminate in his run to his death on the gallows. Remarkably, instead, considering his background and the evidence against him, he took on the role of the injured party – an innocent who had been framed by the police.

His birthplace no doubt accounted for some of the lurid fantasies he spun while in Peterhead. He boasted that his father had been an American gangster who had died in the electric chair and claimed that he himself was involved with the British Secret Service. If nothing else, his brief sojourn in the Land of the Free had imbued him with Walter Mitty tendencies. More seriously, the belief that he had been framed by the Lanarkshire police is thought to have contributed to a lifelong desire for revenge and the perverse pleasure he took in taking on the authorities and defending himself in court. This notion that he was better than his legal team was perhaps fuelled by his success in a 1955 incident when, charged with yet another assault on a woman, he won himself a not proven verdict.

A few years later, there was to be a court appearance during which he faced much more serious charges. In May 1958, he was in the dock of the famous old High Court in Glasgow charged with eight murders. The victims were: Anne Kneillands (17); Mrs Marion Watt (45); Vivienne Watt (16); Mrs Margaret Brown (42); Isabelle Cooke (17); Peter Smart (45); Mrs Doris Smart (42); and Michael Smart (10).

The background to this trial is intriguing. Often, when there is a public outcry about a sensational murder or series of killings, the police are under enormous pressure to come up with results – to find a scapegoat and let the public get back to their cosy lives. And life in Glasgow and the surrounding areas was far from cosy when Peter Manuel stalked the streets and lanes. The number of unsolved murders was causing great unease. It was the topic of conversations in pubs and homes. There was a boom in home-security items like padlocks and window locks. Many in the areas near the scenes of the killings felt unsafe and walking alone at night, in the dark, was not the thing to do. Operating in such a climate, the police do tend to take a look at the usual suspects. It is clearly a prudent approach but often it earns them criticism from the liberal lobby. What is more concerning, however, in the Manuel case was the fact that, early on, he was indeed investigated but he was not charged and he went on to kill again. The police did, in the end, nail this evil man but it seems incontestable that some early opportunities to stop him in his tracks were missed – as was another opportunity later in the saga.

The Anne Kneillands murder made headlines when her body was found on a golf course in **EAST KILBRIDE** in 1956. Nothing came of the police investigation into Manuel in this case although his record made him an obvious suspect. (Interestingly, he was found not guilty of her murder at the trial two years later when he was convicted of seven killings.) But, in the years before his final trial, there was an astonishing episode in which an innocent man, William Watt, was accused of killing his wife, his sister-in-law and his daughter. The three women had been slaughtered in a break-in at their bungalow in **BURNSIDE**. In hindsight, it was just the sort of crime that matched the Manuel modus operandi – burglary and murder. Once again, he must have been the most appealing of the usual suspects. But, no. An astonishing chain of coincidence led to Watt, a master baker, being accused of killing his own family.

For a spell, Watt looked the scapegoat the public had been clamouring for but, from the outset, the case against him was a nonsense. Indeed, it is truly scary that this man spent sixty-seven days in Barlinnie, accused of the most horrendous crime of killing his own family.

On the night of the murder, Watt had been away on a fishing holiday in Argyll, staying in a hotel near Lochgilphead. At 8 a.m., he had breakfast in his hotel in front of witnesses. The victims had been shot at 6 a.m. The cops believed that he had driven from Argyll to Burnside to carry out the killings and then returned to the hotel to establish an alibi. The timescale itself made this notion suspect from the start. Even today, in a modern car on much improved roads, it is a hard two-hour journey, each way. To do it on a dark autumn night, over twisting roads, all these years ago, would have required a remarkable car and a remarkable driver. Reports that he had been seen on the Renfrew ferry and driving around Loch Lomondside were also suspect. There was disagreement about what type of car he had allegedly been seen in. Worse he was picked out at an identity parade *after* his photograph had appeared in the papers. And the car that was supposed to have made this high-speed trip of around 200 miles was seen covered in frost at daybreak in Lochgilphead. It was truly one of the most bizarre episodes in the history of crime in this city. In the end, of course, the police had to face the fact that they had banged up an innocent man and William Watt was freed.

By coincidence, while Watt was in the Bar-L, a neighbour in a nearby cell, accused of housebreaking, was Peter Manuel. Laurence Dowdall who played such a major role in criminal cases in the city was representing Watt. Hearing of this, the cocky Lanarkshire killer wrote to Dowdall, asking if they could meet to discuss the case. This was arranged and, during the meeting, Manuel let slip inside knowledge of the Watt family home in **FENNSBANK AVENUE**. Also amazingly, he told Dowdall that Watt's sister-in-law, Mrs Brown, had been shot twice. This was something that the lawyer himself did not know and the police were later to confirm it as being true. Dowdall immediately informed the police about the details of this meeting. You might have thought that this would have resulted in Manuel being charged. Some people at the time thought so and so have many investigators and commentators since. But, no. There was a tragic misjudgement – perhaps in the belief that more evidence was needed.

On his release in 1957, Manuel met Watt and, because of what transpired, Watt was even more convinced that Manuel was the killer. But no matter what suspicions were swirling around him, the woodworker from Lanarkshire remained free to kill. Later that year, he was believed to have murdered a Durham taxi driver, Sydney Dunn. And an attractive **MOUNT VERNON** teenager, Isabelle Cook, was strangled on a footpath near her home. At New Year time, the manager of a civil engineering firm, Peter Smart, and his wife and young son were shot in their **UDDINGSTON** home.

This last killing brought Manuel's bloody orgy of violence to an end. His own self-confidence, which had been boosted over the years by his successes as an amateur lawyer and in dodging arrest for crimes in which he was clearly implicated, led him into an act of colossal stupidity. He stole the Smarts' car and gave a policeman a lift into town in it! When arrested, he confessed to eight murders, including the slaughter in Burnside for which William Watt suffered so much.

The trial of Peter Manuel opened on Monday 12 May 1958. It

was to last a fortnight. For those fourteen days, it dominated the headlines and was, to a large extent, the only serious topic of conversation in the city. The indictment listed 228 productions and 280 witnesses were cited to appear. Housebreaking, as well as serial murder, was alleged. Lord Cameron was the presiding judge and Mr M G Gillies, advocate depute, led for the Crown. The head of the defence team was Harald Leslie QC who later became Lord Birsay. Press interest was almost unprecedented with sixty-eight seats reserved for reporters who had been issued with identity cards and tickets for a front-row view of justice in action. The scribes came from local papers, English-based publications and even foreign news agencies.

It immediately became clear that the ordeal of William Watt was not yet at an end. Harald Leslie rose to intimate a plea of not guilty and a special defence. Peter Manuel claimed the Burnside murders were the work of Watt and he claimed he had an alibi for the Smart killings. But the first case to be dealt with was that of Anne Kneillands. Although Manuel had confessed to this crime it was ruled that there was no supporting evidence and the judge told the jury to acquit him on that charge. This highlighted one of the many intriguing differences between the legal systems of Scotland and England. Down south, such a confession, even without corroboration, could result in a conviction – not so in Scotland. Press and public alike revelled in this sensational start but more was to come.

That pre-trial confession threw up another issue – in it, Manuel had admitted to killing Isabelle Cooke and, in this case, there *was* corroborating evidence. The confession had included facts that only the killer could have known, including where the victim's clothing could be found and where the body lay. The confession also went against his claims of alibi in the Smart killings as he had indicated to the police roughly where the gun used to kill the family would be found. And he also knew details of the inside of the house where their deaths had taken place.

Attention grabbing as all this was to the reader or juror, further sensations awaited. Later in the trial Manuel decided to sack Harald Leslie and conduct his own defence, albeit with some legal assistance. Now he wanted William Watt brought to court. But, before this happened and with the defence team intact at this point, the jurors heard details of the meeting between Manuel and Laurence Dowdall and this underlined the appalling way the police had reacted to this information. Basically, Manuel told the lawyer at the meeting that Watt was innocent and the reason he said this was that he knew who *had* done it – indeed, he did. There were other meetings and Mr Dowdall pressed Manuel to tell the police what he knew but the accused would have none of it. Eventually, Laurence Dowdall said to Manuel, 'What will you do if I go to the police?'

Manuel replied, 'I shall deny that I said it.'

The scene was set for William Watt to meet Manuel in court – it was to be the first of two face-to-face confrontations. An added emotional factor in this highly-charged meeting was that the master baker had to give evidence from a wheelchair after being injured in an accident before the start of the trial.

Mr Watt detailed the chain of coincidences that had resulted in him languishing in Barlinnie, accused of murders he did not commit. On the Sunday before the killings, he had had some work done on his car in Lochgilphead. This appeared to be an insignificant action but it was to lead to the suggestion that he was getting it ready for a fast return trip to Glasgow. That night, he returned to his fishing hotel, which was actually in Cairnbaan, a few miles north-west of Lochgilphead. There, he pared a corn on his toe to ease some pain and left a few drops of blood on the bed sheets – something else that could be construed as evidence against him.

He then told the court of how he had come to hear of the murders when out fishing. The police had informed the hotel of what had occurred in Burnside and someone was sent out to the edge of the pool, where he was waiting, in tweeds, for the fish to bite, to tell him that 'something had happened and he should phone the hotel'. He said that, at first, he couldn't take in what he had been told of the tragedy in his home and phoned his brother in Glasgow for more details. At this point in his testimony, he broke down and was given water by court attendants as a doctor stood by.

He recovered his composure and, under defence questioning, he made a significant remark. He said he asked the police to supply a driver to take him to Burnside and that:

> On the way down, I was able to make myself contained. I made up my mind that this was done and that breaking up would not do me any good whatsoever. I would go to the police and help them get the fellow who had done this terrible deed.

This worked against him in that some of the original investigators felt that this attitude suggested an involvement in the crime rather than an exhibition of strength of character. But, from the witness box, he was able to detail the faults in the case against him and dismiss Manuel's accusations as 'a load of nonsense'. The jury believed him.

After this, the prosecution case moved to the killing of Isabelle Cooke and the Sharp family. As previously mentioned, the confessions to these killing were accompanied by several pieces of corroborative evidence – witnesses had seen him near the scene of the Cooke killing and his alibi for the Sharp murders was dismissed.

All this was a bit of a preliminary to the real sensation of the trial. The famous Glasgow detective Tom Goodall (a sleuth who features in several of the famous cases in this book) was about to be examined by the advocate depute for the prosecution when the prisoner stood up and said, 'Before the examination of this present witness, I would like to confer with my counsel.' The ensuing silence in court was broken when the urbane Harald Leslie announced, 'I think it would probably be desirable.'

The jury withdrew. Lord Cameron went to his chambers and

Manuel headed to the cells. After forty minutes filled with buzz and speculation, the court reassembled. Manuel carried a file of papers and the blue notebook he had used throughout the trial. Harald Leslie rose to his feet and, in a quiet voice that could barely be heard at the back of the packed courtroom, he said, 'I have to inform your Lordship I am no longer in a position with my colleagues to continue in the case and the panel is desirous of conducting the remainder of the trial. I would accordingly withdraw.'

Lord Cameron turned his attention to the prisoner. 'Manuel,' he said, 'do you now wish to conduct your own defence for the remainder of the case or would you like an adjournment to allow you to appoint another counsel?'

Manuel now had no doubt that he was in charge of his own destiny – he would lead the defence although he retained a couple of solicitors for advice on procedure. He was having his day in court, free to tackle the evidence of his old enemies – the police. He started by questioning a number of police witnesses and his knowledge of how the force worked and thought gave him a few minor successes though, by now, the case that had been painstakingly built against him was emerging as almost unchallengeable. However, Manuel was not to be denied one last face-to-face with William Watt. He had the injured baker brought back into court in his wheelchair but the judge restricted him to questioning the witness on certain issues only.

At one point, it almost descended into farce with Manuel claiming that Watt had told him that he (Watt) was a faster driver than Stirling Moss. More emotional was a question or two about allegations that Watt had said he could have turned the gun on himself after killing his daughter. All this was strongly rebutted by the baker as lies and fantasy. During this bizarre episode, Manuel indulged in all the legal niceties, making a particular point of addressing the judge as 'His Lordship'.

For William Watt, however, it was all over. His long nightmare – at least as far as court appearances were concerned – had ended and, as he was wheeled backwards out of the court, he allowed himself, for the first time, a relaxed smile at the reporters who had followed his ordeal and who, by then, knew him well.

Peter Manuel liked to think of himself as a bit of the legal eagle. But, despite his undoubtedly comprehensive experience in court, he failed to take into account that old lawyers' adage – never ask a question if you don't know, or don't have a good idea of, what the answer is going to be. This was dramatically shown in one exchange in the High Court when the serial killer asked, in his best, clipped legal manner, if a detective was sure that he, Manuel, had killed Isabelle Cooke. 'I have no doubt whatsoever.' was the succinct reply. There was a similar streak of curious naivety in Manuel's three-hour final address to the jury. Despite its length, it was all pretty pointless as the prosecution's own final address was devastating. The confessions, the absurdity of his accusations about Watt, the fact that the Webley gun, used to kill the Smarts, was found at a place he had shown to the police, the fact that he had indicated where the body of Isabelle Cooke had been buried – all of these things pointed to guilt. His claims of alibi in the Smart case and his accusations that his family were threatened by the police were all dismissed.

Lord Cameron's handling of the case was scrupulously fair. He told the jury:

> For the past fourteen days, you have been listening to evidence which has covered a catalogue of crime that, in gravity, is certainly without precedent in this country, for very many years indeed. And there is one unusual feature in this case which is possibly unique in trials for murder in our courts in Scotland, in that the accused himself has elected, some distance through the trial, to conduct his own defence.

The eminent judge went on to point out that, by taking this decision, Manuel had denied himself the distinguished forensic abilities and skill of the counsel who had earlier appeared on his behalf. Striving for the utmost fairness, the judge said that the jury needed to scrutinise the evidence to see that all points which could properly be made in favour of the accused were given due weight. He then paid something of a tribute to Manuel. 'I should add this – that, from what we have heard in the past days, particularly today, the accused has presented his own defence with a skill that is quite remarkable.'

That was generous but the jury had no difficulty in concluding that Manuel was guilty of seven of the eight murders he had been charged with. And, despite the words of Lord Cameron, at least some of Manuel's final submission was distinctly lame. He had closed his address to the jury, saying, 'I can only say I have not murdered any of these people. I have got no reason to murder these people.' Not quite Perry Mason – or Laurence Dowdall!

The jury left the courtroom to consider its verdict and those left behind on the public and press benches endured an hour of tension and speculation before a buzzer sounded. The reporters scrambled to attention in their seats, notebooks and pencils at the ready. But it was a false alarm, a courtroom attendant explained the buzzer was not a call for the resumption of the court sitting. It was two hours and twenty-one minutes after the jury retired when a bell announced an unmistakable return to the court. Manuel was brought back to hear his fate, showing composure and sitting in a relaxed position with one knee lifted and clasped between his hands. The verdicts came one by one. First was the formality of acquittal as directed by the judge on the Anne Kneillands case. Then there was a guilty verdict on all other capital charges – although one minor housebreaking charge was found not proven. On the Watt killings, the slaughter of the Smarts and the death of Isabelle Cooke, the jury was unanimous. There could be only one outcome – the production of the black cap and the chilling sentence of death by hanging. Lord Cameron was reported to have been 'visibly moved' as he told the Lanarkshire woodworker his fate.

Given his predilection for legal argument, it is no surprise that Manuel tried an appeal, claiming that the confessions, written and verbal, should not have been submitted as evidence. He also claimed misdirection of the jury by the judge. Lord Clyde, Lord Carmont and Lord Sorn dismissed the appeal and there was to be no escape from the rope for this evil man. When he knew of the inevitability of his death, he confessed to sundry other murders.

As far as the death penalty was concerned, it was clear, in the climate of the time, that there would be no reprieve. And so it happened. On 9 July, Bailie Blas, who had travelled to the Barlinnie with the town clerk depute Joseph Dickson, told Manuel his fate was sealed.

On the actual morning of the execution, the eleventh of July, there were few in the city who did not glance at the clock and wonder about the grim scene taking place in the old hanging shed at Barlinnie as Manuel breathed his last. But, strangely, there was no huge crowd outside the gates as the hangman carried out the grim ritual. It is said that only twelve people were outside the prison as the monster died at one minute past eight. This had swelled to around thirty when the official confirmation of his death was announced at 8.50 a.m. Bailies John Paterson and John McDougal said Manuel had made no reference to anything before he died and they then confirmed that the hanging had been carried out in a satisfactory and expeditious manner.

Many years later, there emerged a footnote of interest to those who oppose the horrors of society ritually murdering those who themselves have taken life. It transpired that Manuel had come a bit closer to escaping the noose than had been expected. Right up to the end, he had displayed the kind of ingenuity that had made him so hard to cage – even when he was suspected of such major crimes. In 1995, documents were released, under an open-government initiative, and they told a story only a few insiders had known about.

Before the execution, there had been doubts, at the highest level, about the sanity of Peter Manuel. The papers revealed that, in prison, shortly before his appeal, Manuel had begun to show signs of madness that the authorities believed to be feigned. Before the trial, Manuel had been examined by three psychiatrists and one of them had described him as having 'psychopathic' tendencies. This was at a time when a Royal Commission had advised that the courts should take more account of psychopathic behaviour when considering whether or not an accused should be put to death. Against this background, the Scottish Secretary and the Lord Advocate were so fearful of public criticism if the monster had escaped the noose, on the grounds of insanity, that they made plans to brief a sheriff to invoke a disused legal power should this happen and let the execution go ahead.

The documents, which had been created twenty years earlier, revealed that, after the trial, the home office and the Lord Advocate were awaiting further medical reports. The reports showed that, shortly before a meeting with his solicitor, Manuel was found on his prison bed frothing at the mouth. His stomach was pumped but nothing was found that could have caused these physical symptoms. Manuel was refusing to talk to anyone. However, two medical commissioners who tried to interview him said that, in their opinion, he was faking madness. 'We consider the symptoms he is presently displaying are consciously motivated,' their report said. There was also the suspicion that Manuel was using knowledge of mental conditions. He'd garnered these from his sister who was a nurse in mental institutions. While being examined, he sat huddled in a chair, pouting his lips, shrugging his shoulders, clutching his stomach and moving his head from side to side. The commissioners were not impressed. It was concluded that 'it was well within his capacity to produce a convincing and suitable display of mental disorder'.

There was to be one final last-minute plea to save his neck. But his mother's pleadings that he should be examined by an independent psychiatrist were rejected by the Scottish Office. The law took its course.

McARTHUR, ALEXANDER

McArthur is the author of perhaps the most controversial book ever written about Glasgow, *No Mean City* (London: Longmans, 1935). A baker, who was born in the **GORBALS** in 1901, he lived for many years in **WADDELL STREET** with his mother and brother. Away from the flour-splattered whites, nightshifts and hot ovens, he dreamed of becoming a writer. Like millions before him he used his own experiences as a basis for his writings. He sent a couple of novels to Longmans, the London publishers. The publishers' readers deemed them unsuitable for publication but the subject of life in perhaps the worst of the slums in Britain seemed to offer scope. The journalist H Kingsley Long was commissioned to ghostwrite a novel with McArthur. McArthur may have provided the inspiration but the perspiration got the bigger slice of the cake with a royalty split of 75 percent to Long and 25 per cent to McArthur who, at the time, was unemployed.

The publication of *No Mean City* in 1935 started a row that splutters briefly to life from time to time, even to this day. But the reviewer in the then *Glasgow Herald* was in no doubt. He wrote:

> It is a novel of tremendous power, a horrible story that holds one enchained in a shocked fascination from the moment of the drunken father's awakening in the first chapter to the razor-king's death at the iron-shod boots of his supplanters in the last . . . The author is unfalteringly realistic.

A book to be proud of you might think. Well, er, not exactly. The response of the despotic and ostrich-like Glasgow council was to ban it from the city public libraries – no room for realism there. The use of the word realistic to describe the novel is undoubtedly correct for it was an accurate view of life in the Gorbals slums – if a tad sensationalised. This is confirmed by the fact that, down the years, Glasgow newspapers repeatedly sent feature writers on assignments to the Gorbals to find out if McArthur had got it right. Almost invariably, they could find folk alive at the time who agreed with the picture painted by the ex-baker. The view of life in the Gorbals is valid enough to be powerful piece of social history. Some of the same sort of blinkered thinking indulged in by the city fathers of the 1930s was still around in the 1990s when the suggestion was made that McArthur should be belatedly honoured in his native city. Labour group leader Pat Lally, who grew up in the Gorbals and made it to Lord Provost, albeit a controversial one, described the book as 'a distorted work of fiction'.

The book, however, has remained in print for more than fifty years and has been a huge best-seller. And Johnny Stark, the razor-king leading character, whose fictional life centres round **RUTHERGLEN ROAD, THISTLE STREET, HOSPITAL STREET** and **CROWN STREET**, has sparked many similar characters in other books. And he has even featured in a contemporary ballet by the Russian dance group Do Theatre, with music by the young Edinburgh composer Stephen Deazley.

For McArthur, the success of the book did not do much to improve his life. He earned little from his writing and a further literary slog which produced four more novels, two plays and twenty short stories seems only to have resulted in one further piece, a short story, making it to publication. Masses of material he sent to the local newspapers also failed to make it into print. He had an ear for dialogue but was not a particularly successful writer and it seems that the old pro H Kingsley Long deserved the larger share of the royalties after all.

They say everyone has a book in them and undeniably *No Mean City* was McArthur's – no matter what help he got – but his life ended in shabby circumstances. In September 1947, two beat coppers came across the dripping-wet body of a man on the banks of the Clyde near Rutherglen Bridge. Early guesses that he had clambered out of the river proved wrong when he was taken to hospital and was discovered to have drunk disinfectant. The vomit and sickness that resulted led to the erroneous belief he had fallen into the river. He was identified by his ration book and had only a few pence in his pocket. A false rumour went around that he had drowned himself by jumping in the Clyde and that he'd been driven to such an act because he was full of remorse for what his book had allegedly done to the city.

I believe the more accurate interpretation is that his failed literary career, following his initial success, was a more likely reason. And, in my view, rather than feel remorse, he should take credit for exposing the reality of the misery of life in Glasgow's slums during the 1920s and 1930s. This was misery that, perhaps, was perpetuated by those politicians of the time who banned the book and tried to sweep the reality of that misery under the carpet.

McAULAY, JOE

This associate of Paul Ferris played a role in the conviction of his boss on gunrunning charges at the Old Bailey, in 1998.

The sleeper train between London and Glasgow is something of a tradition. If the train selected, leaving from Glasgow Central or Euston, had a bar, that made it all the better to while away some hours as the carriages rocked their way to the destination. If there was no bar, there was always the steward with a friendly miniature or two or a suitable 'carry oot' could form an indispensable part of the luggage. It was normal for passengers on the late night InterCity service to enjoy a nightcap or six – it helped you sleep!

The staff were well used to such habits and it took some doing to get into trouble with the railway police. But McAulay managed it. Blind drunk, he was being abusive to other passengers and, when his night train halted at Preston on its way to Glasgow, the Transport Police were called. They got a shock when they looked in the troublesome passenger's holdall. Inside, they found a .22 Ceska handgun.

On this particular night, Paul Ferris was staying in London with associates and, while McAulay languished in a cell in Preston, Ferris made frantic phone calls to try to find out what was happening to him. He told the cops he was just trying to let his friend know how he was getting on. He said he was down in

London trying to get that year's hot Christmas toy, a Buzz Lightyear doll. He also told the police that McAulay had a gun because someone was hassling his daughter. Ferris was right to be worried. McAulay coming to the attention of the police was bad news.

A senior police officer had been working for months trying to get evidence that Ferris was involved in gunrunning. He told the *Evening Times* that 'the link with McAulay was vital. It showed that there was a system going on.' The police allegation was that McAulay had been sent to London by Ferris and there he bought a gun. Aware of the risk in trying to get through security at Gatwick, he had decided to take the train home. In Preston Crown Court, he admitted that the weapon, which had a silencer fitted, and the thirty-nine rounds of ammunition in his luggage were intended to cause 'fear or violence'. The judge said he was plainly carrying the gun for someone else. The nightcaps McAulay had consumed so vigorously on his way north were expensive – they provided a valuable piece of the jigsaw for the police hunting Paul Ferris, gunrunner.

McCANN, JOHN

This small-time criminal of the 1970s ended up in Peterhead and was distinguished by the nickname 'The Aga Khan'. Among the city's criminal fraternity, nicknames are common and often quite ingenious. The 1991 trial in which Paul Ferris was cleared of murdering Arthur Thompson Jnr – himself known as The Fat Boy or The Mars Bar Kid – featured a string of nicknames for those involved as witnesses or otherwise. There was Brian 'Square Go' Graham, William 'The Rock' McLeod, 'Snazz' Adams, William 'Tootsie' Lobban, John 'Blind Jonah' McKenzie, William 'Gillie' Gillen, David 'Soagy' Logue and Joe 'Bananas' Hanlon.

Also on the scene, at one time, was the famous 'Saughton Harrier' which was the soubriquet given to Willie Leitch. Leitch had effected a masterly escape worthy of a theatrical farce or comedy film. Spending time tending the governor's garden at Edinburgh's

Saughton Prison, he noted that a marathon road race was due to pass nearby. With a bit of quick thinking, he fashioned himself a number on his vest, jumped through the governor's prized roses and out on to the street, where he started trotting into the distance in the company of the genuine harriers. His was a nickname was definitely well earned!

McFLANNELS, THE

One of the earliest and most popular of radio soap operas, *The McFlannels* was set up a close in Glasgow and featured the doings of a fictional working class family, the McFlannels. It attracted a huge audience. On a Saturday night, it was a must for Glasgow folk and it was indeed an accurate, if somewhat cosy, view of life in the city in those days. The listeners could relate to the everyday concerns of the radio family and the scripts had a strong seasoning of humour as well as drama.

But, curiously, *The McFlannels* got mixed up in real-life murder and mystery. One of the cast, George McNeill – who played Mr McZephyr, for those old enough to remember the show – was murdered by a 'friend', John Gordon. McNeill had been a lay preacher and, at Fairfield Shipyard, he had been a welfare worker. Given the enormous audience the show attracted and the affection most felt for it, the murder became the talk of the steamie, as they say.

The killer added to the infamy of his crime – and to newspaper sales – with an imaginative attempt to escape the arms of the law. Big John Gordon fled **GOVAN** for the more exotic pleasures of Barcelona from where he was eventually extradited to Scotland to stand trial. Maybe Gordon had done too much adventure story reading in his childhood – when in the Mediterranean sun, he made failed attempts to join both the Spanish and French foreign legions. Convicted of the murder, he spent years in the more down-to-earth confines of Peterhead – a far cry from wearing a kopi, the hat worn by the Legionaires, and tramping the sands of the Sahara.

Even when he was released from his life sentence, John Gordon, a smooth talker, made headlines. Not too long after the gates had banged shut behind him, he found work of a remarkable nature. He got a job as part of a security group guarding Princess Anne – at least he did until the *News of the World* exposed him in a scoop showing how careless those charged with guarding the royal family could be. This was to be only the first of other big-time failures to screen the royals from danger. Tabloid readers will recollect the intruder Michael Fagin who managed to get into the Queen's bedroom and the comedian Aaron Barschak, dressed as Osama bin Laden, who gatecrashed a private party to celebrate Prince William's twenty-first birthday in Windsor Castle.

McGIBBON, BILL

Bill was one of the founding members of the Scottish Offenders Project, a group that bought a flat in Glasgow's south side to help rehabilitate ex-prisoners, especially lifers. His own life was something of an example of what can happen despite an off-the-rails start. He grew up in Bridgeton and was variously a member of the Baltic Fleet and the Brigton Derry. Speaking of those days, he says, 'Your razor went everywhere with you.' He served time in Barlinnie for attempted murder but, one night, as he lay in his cell, he had a dream that some day he would spread the word of God, as a free man, among prison inmates.

In 1993, he told his story to the papers. He spoke of how his conversion had started with Bible classes in the Bar-L and how he returned to prisons to tell hard cases 'that Jesus loved them even if their mothers didn't'.

McGRAW, TAM

Known as 'The Licensee', he is one of the foremost figures to feature in newspaper stories of crime and the underworld in the city. He is also the most financially successful of a dangerous

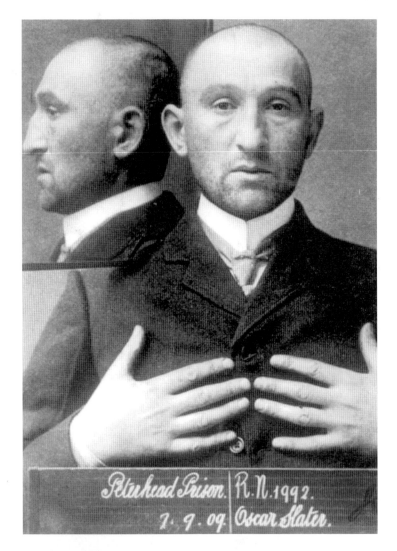

Peterhead Prison. R.N. 1992.
7. 9. 09. Oscar Slater.

ABOVE: Oscar Slater, the victim of one of the most outrageous stitch-ups in the history of crime in Britain. This photograph comes from the Peterhead Prison files. Slater was innocent of the murder of which he was convicted but escaped hanging by a few hours, itself a mysterious decision, and spent almost nineteen years in prison.

LEFT: Detective Lieutenant Trench who exposed the false nature of the case against Slater – and paid for it by being dismissed from the police!

Mrs. Jessie M'Lachlan.
(From the portrait published after the Trial.)

Jessie McLachlan was described as 'the much wronged heroine of the Sandyford mystery' by the legendary writer on criminal matters in Scotland, William Roughead. This portrait, published after her trial and conviction, shows a sad-eyed woman who was, in the view of most students of the case, wrongly convicted. She escaped hanging but spent long years in jail as a model prisoner, always protesting her innocence. Despite her demure look, the trial was a sensational affair with sex, drink and drugs involved.

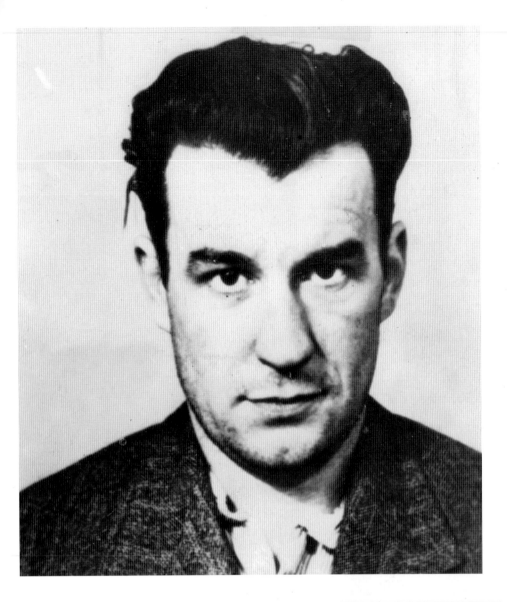

ABOVE: One of the most used newspaper photographs of mass murderer Peter Manuel who died on the gallows in Barlinnie on 11 July 1958, reputedly running the last few steps on to the scaffold. The Lanarkshire woodworker was sentenced to hang after being found guilty of seven killings but it is now thought that he killed at least twice that number.

RIGHT: Manuel's trial was perhaps the most dramatic heard in Glasgow High Court. He defended himself for much of the time and insisted on interviewing master baker William Watt who was brought to the court to give evidence on a strecher after an injury. Manuel killed Watt's family and then tried to implicate him, an innocent man, in the murders.

THE VICTIMS

Patricia Docker

Helen Puttock

Mima McDonald

ABOVE: This is the face that no one who lived in Glasgow in 1968 and 1969 can forget – the haunting indentikit police poster of the killer they called Bible John. Still unsolved, the murders of three young women who'd been at the dancin' are an intriguing mystery and talking point to this day. Now, some believe there was more than one killer.

LEFT: The newspaper interest in the Bible John case was immense with squads of reporters following every twist and turn in the investigation. Here, one of the top detectives involved, the late Joe Beattie, emerges from the incident caravan to brief waiting hacks.

The history of crime in Glasgow is peppered with injustices, perhaps none worse than the wrongful conviction of Joe Steele and Thomas 'T C' Campbell of the Ice-Cream Wars murders in 1984. It took till 2004 to overturn the verdicts after appeals and reinvestigations. Over the years, the faces of those involved became familiar to newspaper readers who were able to see how dramatically their appearances changed as time passed. This photo shows Thomas Lafferty, on the left, who featured in the original trial and a young 'T C' is on the right.

Down the long years of wrongful imprisonment, Campbell, seen here on the left, and Steele took on authority as they fought to prove their innocence. Their attempts to secure justice involved more than beards and T-shirts. At one stage, after an escape from prison, Steele chained himself to the railings of Buckingham Palace and, in another stunt, he climbed a security tower at Barlinnie.

The two victims of a police stitch-up had some false dawns. Released on appeal, they were rejailed again before their final release. They were no strangers to a walk down the court steps in suits and ties. But there was to be no truimphalism when they were finally released. Instead, there was a considered plea for justice and a detailed look at the procedures that had led to them being wrongly convicted of the hideous murder of a family, including a young baby, all these years ago.

LEFT: This is the face of one of the hardest of hard men in a hard city – Arthur Thompson Snr. Thompson was one of a series of Godfathers who continue to blight the city. From his home near Hogganfield Loch, the legendary and much guarded Ponderosa, he ruled an evil army that once included the likes of Paul Ferris. Arthur Snr survived assassination attempts to die in his bed. But his son, also Arthur, was mown down in the street in a gangland killing.

RIGHT: The hearse that took old Arthur to his final resting place was covered in flowers and the police were out in force to control the traffic at Glasgow's equivalent of a Mafia send-off.

ABOVE: The bad old days of chequebook journalism as reporters fight over Walter Scott Ellis outside the court when he was freed after facing a charge of murdering a taxi driver. This undignified and distasteful mini riot resulted in the authorities taking a close look at how newspapers were allowed to cover trials and led to changes being made to the law.

This is Walter Norval, the city's first Godfather. A hard man who grew up in the Garscube Road area, he was a teenage tearaway and leader of a gang known as the Wee Mob. He matured into a feared man of violence, an audacious bank robber and criminal mastermind whose career was brought to a sudden end when he was betrayed by a gang member. As Godfather, he presided over the unification of several gangs and, for a spell, large areas of the north side of the city were under his control. Here, in his heyday, he is seen celebrating a court victory with Agnes Delacorti who had been accused of killing his hated step-father but was found not guilty.

CRIME BUSTERS

LEFT: The 'Captain' of police legend, Sir Percy Sillitoe the Chief Constable who came to Glasgow to tackle the problem of gangs. Using force, he had many successes in defeating them in violent street battles.

RIGHT: Sir David McNee, perhaps the most influential of Sillitoe's successors. Nicknamed the 'Hammer', he was a different sort of policeman – he was still no soft touch but he was more thoughtful. Keen to improve life for Glasgow's citizens, he was not just interested in hammering the neds – though he did do that too!

The Barlinnie Special Unit was a remarkable experiment in penal reform. It had some considerable successes before it was closed down, amid lurid tales of sex and drugs behind bars and a general feeling that its policy of redemption rather than retribution had lost its way. But it still influences the penal system for the good. Two of its most well-known occupants, who both went on to make names for themselves in the world of arts, were novelist and sculptor Hugh Collins (left) and Jimmy Boyle. Collins seemed, in public at least, to be the more reflective about having lived two very different lives – a murderer who regretted his past and wrestled with the intellectual challenges of living as a changed man with a changed life. Here, he reflects before one of countless interviews.

The most flamboyant of the new gangland characters is Paul Ferris who, from time to time, claims to have left his past behind him. He featured in some memorable trials and made an indelible mark on the history of crime in the city. Cleared of killing Arthur Thompson Jnr, he went on to do time south of the border for his involvement in the supply of guns. Once an associate of Arthur Snr, he took on his old mentor's liking for expensive suits and silk ties – hardly the normal uniform for a Glasgow hard man.

breed that emerged from the east end in the post-war years. As a young man, he worked as an enforcer and general hard man for what was known as the Barlanark Team. He is also said to have had associations with the Thompson clan at one time. His long career, battling with the law, took him to the point, in August 2004, when it was reported that he had a fortune which was said to be estimated at £20 million. He was at odds with the income tax authorities who were pursuing him for large sums of money – as high as several hundred thousand pounds in some reports but much lower in others – they claimed he owed them from the profits of a taxi cab firm he used to own.

Aficionados of real-life crime will recall that it was trouble with the tax guys that took 'Big Al' Capone across America in 1931 from his Chicago fiefdom to the cells of Alcatraz out in the bay of San Francisco. Sentenced to a ten-year stretch for tax evasion, he served eight years. It is worth noting that, when Alphonse was arrested, it was thought that his crime syndicate was making profits of $100 million a year – and that was more than seventy years ago! But it would not necessarily be a good move to bet on the taxman beating Tam McGraw.

The Licensee and Paul Ferris are often linked in the crime pages of the tabloids and there are similarities in their careers – not least of which is the fact that McGraw, like Ferris, 'walked' after a long-running trial. During it, Donald Findlay QC gave an interesting indication of McGraw's attitude to tax. 'Mr McGraw does not pay tax and he doesn't like paying tax,' he said. But that was just one aside in a complex trial.

The Licensee stood trial in July 1988, accused of bankrolling a major drug-running operation. The charge was found not proven by a majority of the jury and he walked free.

McGraw's release came after another masterful performance by Donald Findlay who, at one stage in the proceedings, described his client as an Arthur Daley figure, 'ducking and diving'. McGraw has little of the verbal flamboyance of Paul Ferris and feels no need to feed good lines to the press. On this occasion, when he was leaving the High Court in Edinburgh and about to get into a black Merc, he contented himself to telling the hacks who were looking for juicy comments on the case to 'fuck off'.

It had been an untidy and disappointing prosecution for the police and the Crown since, of the original eleven men charged, only three remained in the dock at the close of play. But it was yet another triumph for Findlay. The judge told the three men, one of whom was McGraw's brother-in-law, who were convicted that 'the jury have found you guilty of playing various roles in what was a major drug importation operation, which has been a disturbing example of organised crime in the midst of needy Glasgow communities.'

But the trial did offer some interesting insights into the business life of Tam McGraw. Donald Findlay hammered home the point to the jury that the case against his client was flimsy and there was not one scrap of evidence to show that his money was going to Spain to buy the drugs. Findlay told the jury that Thomas McGraw was a character who did a bit of this and a bit of that and that he didn't pay tax or VAT. He told the court that, coupled with his legitimate business activities, his client's objection to paying tax explained why he was in possession of huge sums of money. His cash came from a cash-and-carry business, ice-cream vans and the Caravel public house. It was said that, at one stage, he had handed over £100,000 to the taxman but was left with more than £300,000 of legitimate money. It was all vintage Donald Findlay. While deliberately evading paying tax was not an admirable way to behave, it did not make McGraw a drug smuggler. The QC went on, 'There is not a single scrap of evidence in this case which in any way connects Thomas McGraw with the bus [the vehicle used for conveying the drugs, it was alleged], holidays in Spain or anything else.' He warned the jury that the Crown case was based on suspicion and possibilities – and *that* had never been enough to convict a man of a crime in Scotland. He believed that, if ever there was a case of the Crown adding two and two together and coming up with seven and a half, this was it. So McGraw, who has always denied wrongdoing, left the court a free man.

He has not been convicted of any offence for twenty years. The next The Licensee was heard of, in the press, was when news broke that he was selling his business empire. This included a car-hire company that was alleged to have been at the centre of a police and customs operation over whispers about the laundering of drug money. McGraw said he was giving up his business interests in order to spend more time in Tenerife where he owns property.

There followed some years out of the headlines at home but McGraw was still in the money in a big way. The spell of obscurity ended spectacularly in the spring of 2002 when there was an outburst of street violence involving some big gang names. The police believe that much of this wave of infighting was down to various factions warring over drugs and territory, in particular, the remnants of the territories once controlled by the Thompson empire. At this time, T C Campbell, once of the feared Gaucho gang and the self-styled Emperor of Carntyne, was out of jail, waiting for his Ice-Cream Wars conviction to be finally overturned, and a certain Paul Ferris was back strutting the streets in his pinstripes. All the ingredients for trouble were on hand. It was reported that McGraw, back from the sun in Spain, was attacked in the street, by a knife-wielding assailant, in broad daylight. It was said that he was patched up in Ross Hall private hospital and that a bullet proof vest, the so-called Kevlar coat of gangland, saved him from more serious injury. McGraw then took what was for him an unusual step. He issued a statement, through his lawyers, denying the press reports about the attack and adding that he was alive and well at home and that he had not been stabbed.

Around the same time, T C Campbell was attacked in **HALHILL ROAD** near his **BARLANARK** home and whacked over the head with a golf club. This was a much more upmarket weapon than the traditional baseball bat or knife. It was speculated that the use of golf clubs as weapons was because they were legitimate sporting equipment that wouldn't look out of place in the back of one of the trendy 4x4s so favoured by the wealthy criminal elite in the drugs business. But make no mistake, a whack over the head with a wedge is no joke.

There were other incidents on the streets. All this activity resulted in a new splurge of press interest in the doings of the modern gangs. Public concern was so strong that Chief Superintendent Kevin Smith of **LONDON ROAD** Station, as near to the front line as you can get, told reporters, 'It is important to stress that these types of incidents generally involve a certain circle of people and not the community at large.' The names of those in that circle were well known to every one who read a newspaper in the city!

Campbell, who had got used to talking to the press and using them for his own ends in his battle against the injustice of his fire-raising conviction, was almost eloquent in his description of the attack on him. It gave some real insight into what was going on. He said, 'The attack had come out of the blue. I had just got out of the house and got to the gate of the community centre [not far from a school], when a car pulled up and two men jumped out with murderous intent.' He went on to say that he told the attackers, 'Leave it out, look at the witnesses. You are going to jail – don't be stupid.' The assault went on for around ten minutes with attackers and victims rolling on the ground. Campbell was not immodest about his role. 'My training as a boxer when I was younger helped me ward off and sidestep the blows. It definitely helped save my life,' he said. It's tough on the streets.

All this was to be followed by even more sensational claims. The *Daily Record*, which is always quick on the case in gangster matters and usually on the inside track, ran a remarkable story under headlines like 'Contract of the Devils' and 'Gangsters' Hit Man Pact'. The paper told of McGraw and Paul Ferris going to a lawyer to draw up a document that would guarantee them both personal safety for some years. It looked as if the underworld was becoming a bit too hot for comfort for all concerned.

Unlikely as it seems, these 'sworn enemies' were said to have made a pact to save themselves from gangland assassins. If either were to be killed, the story goes, and the finger of suspicion pointed at the other, the survivor's interests would pass to the victim's associates. It was the sort of arrangement that would have tested the ingenuity of a Hollywood scriptwriter. Incidentally, the interests referred to include properties, leisure industries, car hire and valeting, among others. The tale even intrigued the police who commented, 'This pair have been at each other's throats for years. It is pretty amazing if they have entered into an agreement like this.'

Did it happen? What happens next? Who knows? What is for sure is that there are some new wars being fought.

McKENZIE, JOHN 'BLIND JONAH'

This thug led a life seeped in violence and provided an unusual footnote in the city's criminal history. He has the dubious distinction of being accused of a gangland murder while being blind in both eyes. He had lost the sight of one eye in his youth and the other when he was said to have been stabbed by a gangland rival. He died of a heart attack but drug abuse was suspected – he was jailed for five years in 1985 after being caught in the east end with a massive consignment of heroin.

McLACHLAN, JESSIE

One of the most remarkable and sensational trials in the city's history began on Wednesday 17 September 1862. It was heard before Lord Deas, a judge so partial to wearing the black cap that his nickname in legal circles was 'Lord Death'. The defendant was Jessie McLachlan who was accused of killing a friend, a domestic servant called Jess McPherson. Jess had worked for a nasty character called James Fleming, a modestly-wealthy retired weaver who was known to the newspapers of the time as 'Old Fleming' – mainly to distinguish him from his son John, who was a respectable accountant.

Poor Jess had been hacked to death with a cleaver. Like Lizzie Borden's father and stepmother, Jess was whacked about the head – although the number of times the cleaver was wielded in this case could not match the Massachusetts case which is immortalised in the rhyme:

> Lizzie Borden took an axe
> And gave her mother forty whacks.
> When she saw what she had done,
> She gave her father forty one.

Glasgow's meat-cleaver murder didn't quite make it into folk memory in the same style as Lizzie's crime did but it did precede the American killing by thirty years. And it did attract the attention of two of the city's most respected writers on crime, Jack House and William Roughead. To Roughead, who edited a massive tome on the case in the *Notable British Trials* series, Jessie was a 'much wronged heroine'. Jack House, in his celebrated book, *Square Mile of Murder*, was also convinced of her innocence. However, he does suggest that, although not actually the killer – Old Fleming did it was his verdict – she may have played a role in the crime.

Before the turn of the twentieth century, the press more or less had a free hand to speculate on crimes without any great fear of libel or being accused of contempt of court. I am in no doubt that poor Jessie suffered greatly from this 'freedom'. Long before she stood in the dock, her name had been blackened in the local press. As the whole city worked itself up into a lather over the savage killing, rumours were invented or presented as fact. Many pertinent facts pointing to Old Fleming, rather than Jessie, as the murderer were ignored.

We tend to think of pre-trial publicity and the ready ability of the public mind to convict the accused without recourse to trial or, sometimes, despite any real evidence, as a modern phenomenon that is fuelled by the excesses of the red-top tabloids. The pre-trial hysteria about the Soham murders and the hounding of Maxine

Carr is a modern case in point. Newspapers walk a tightrope every day – they have to balance feeding the public appetite for detail piled on detail of horrific crimes with ensuring they don't prejudice any eventual trial.

In Scotland, the law regarding this is – as it is in most respects – more sound than that operating in England, where newspapers have gone over the score in many recent cases. But, in the nineteenth century, our papers were as bad as the worst today. It has to be said, however, that the Jessie McLachlan trial would have tempted any editor, no matter how circumspect. It would also have tried the patience and skill of a top team of newspaper night lawyers, the legal eagles hired to keep editors out of jail!

The scale of the interest in the case was almost unprecedented.

Long after the conviction, Sir Archibald Alison, Sheriff of Lanarkshire, wrote the following in his autobiography:

> Such was the public anxiety for intelligence that the newspapers for a month were daily filled with these details – [like the story that Jessie's hands were scratched] – accompanied by the most violent declamations against the woman, as each successive article of evidence was revealed. To such a pitch did the public excitement on the subject rise that the editors of some of the daily papers told my clerk, Mr Young, that their circulation since the precognitions began to be published had risen from 10,000 to 50,000 a day; and that if only they could secure a Mrs McLachlan a month, they would soon be in a situation to retire from business with handsome fortunes! I myself was obliged, when the trial of the prisoner was fixed, to write a circular to the editors requesting them to abstain from any further notice of the case, as, if the incessant discussion went on, the prisoner could never have a fair trial.

For circulation boosts like that, I suspect some modern tabloid editors would send out for a meat cleaver themselves!

The case itself had every sensational ingredient you could wish for – class warfare, family infighting, violence, theft, drink and even a hint of drugs. Saturday 5 July 1862 dawned fine and warm. It was four in the morning and three sisters, Margaret, Jessie and Peterina McLean who had been to their brother's wedding in Partick were walking home along what was then known as Sauchiehall Road. There were respectable terraces on either side of the road and, in the many trees and bushes, the birds sang. The sisters noticed that in one house a gas light was burning brightly. They wondered if someone was sick or if there was perhaps a very late party going on. The light shone from 17 **SANDYFORD PLACE**. It also attracted the attention of other passers-by who were discussing something they had heard. But the groups moved on before another stroller, Mary McIntyre, a dressmaker, reached No. 17. She heard a low moaning noise. She wondered for a moment if she should go to the house to see what was wrong but, for one reason or another, decided against it. Jack House observed that, had she done so, the murder might have been avoided or solved.

The house was home to the weaver Old Fleming, his accountant son John and a grandson, also called John, who worked in his father's office. It was said that the accountant was somewhat ashamed of his father who spoke roughly, was too fond of a dram and liked the company of the servants overmuch. That particular weekend, the accountant and his son had gone to their house in Dunoon, leaving the old man and the servant, Jess McPherson, alone. They were sure the old fellow would be looked after though they might not have been so confident if they had known more of Jess. At thirty-five, she had had two illegitimate children and had been telling her friends that Old Fleming was an 'auld deevil' who was always asking her to marry him. Old Fleming himself was either seventy-eight or eighty-seven. He gave different ages at different times and the truth was never established, other than the fact that he was a grandfather and no youngster.

The son and grandson returned to town on Monday 7 July, worked in their office in **ST VINCENT PLACE** till around 4 p.m. and then headed home. The older man went to the butcher's to

168

collect some meat and John Jnr, the grandson, went to Sandyford Place. His grandfather opened the door. 'Where's Jess?' said the young man, surprised that she hadn't been the one to let him in.

His grandfather informed him that he hadn't seen Jess since Friday, adding, 'She's away. She's cut.'

Her room was locked but, when the accountant returned from the shops, he and John Jnr managed to get into it. The door opened on to a shocking sight. Jess McPherson's bloody body was lying alongside her bed. She was naked from the waist down and some clothing obscured the upper part of her body and head. This seemed to affect John Fleming's common sense for he ran around the area in something of a panic. A delivery boy from the butcher's who had arrived on the scene called the police. Young Fleming had managed to summon a doctor who found that Jess McPherson's savagely attacked body was 'quite cold' and declared that she had 'been dead for some time'.

To this confused scene there was added another witness, a neighbour named Mrs Walker. This woman was something of a busybody who kept an eye on what was going on in the neighbourhood but her observations were to prove useful. She had been attracted to the murder scene when looking out of her window over some waste ground at the back of Sandyford Place. The area was frequented by prostitutes and drunks so she knew something unusual was going on when she was confronted by the sight of a policeman running. On the Monday afternoon, she turned up at the house where Old Fleming was telling everyone who would listen that the last he had seen of Jess McPherson was on Friday night at half past nine and he found her door locked on Saturday morning.

In his classic *Square Mile of Murder*, Jack House wryly observed that Mrs Walker's true vocation seemed to be that of a detective. In the event, she was the one who asked the obvious question about Old Fleming when she wondered why he hadn't thought of enquiring about the girl, given that she had been away for so long. 'No,' replied the old man. Mrs Walker pressed on, asking whether he had thought of getting the locked door opened and if he had checked to see if anything had been stolen. When questioned if he had heard anything, Old Fleming said he did hear some moaning at around four o'clock on the Saturday morning. 'Detective' Walker probed further, asking the old man why, if he was awake and had heard moaning, he had not even shouted down to find out what was the matter. 'I didnae think,' was the answer.

By now, the police surgeon had arrived and found that the victim had been killed with an axe or cleaver and that the bedroom floor had been washed. So had an area of the kitchen near to the bedroom. But there were still three footprints in blood beside the bed and these may or may not have been left by the killer. There were bloodstains in and around the kitchen and basement. And some of Old Fleming's shirts, stored in nearby room, also had spots of blood on them. Some silverware of no great value was missing and so were the best dresses belonging to Jess and, according to the investigators, her clothes chest looked as if 'some bloody hand had been working in it'. Mrs Walker had been shrewd in her questions – one of the oddest aspects of the case is that Old Fleming apparently did nothing when the servant went missing. He even went to the kirk twice on the Sunday and never mentioned her to anyone.

The post-mortem pointed to the fatal blows being delivered lightly. This was consistent with the kind of force used by a woman or a weak man. The size of the bloodstained footprints proved they were neither Jess's nor Old Fleming's.

While the efforts of the newspapers may have tended to prejudice a fair trial, their keen reporting of every detail of the crime did have some positive effect. A pawnbroker read of the missing silverware and found he had what looked like it. His books showed that the silverware had been pawned by a Mary McDonald of 5 **ST VINCENT STREET**. No such person stayed at that address. The same day this happened, the police arrested Old Fleming in connection with the killing and he was committed to prison for further enquiries. No one knows what the old rascal told the police

170

when he was incarcerated but, somehow, the police became interested in a twenty-eight-year-old woman who lived with her husband at 182 **BROOMIELAW**. This was Jessie McLachlan who had been a servant in the Fleming household for two years and was close to Jess. She knew Old Fleming as well and met him when she visited Jess at Sandyford Place. Old Fleming was also known to have called at the McLachlans' house in Broomielaw. Jessie's husband, James, worked as a mate on a cargo ship on the Irish run and his job kept him away from home for periods. A hint of trouble ahead came when James came home from sea to read in the papers the pawnbroker's description of the woman who pawned the silverware. 'That's unco like you,' he said to Jessie. The police seemed to be on the same scent and, on 13 July, Jessie and James were both arrested. James had been at sea at the time of the crime and Jessie protested she had nothing to do with it. The husband only spent one night in jail but for Jessie it was a different story.

In the course of the case, Jessie made a number of 'statements'. The first came after her arrest. In it, she told of a visit to Jess in Sandyford Place but said:

> I was not in or near Mr Fleming's house on the evening of Friday the 4th or the morning of Saturday the 5th and did not see Jess McPherson that night or morning and I was in no way concerned in assaulting or murdering her, nor was I concerned in stealing any silver plate from the house on said night or morning.

She then gave a convoluted account to her movements on the night of the killing but said that, on the Saturday, around midday, she had gone to the pawnbroker in **EAST CLYDE STREET** with silver plate. She said Old Fleming had brought the silverware to her house and asked her to pawn it for him, telling her she should use the name of Mary McDonald.

According to her, Fleming was short of money and said he

wanted the £3.10s he thought it would raise for a trip to the Highlands. In fact, the silver plate raised almost double that sum. The statement, which took four and a half hours to wring out of her, went on to say that Old Fleming had come round to collect his money. He gave her five pounds for doing the message and said that she was to tell no one about it. Jessie also went into great detail about the clothes she wore that weekend and detailed other clothes she had had altered or dyed. She also mentioned a mysterious black box.

Most of this extremely long statement was nonsense and the police knew it. They could prove she had been out of her house most of the night of the 4th–5th and a tip-off had resulted in a black box being found in **BRIDGE STREET** Railway Station. It contained the clothes missing from the chest in Jess McPherson's bedroom. Jessie's explanation for this was that she had been asked to get the clothes altered for Jess.

Then came another intriguing twist. Jessie was visited in jail by a Dr George McLeod who asked for her assistance in an experiment. He had wax cloth and bull's blood with him and asked Jessie to stand on the blood and then stand on a plank of wood. The prints corresponded closely to those found on the floor at the scene of the murder. This was seemingly enough to get Old Fleming released. This event triggered a new frenzy of speculation in the newspapers. The then *Glasgow Herald* in particular seemed pleased that a shadow had been lifted from a 'respectable' family. In their opinion this 'auld deevil', as his servant put it, was entirely above suspicion and they took a swipe at their newspaper rivals, saying:

> It is no small satisfaction to us, we must declare, that, in spite of the strongest prejudice and gross perversion of facts, we stuck to the side of the old innocent – and we believe we were the only paper in the city that did so without the least equivocation.

So much for waiting for the trial and an independent analysis of the facts!

The modern reader may agree with Jessie who, on learning Old Fleming had been freed, told a fellow inmate, 'He's an old murderer. He did the deed. The guilty has got out and the innocent kept in. If I had the money I would have got out as well as him.' It was an understandable reaction.

But this was an incredibly complex case. Around this same time, bloodstained clothing was found in a Lanarkshire field and some of it matched clothing found at Jessie McLachlan's house in Broomielaw. Jessie simply denied knowledge of the clothes but went on to make another of her sensational statements which all seem to be a strange mixture of truth and untruth. This time, she admitted she was in Sandyford Place on the night of the murder. Her lawyers advised her against making this statement as they were sure the Crown could not prove she was there at the time. During her time in jail, Jessie, unaware of the detailed evidence against her, had been discussing the case with lawyers and fellow prisoners and was getting her side of the story into a fankle.

With a fanfare of trumpets, the trial began on 17 September in Glasgow High Court. Shifting the trial to Edinburgh might have offered a less passionate arena for the search for the truth but that option was not taken. The first witness was Old Fleming who told of Jess serving him his breakfast on the fateful Friday morning. He had told Mrs Walker that after having breakfast he'd been lying abed when he'd heard noises coming from Jess's bedroom and he later told the court the same tale. He went on to say he thought she had a friend with her and that was why he didn't pursue the matter. He then went into great detail about how he had spent the rest of the weekend, even down to telling how he had made himself a boiled herring and tea for breakfast. He was of the opinion that Jess had left with her friends or acquaintances.

The bloodstains on the shirts he explained happened when he had dried them on screens near the murder bedroom. He stuck by that version of events though he did admit that he knew Jessie

McLachlan and had visited the house. This went against previous newspaper reports that he said he didn't even know her. He also denied Jessie's pawn story.

Contemporary reports indicate that the Judge, Lord Deas, made cross-examination of the old fellow difficult making many interruptions and did not himself question the witness in any depth.

But the old rascal did say some odd things in the witness box. There was speculation about why he, rather than Jess, had answered the door to the milk boy on the morning of Saturday or Sunday. This was made all the more unusual by the fact that he had been fully dressed so early in the day. Asked about this, he said something along the lines of, 'We kent it was a' ower wi' Jess afore that.' The various newspapers reported the words slightly differently but the nub was that he seemed to be saying he knew she was dead.

But it was to get even more sensational. Andrew Rutherford Clark, Jessie's chief defence counsel, asked the same question in another way and got three answers. 'There was no Jessie to open the door that mornin'.', 'She was deid before that.' and 'On Saturday morning, ye ken, she was deid – she couldna open the door when she was deid.' But, when Mr Clark zeroed in to ask if he knew, when he had answered the door to the milk boy, that Jess was dead, he suddenly replied loudly that he did not. And then the judge cut short that line of argument. Old Fleming made a plea for pity, saying, 'I can say no more than I have. I have told you everything in my heart. The memory of a man of seventy-eight years is not so fresh as a young man's. Be as easy as ye can.' At this point, a member of the jury pointed out to the judge that he had already given his age as eighty-seven. Fleming was again asked his age but this time said eighty-seven! Lord Deas kindly told the old man, 'You can go now.' and the jury was denied any real insight into his involvement.

Next up was Jessie herself. Guilty or not, her lies in statements made to fellow prisoners had eased the Crown case. But there was to be another twist. The defence produced a witness who said Old

Fleming had been called before his own Kirk Session to explain amorous activities. But Lord Deas seemed to show his prejudice in favour of Fleming by again ending a line of questioning that might have helped Jessie. And the defence's closing was hampered by the fact that Mr Clark felt that he should major on his belief that the Crown could not prove that Jessie McLachlan was in Sandyford Place on the night of the killing – even despite that statement by Jessie herself saying that she was there. The defence counsel actually had the statement admitting she had been at the scene on the night of the killing in his pocket. Lord Deas's summing-up was said by many to be more like the address for the prosecution than the address for the prosecution had been. Incidentally, he arrived in court for that one-sided summing-up ostentatiously carrying the black cap in his hand. The jury took the hint and, after a mere fifteen minutes, the verdict was guilty. Considering the complexity of the case and the contradictions that peppered the evidence, this was quite remarkable.

Asked if she had anything to say, Jessie declared her innocence and was then allowed to read a lengthy statement. In essence, it told of Jessie, Jess and the old rascal, at home without the influence of his son and grandson, getting involved in something of a drinking session. So much alcohol was consumed that Jessie said she went out to a whisky shop in **NORTH STREET** for more. On her return, she exchanged some words with Fleming and then she heard moaning coming from Jess's bedroom. She said she went into the bedroom where she found Jess 'stupid or insensible', with a bleeding wound across her brow. According to her statement, she then asked Fleming why he had done this. He replied that it was an accident and he had not meant to hurt her.

Jessie claimed to have then ministered to her friend's injuries but could not get much sense out of her. In her statement to the court, Jessie indicated that Fleming had attacked his servant in a sexual way after all concerned had been drinking. There was discussion about sending for a doctor but, in the drunken confusion, nothing was done. According to Jessie, Old Fleming came back into the room to help mop up blood and water was spilled everywhere. Jessie asked the old man to help her and together they put the roughly bandaged Jess to bed. It must have been a hellish scene as they both attended to Jess and mopped up the blood.

After a while, once Fleming had left the room, Jessie said Jess told her of an occasion, a few weeks earlier, when the two younger Flemings had also been away. Jess said the old man had gone out and got fu'. He came home and tried to get into bed with her and take liberties. The next day, he blamed his behaviour on the drink and made her promise not to tell his son. From then on, Jess apparently felt that Fleming saw her as a threat, a woman able to destroy his façade of respectability.

Jessie McLachlan then asked how Fleming could have struck Jess 'after his own doings with her'. He said he was sorry and would make it up to her. A doctor was to be called in the morning he said but it was clear he was worried that the happenings of that dreadful night would come out. Jessie says she was made to swear on the Bible that she would never tell of it.

This truly sensational statement went on to say that Jess took a turn for the worse and that Fleming was obstructive about summoning a doctor. She seemed to be dying. Jessie left the room at one point and returned to see the old man striking Jess with a meat chopper. Jessie, fearful that she too would be murdered, ran. But the old devil didn't attempt to harm her and merely said, 'Help me!' He went on to tell Jessie that he knew from the first that Jess would not live. The pair knew they were both in trouble should anything come out. The statement continued:

He said it was as much as our lives were worth if either of us would say a word about it. So he bade me help him and wash the blood from the floor, but I said I could not do it if I should ever move. He took the body by the oxters and dragged it ben into the laundry, and took the sheet and wiped up the blood with it off the floor. The sheet and the blankets he had thrown up off the floor on to the end of the table; and, when he took off the sheet to wipe up the blood, I saw the chopper all covered in blood lying beneath it. I beseeched and begged him to let me go away, and I would swear never to reveal what I had seen, in case of being taken up for it myself as well as him. He said that the best way would be for him to say that he found the house robbed in the morning and to leave the larder window open. He brought the dresses from Jess room into the kitchen, and said that if I would take them away, and buy a box, and take them by some railway out of the way to some place, or to send the box to some address by the railway to lie till called for, that it would never be found out what had become of the clothes.

Jessie McLachlan went on in her statement to clear up points about the pawning and the meeting with the milk boy. She also acknowledged that her friend Jess had a provoking tongue and could use it in her verbal jousts with Old Fleming. Her defence counsel read the statement to the court and it took forty minutes. According to Jack House, it had a remarkable effect on everyone in court – with the exception of the black-hearted judge. He went on to sentence her in such a way that House could write, 'I know of no other convicted person who was sentenced in so cruel and vindictive a manner as Lord Deas used to Jessie McLachlan.' Part of the sentence read as follows:

In the course of that night, at precisely what time and in what precise manner we do not know . . . probably when she was asleep, you did attack her with that cleaver we saw here, or some other deadly instrument . . . upon that night you did most barbarously and most cruelly murder that unsuspecting woman, who believed you were up to that hour the best friend she had in the world.

He went on in similar vein for some, time saying, 'There is not upon my mind a shadow of suspicion that the old gentleman had

177

anything whatever to do with the murder.' On went the black cap and Jessie was told that she would dine on bread and water till 11 October when she would be hanged. 'And may God almighty have mercy on your soul,' the judge said in conclusion. Jessie's response was to say, 'Aye, he'll hae mercy for I am innocent.' And many people who had followed the case agreed. It seems certain that she did play some part in the crime but it seems equally certain that Old Fleming was far from being an innocent old man and there is much to point to him as the actual killer.

Strangely, it was an English newspaper that summed up what had happened. In a leader, the *Daily Telegraph* highlighted the fact that no evidence was presented to the jury to show the previous relationships between Old Fleming and his family and servants, including Jess. According to the newspaper, the only real evidence against Jessie was that she was in possession of the victim's property and there was nothing else of importance to link her to the killing. Admitting that she may have been involved in some way, the *Telegraph* said it seemed impossible to believe that Jessie McLachlan had left home that night to kill Jess McPherson. They asked for an inquiry into this strange trial before Jessie went to the hands of the hangman.

A petition to delay the execution until more inquiries had been made was started and it found support in all parts of Britain, with 50,000 in Glasgow alone signing it. Old Fleming was hounded by mobs of folk convinced of his guilt. The Lord Advocate ordered an inquiry and the hanging was delayed till 1 November. Not long after the inquiry, the sentence was reduced to penal servitude for life and Jessie spent fifteen years as a model prisoner in Perth Prison.

She always insisted she was innocent. As for the Fleming family, they felt the alteration to the sentence damaged their respectability and John Fleming wanted the Crown to admit that the change in the sentence was not intended to infer that Mr Fleming was other than innocent of the murder. He got no response.

But this bizarre case was to have further surprises. A year after the trial, news came of a 'confession'. Jessie, who had become famous for her inability to stop lying, at least some of the time, had made another of her famous statements. Her lawyers had given it to *The Glasgow Herald* in order, they said, that the correct statement should be known rather than a hearsay version. It was intensely detailed and, at times, rambling. It said that, when Jessie was interviewed in jail, after being accused of the murder, she appeared to be hysterical – sometimes crying, sometimes laughing and giggling – as she made statements contradicting some of her earlier claims. It was said she was not insane and seemed to know what she was speaking about. In the midst of her statement, she said that, on the fateful night, 'the auld man wasnae there at all'. So much for watching him use the cleaver!

It should be remembered that, in the annals of crime, it is not unusual for an accused person, at some stage, to falsely confess to the crime. But the fact is that what really happened on that drunken night will never be fully known. The mysteries thrown up by Jessie's talent to make conflicting statements could be explained by the quantities of drink taken. She tells that Jess had got sick with the drink and was lying on the kitchen floor vomiting. Then she washed the vomit from Jess's face and brought in blankets. In this version, the blankets were not washed to remove bloodstains.

Into this powerful mixture of three folk, all the worse for wear because of drink, came a new element – laudanum. The fuss had left Jessie McLachlan herself sick from drink and feeling nauseous. Jess McPherson gave her a large dose of the drug to help her. This made her delirious. She remembered nothing else till the body was found in the morning. On hearing all this, her counsel said it put them in a difficult position. But, having said it, the prisoner quickly changed her mind. She said it was a load of nonsense and she had made it up to see how the lawyers would take it. She went back to the stance that what she had said at the trial had been the real truth about what had happened.

All this, and the effect it had on the defence lawyers, led to the Dean of the Faculty of Advocates in Edinburgh being brought in to the controversy. He suggested further interviews and pointed to the injustice that would be done to the Flemings if the old man was innocent. The interview took place and Jessie was told to be completely honest – she couldn't be hanged now the sentence had been reduced. Amazingly, she denied ever having talked about laudanum and reiterated that Old Fleming had 'done the act'.

For once, the papers gave the earlier statement and the hysterical 'confession' short shrift. Indeed, now the trial was over, they began to look at Old Fleming differently. He had fathered an illegitimate child by a domestic servant, when in his seventies. The police had not properly investigated his wardrobe – he would have had plenty of opportunity to burn any bloodstained clothes. The light seen by those homeward bound party-goers was also not probed and there was the mystery of the milk boy who insisted that the old man had come to the door fully dressed at before eight on the Saturday morning.

But perhaps the most telling proof of Jessie's innocence was highlighted in a book by Christianna Brand, which was published many years after the case. In *Heaven Knows Who* (London: Joseph, 1960), Brand pointed out that all the evidence showed Jessie had been seen outside in the street when the first moaning from Sandyford Place had been heard. Jess, it seems, had been attacked before Jessie arrived. The attack witnessed by Jessie was the second one according to this version. Other bits of the police evidence, like the washing of the head and neck of the body, confirm Jessie's trial statement. *Heaven Knows Who* is a splendid title and serves to confrim the idea that no one will now know the full truth of the case. But, looking back, it seems to me that Old Fleming had indeed 'done the act' – perhaps after his sexual advances had led to a row with Jess. Even if Jessie McLachlan was involved at some level, she was still the victim of a prejudiced trial.

She was given a ticket to leave Perth in October 1877, by which time old Fleming had died and been buried in **ANDERSTON** Kirkyard which has now disappeared under motorways. There was some happiness for Jessie when she was released and reunited with her son who, by that time, was eighteen. However, her husband James had disappeared. To escape the controversy still around her, she fled to America to seek anonymity and there she married. She died at Port Huron, Michigan, in 1899 of a heart attack.

McNEE, SIR DAVID

Along with Sir Percy Sillitoe, he is the most remembered and distinguished of the city's chief constables. He succeeded Sir James Robertson in 1971 and then went south to serve as Commissioner of the Met in London from 1977 to 1982. A committed Christian and, in particular, an enthusiast for Billy Graham-style evangelism, he was far from the stereotyped concept of the hard-nosed cop at war with the neds, ready to fight fire with fire and to retaliate first. That sort of policing had largely died with Sillitoe. David McNee was motivated by his religious and social beliefs. He held that, as well as having a duty to nail the guilty, Strathclyde Police was part of the social support mechanism in the region. He embraced the views of the late Geoff Shaw, a man who contrived one of the most remarkable doubles in life – a kirk minister, he lived with and worked for the deprived in the city and still, driven by his beliefs, went on to high-profile success in local politics.

Like Sillitoe, McNee became chief constable at a remarkably young age – they were forty-three and forty-five respectively. David McNee was educated at **WOODSIDE** Senior Secondary and joined the navy in 1943, serving on the lower deck and taking part in the D-Day landings. On leaving the armed forces in 1946, he joined the police force and worked as a constable in **PARTICK** and **ANDERSTON**.

His was a classic progression to the top. Five years into his police service, he was a detective constable in the Marine Division and, by 1964, he was a detective inspector in the Flying Squad. He later served in the Special Branch. Sillitoe was known to his men as either 'The Captain' or 'The Big Fella'. McNee's nickname of

'The Hammer' came about as a result of his success in tackling the tallymen. These illegal moneylenders blight the city by preying on the out-of-work and anyone down on their luck and needing money to pay the bookie or to buy drugs, clothes for their children or whatever. In financial desperation, thousands turn to this evil trade and it is still a concern of the police and social workers today. But, in his day, McNee had some spectacular successes against the tallymen.

The nickname was first used in the old *Scottish Daily Express* in 1968. Reporter David Scott told the tale of McNee's part in one spectacular investigation that involved illegal moneylending and murder. The newspaper sub-editor handling the piece plucked the phrase 'The Hammer of the Neds' from the air to use as an eye-catching headline and the nickname stuck. McNee was no soft touch but 'The Hammer' hardly told the whole story. One writer in the *Evening Times* felt that the tag was a misnomer as the chief was basically a gentle man, comfortable in his beliefs, who enjoyed family life and music. As well as his association with Billy Graham, David McNee was an elder in the St George's Tron Church in the city centre. This was the base of the well-remembered kirk minister Tom Allan.

But McNee didn't object to the shorthand description of him implied by the nickname. In response to being asked what he thought of it, he said:

If people want to call me 'The Hammer' when I am dealing with lawbreakers, I have no objection whatsoever. My job is to maintain law and order and that's what I have always and will always try to do during my career, wherever I am.

His career meant that he had moved around a bit. Before taking up the top job in Glasgow, he had been deputy chief constable in Dunbartonshire. His potential to become a nationwide lawman was obvious when he became the first Glasgow officer to take a higher command course at Bramshill Police College in England.

In his time in charge in Scotland, David McNee showed other similarities to Sillitoe. He was an imaginative and responsive policeman who was not afraid to apply new thinking to old problems. His success on his home patch was based on saturation policing in problem areas and mobile support units. When technology could help, he embraced it and he was an early advocate of the use of helicopters – although it was one of his successors, Andrew Sloan, who actually got the cash to deploy the first one. Few who had been following the career of this remarkable cop were surprised when he became Britain's 'supercop', Commissioner of the Metropolitan Police in London.

But there were surprises around the corner for David McNee. Commissioner of the Met is the toughest of jobs. There is a vast area to police, the patch is a veritable Mecca for all sorts of villains and there is a constantly shifting cosmopolitan population. The McNee years were turbulent ones with race riots to deal with, IRA terrorism and accusations of corruption in the force. Eventually, there came the trauma of the discovery of an intruder in the Queen's bedroom. This incident was a low point in his career and he had to muster up all his strength of purpose to continue in the face of controversy and calls for his resignation. The Buckingham Palace break-in led to further embarrassing discoveries of homosexual indiscretions in the Queen's bodyguard. It seems that the then head of the Police Federation, Tony Judge, said it all when he observed:

> Sir David didn't have the luck. It could have been any commissioner at the top – there was nothing he could do about it. He has done a good job in difficult circumstances. His reign was overshadowed by Operation Countryman's investigation into corruption and rumours surrounding it. He also had to deal with the Brixton riots and the growing problem of policing the inner city.
>
> On the other hand, he conducted successful operations against major criminals and terrorism and he encouraged

local commanders to get to know the public more. The force has become less remote under his leadership.

The Times which had followed his career in the Met with meticulous detail was in a good position to sum things up when he left to return to Scotland. They wrote: 'His legacy is a fine one . . . all in all, it is not a bad record for Commissioner McNee to take home with him to Glasgow – no mean man returning to no mean city.'

McPHEE, BILLY

A henchman of the so-called 'Licensee', Tam McGraw, McPhee died aged thirty-eight after being stabbed in a crowded pub and restaurant in **SPRINGCROFT DRIVE** in Baillieston, in March 2003. A well-known figure in modern Glasgow's gangland, McPhee had admitted a knife and golf-club attack on Thomas 'T C' Campbell, the previous year. At the time, T C had not long been freed after his conviction for the Ice-Cream-War murders in 1984 had been challenged and eventually overturned. The day McPhee died was a big one in the sporting world. Rangers were playing Celtic and the game was being shown on TV and an international rugby match, featuring Scotland and Wales in action at Murrayfield, was also being played. McPhee may have added a footnote in the history of weapons in Glasgow with his use of a golf club to whack Campbell but he himself died after repeated stab wounds that were possibly inflicted by that old-fashioned Glasgow weapon, the 'ornamental sword'.

Thirty-three-year-old Mark Clinton was accused – but cleared in court – of the killing which took place in full view of customers who were there to eat, drink and watch the sport. However, the live action was to be of a more bloody kind than the patrons had bargained for. It was said that the killer, whoever he was, calmly walked into the restaurant with murder on his mind. The scene was described as horrific and surreal with not a word spoken. One customer thought he was watching a madman at work. Clinton's trial lasted barely a day before the Crown prosecutor announced that the indictment was being withdrawn because crucial identification evidence from two eye-witnesses was insufficient for the case to go ahead. Clinton had lodged special defences – one claiming he was elsewhere at the material time and the other blaming two men and an unnamed man of Arab extraction for the killing. Mark Clinton walked free.

MEEHAN, PADDY

Meehan was the victim of one of the most famous of all Scottish miscarriages of justice. Sentenced in 1969 for the murder of a pensioner, Rachel Ross, in Ayr, he was freed after seven years in solitary in Peterhead – where he had always insisted on his innocence. Following a campaign by top names in the law and the media to overturn his conviction, he was given a royal pardon and £50,000 in compensation.

The convoluted story of his conviction began when newspaper buyers woke up to read of the horrifying murder of Mrs Ross. Aged seventy-two, she had been killed in the house she shared with her ex-bookmaker husband, Abraham. Before it was over, there were to be notorious accusations of the police planting evidence, of an establishment cover-up and even allegations of secret service involvement.

The house the old couple slept in had been broken into and they were both tied up and cruelly left while the intruders made their escape. Mrs Ross had been bludgeoned, sustaining horrific head injuries, and she later died in hospital. Her husband was left beside her and the crime was not discovered for twenty-four hours. It was a high-profile crime and, as always, such offences often put intense pressure on the police to make an arrest to quieten the public clamour for action.

As has been noted before, targeting the usual suspects frequently makes as good a starting point as any, at such times, and so it was in this case. Paddy Meehan was well known to the police as a safe-breaker and he was suspected of having been in the area, which is well away from his usual Glasgow patch, on the night of the crime. The police questioned him and set in train a series of events that was to end in a dramatic fatal shoot-out in the city.

Meehan told the cops who quizzed him that he had been in Stranraer, south of Ayr, on that night, in dangerous company. His companion was James Griffiths, a man who was equally well known to the lawmen. Griffiths, a somewhat desperate figure, was a violent man who was said to have a pathological fear of being locked up behind bars. The pair were undoubtedly up to no good in Stranraer that night.

On learning of his involvement with Meehan, the police naturally sought Griffiths out. Perhaps it was the fear of arrest that turned his mind when the cops arrived on his doorstep to question him about the events in Ayr. Whatever the cause, he went berserk. He met the cops with a hail of bullets and then went on the rampage through the streets of Glasgow with a rifle and a shotgun, even firing indiscriminately into a children's playground. He shot nine men, one of them fatally. He also killed two women, a child and a policeman. After a street chase that could have come from a Hollywood movie, Griffiths was cornered and shot in a house in **SPRINGBURN**.

Glasgow police are reluctant to draw arms but there was no doubt that they needed to do so in this case as a virtual madman ran through the streets threatening life. The chase had started at Griffiths's lodgings in a house just off **GREAT WESTERN ROAD**. Here, there was a brief siege, in which one of the first policemen to arrive was caught in the gunfire as the berserk criminal blasted at his attackers. Griffiths escaped out of the back of the house, commandeered a car, went to a bar, took a bottle of brandy and then shot a newsvendor who was later to die from his injuries. He abandoned the car but commandeered a lorry and made his way to Springburn where he broke into a flat and then started taking potshots out of the window at anything that moved.

This was the horrific scene when the police caught up with him. Desperate action was required if more lives were not to be taken by the crazed killer. Two brave policemen, Malcolm Finlayson and Ian Smith, carefully crept up the stairs to where the gunman was holed up. Malcolm Finlayson fired a shot through the letterbox, aiming at Griffiths's shoulder, in an attempt to disable him, but the bullet ricocheted into his heart. The terrifying siege was over and, later, Finlayson was awarded the MBE. His bravery in taking on such a desperate man had undoubtedly saved lives – this was the first time in Scotland that an armed policeman had shot and killed in such circumstances. Ian Smith was awarded the BEM for his part in the incident.

It was a satisfactory end to that particular incident but it led to what looks like, from this point in time, a bit of pre-trial triumphalism that might have had an effect on the wrongful conviction of Meehan. The media was making the most of this compelling story of violence and danger. The police, too, it has to be said, were a bit pleased with themselves at the outcome which, however horrific, could have been so much worse.

Tom Goodall, the chief superintendent who led the CID at the time, was a legendary figure who had caught many of the city's top villains and solved many a difficult crime investigation. After the shooting of Griffiths, he told a news conference that 'the full facts surrounding his death will be reported, as soon as possible, to the Procurator Fiscal'. The policemen were armed to protect the public and 'if they had to use their guns to do that, then that is alright'. His men had acted in a most commendable way and 'I think we can be proud of them,' he told the press. So far, so good.

But then the Crown Office made a later statement that was perhaps unwise and which led to problems after the trial of Meehan. Part of it said:

The Crown Office can confirm that, with the death of Griffiths and the apprehension of Patrick Connolly Meehan, the police are no longer looking for any other person suspected of implication in the incident concerning Mr and Mrs Ross at Ayr.

This seems rather reckless indeed now that we know that neither Meehan nor Griffiths was actually involved!

Griffiths was an oddball who had been disowned by his family in Rochdale after early criminal exploits, including breaking into his own brother's house. As his father had refused to come north to claim his son's body, Glasgow Corporation was left with the task of disposing of this unloved thirty-four-year-old. He was interred in an unmarked pauper's grave in Linn Cemetery in **CATHCART**. There were no flowers, no wreaths and only the undertaker and the gravediggers watched.

To the police, the fact that Griffiths had panicked and reacted so violently simply underlined their belief that he and Meehan had been involved in the Ayr killing. However, they had overlooked something. For months, the Englishman had been on the run for other crimes and was constantly looking over his shoulder and expecting the arrival of the law at any moment. This must have made him jumpy.

Newspaper interest in the case was still at a high and, before the trial of Meehan, the clicking Nikons and Canons of the assorted tabloid button-pushers were focussed on old Abraham Ross. The idea was that he should show his injuries and talk about his ordeal to encourage the public to come forward with any missing details. As he sat up in bed in a screened hospital ward and talked of the crime, he described how his bound figure and that of his wife had been discovered more than twenty-four hours after the break-in by a daily help who arrived on the Monday morning. He said his assailants, both masked, had acted with quite unnecessary force. Mr Ross then showed the burn marks on the skin round his wrists where he had struggled to try to free himself in order to get help for his dying wife.

It was a horrific story and the public was much concerned that the perpetrators were caught and dealt with. So seriously was the crime taken that, at one stage, more than 100 detectives were involved and so it seems very strange that such intensive investigation could come up with a result that led to such a spectacular injustice.

Joe Beltrami represented Meehan from the start and entered a plea of not guilty to three charges at a pleading diet in Ayr. The charges were that, on 6 July 1969, while acting with another person, Meehan:

1. Broke into the house at 2 Blackburn Place, Ayr, and assaulted Abraham Ross, aged 67, punched him in the face and body, struck him on the shoulder and buttock with a sharp instrument, and bound him with rope and nylon stockings to his severe injury.
2. Assaulted Mrs Rachel Ross, aged 72, dragged her from her bed, put her on the floor, placed his knee on her chest, and bound her with rope and nylon stockings, as a result of which she died in Ayr County Hospital on July 8 and murdered her.
3. Stole £2,000 in money and a number of travellers cheques.

To these charges, Joe Beltrami intimated a plea of impeachment and alibi.

Next was to come the first of many spectacular twists in this most intriguing of cases. The trial was set to take place in the High Court in Edinburgh and Meehan was making headlines before it even started. He wanted to be tested with a so-called 'truth drug' and petitioned the authorities to that effect. It was an early indication of his fervent assertion of his innocence. The use of such a drug was without precedence in Britain but it had been used in the United States. Three judges, sitting in Edinburgh, heard this unusual request. Meehan pointed out that, if he was at liberty, he would have had the freedom to administer the drug to himself with witnesses but, in jail, waiting to stand trial for murder, he needed the permission of the authorities. The drug was said to be a cocktail of various chemicals. No matter what the drug was, the judges ruled that it would not be used in this case.

So the trial went ahead. Apart from the involvement of Joe Beltrami, two of the most important legal figures in Scotland at the time were in action. Joe had chosen the flamboyant Nicholas Fairbairn and the future Labour Party leader John Smith to act for the defence. As well as making their mark on the law, Fairbairn and Smith both had successful political careers. Indeed, John Smith was perhaps only denied the premiership by his untimely death in 1994 from heart trouble.

At the opening of the trial, Fairbairn confirmed that Meehan was pleading not guilty to all the charges, except a minor one involving a passport, and he repeated the plea of incrimination. The defence claimed that, if a murder had been committed, it had been done not by Meehan but by two other men – Ian Waddell, then an untried prisoner in Barlinnie, and Samuel Phillips, whose whereabouts, at the time, were unknown.

Abraham Ross appeared in court with a bandage over his right eye, a consequence of the attack. He told the court he was a director of a bingo club in Paisley and travelled regularly between Ayr and the Renfrewshire town in that connection. He tended to carry a fair amount of cash and some of it was kept in Ayr.

He said that, on the Saturday night of the attack, he had fallen asleep and the next thing he remembered was someone coming at him and diving on top of him. He told the court his wife was screaming and moaning. In the struggle, he said he noticed that the assailant was wearing a black nylon hood over his head and this prevented him from recognising whoever was attacking him. A blanket had been placed over his own head, further hampering his ability to see who was there, but he was aware that there were two men in the attack. He said he heard the man who was assaulting him cry out, 'Pat, get this ****** off me!' He then got a knock on the head and was unable to continue his resistance.

In reply to a question from the prosecution, he said the assailant was called Jim by the other man. Before they left, the two attackers bound Mr and Mrs Ross by the hands and feet with ropes and

190

nylon stockings. They were left lying on the floor. Mrs Ross was able to reach the phone but found it was out of order. He further described their horrific ordeal:

> We were unable to free ourselves and shouted all day long on the Sunday for help. We heard people passing but no one heard us and we were in a pretty bad state. Eventually, the daily help came in on Monday and we were taken to hospital. I did not see my wife again.

Nicky Fairbairn started off on a robust cross-examination of the retired bookie. He had been given permission to call Ian Waddell into court. He handed Waddell a piece of paper and asked him to repeat various phrases like 'Shut up, shut up!'. The reasoning behind this was to discredit the previous identification of Meehan's voice by the witness. Mr Ross agreed that Waddell's voice was similar to the one he had heard in the identification parade (Meehan's) but, because of the interval of time, he could not be certain.

The court then heard more of this parade. Detective Superintendent David Struthers said that, when a warrant was presented to Meehan at his home, he had said, 'You are making the biggest mistake of your life.' He also wondered why he had to go to an identification parade since 'there were only the two girls I picked up'. (This was a reference to two girls Meehan and Griffiths had given a lift to in their car near Kilmarnock, on the night of the murder. This was when they were returning from 'business' in Stranraer, Meehan claimed.) Indeed, it is striking how strident Meehan was in his claims of innocence right from the start of this affair. Later in the day, when charged, he again told the police they were making a 'horrible mistake – I know absolutely nothing about it.'

The story of the identification parade is intriguing. There were six men in the line-up, the first being Meehan. The men in the parade were asked to repeat the words 'Shut up, shut up! We'll call an ambulance.' Mr Ross had said he had heard one of the attackers say this in response to his wife's pleadings. When Meehan spoke, the old man staggered back shaken and declared, 'That's him!' He was said to be on the point of collapse.

Meehan's reply was 'Oh, sir, you've got the wrong man, honestly.'

Identification parades are often the subject of much dispute and it was no different in this case. After the trial, Meehan supporters, campaigning for a pardon, claimed that old Mr Ross had been tipped the wink by the police as to who they thought was the guilty man. It would not be the first time such a thing had happened!

The allegation that the police tampered with evidence was also a thread running through the Meehan case. According to those fighting to free Meehan, scraps of paper that had come from the Ross house were found in Jim Griffiths's car coat. When they were mentioned later in the trial, they were said to have been planted by the police.

However, back in 1969, the two girls who got a lift in Meehan and Griffiths's car did identify Meehan as a passenger and they said that the driver had addressed him as Pat. Mind you, all this seems to prove little other than the fact that Griffiths and Meehan were in Ayrshire, a big county, on the night in question.

In the witness box, Meehan stuck to his story. Asked whether he had had anything to do with the murder and robbery in Ayr on 6 July, Meehan replied, 'I was never, at any time, involved in that robbery and murder and I never set eyes on Mr Ross till I saw him at the identification parade.' Meehan also said that he never set foot in Ayr that night though he might have passed through the town on the early hours of morning – on their way back from Stranraer, Griffiths was driving and he was trying to get some sleep.

He admitted that their trip to Stranraer was made in order to do a recce on a car registration office, with the idea of breaking in and stealing some car registration books. The plan was for the books to be used by Griffiths to recycle stolen cars. However, when they got there, the job did not seem as easy as they had thought it would be so they turned their attention to an attempt at stealing cameras from a hotel. Then, after breaking into a van, they decided to return to Glasgow.

They reached the safety of the city at around 5 a.m. This was after a diversion during which they had picked up a girl who said she had been put out of a white car by the people she had been travelling with. Meehan and Griffiths managed to follow and catch up with the car that had dumped her and she was reunited with her friend and their companions in the wee small hours.

At home, Meehan told his wife of the adventures of the night and claimed he only learned of the murder in Ayr from the newspapers and television. He said the family were shocked at the brutal killing. Meehan's daughter suggested that perhaps the men in the white car had been involved and asked her father to phone the police. Meehan said he didn't want to get involved but he would phone the police and not give his name. He phoned them and said he had a friend who might identify the men in the car. Questioned by Nicky Fairbairn, he said he did not disclose his name because he knew that the police had been searching for his partner in crime, Griffiths, for months.

Although, in the end, he was to lose the case, Fairbairn made more than his share of telling points. On this business of the white car, for example, he asked the accused, 'Supposing, for a moment, you were the man who had committed the murder. Did this mean you made a call to the police disclosing the name of two girls who could probably identify you?'

Meehan indicated that it was his distaste for such a filthy crime that had driven him to contact the police and that was why he had given them the girls' names in a second phone call. He said he left for England with Griffiths that night but denied that either of them intended to flee the country.

At this point in the trial, Meehan was also questioned about the presence of small stones on his shoes. The stones apparently were similar to those covering the roof of the garage of the murder-scene house. Meehan told the court that he had, at one time, been employed in a store selling the sort of felting that was on the garage roof and this is no doubt where they came from. Later, in the campaign to free Meehan, these stones were to become the subject of much interest.

The prosecution then turned their attention to Meehan's way of life. He said he was employed to install security devices in private houses and made about a tenner a day. He was asked about Griffiths's response when the police came calling on him and replied, 'As far as I know, he started shooting.' Meehan denied knowing that Griffiths had a gun. But the court then heard of a preliminary phone call before the raid on his house, between Griffiths and Tom Goodall, in which Griffiths had said that he knew the identity of the guilty men but would not give their names.

Meehan's plea of incrimination was the next thing to be tested. Ian Waddell was brought into the court. A lorry driver cited as a witness said he had been drinking with Waddell from the Saturday night till 10 a.m. on the Sunday, covering the time of the crime. But against this a Robert McCafferty, who was then an untried prisoner in Barlinnie, said that he was in conversation with other prisoners in the exercise yard when there was speculation among the group about what their sentences might be if they were to be found guilty. One of his fellows said to McCafferty, 'You think you are bad – just look at Paddy Meehan in for the Ayr murder.'

McCafferty went on, 'When I turned round, Waddell, who had joined us, said, "How do you think I feel? It was me that done it."' McCafferty claimed that he then asked Wadell, 'Are you joking?' He told the court that in reply Waddell said words to the effect that, if the police had made a bloomer, it was hardly his (Waddell's) responsibility. McCafferty went on to deplore the fact that the couple had been left bound up and said that Waddell claimed Phillips used the phone but that he only 'called the operator', not the emergency services.

Waddell was then questioned. Asked if he had ever used the words 'Shut up, shut up! We'll call an ambulance', he refused to answer. He had already been told by Lord Grant, the judge, that he did not need to answer any question that might incriminate him.

After five days, the trial drew to a close. Despite the telling submissions of the defence that pointed at a hand other than Meehan's being involved, the jury preferred the evidence, particularly the identification parade, that pointed to his guilt. Reading the evidence at this distance, it is surprising that they did so and, of course, the inconsistencies in the case against Meehan were, amongst other things, what attracted the campaigners for his release. But, at the time, the identification by Mr Ross, with whom the public had a lot of sympathy, swayed the decision against Patrick Connolly Meehan.

It took the jury just two hours to reach their majority verdict. Lord Grant had directed the jury to find that, with regard to Waddell, incrimination had not been established and he told them they were not to be concerned with the bloody shoot-out involving Griffiths. He said, 'You are trying the accused on the evidence you have heard in this court and on that evidence alone. Evidence of what a dead man said, not being subject to cross-examination, must be looked at with particular care.' The judge also pointed out that the evidence was largely circumstantial but they must look at the cumulative effect of the evidence as a whole.

Meehan was described by the judge as a sort of Jekyll and Hyde, a man who installed security devices by day but wandered around the country at night on mysterious errands. He was also a self-confessed liar and crook. This was all true but he didn't kill old Mrs Ross and, when sentenced to life, his reaction was direct and understandable. 'I am innocent of this crime and so is Griffiths. You have made a terrible mistake.'

Down the years, commentators on the case have remarked that Lord Grant did Meehan and his defence no favours. An illustration of this comes in a courtroom exchange when Ewan Stewart, for the prosecution, said to Meehan, 'You are a self-confessed liar, aren't you?'

Meehan replied to the effect that, with regard to this murder, he had offered to take a truth drug.

Ignoring the convention during trials of addressing the accused using the title 'Mr', Lord Grant sarcastically said, 'Can you not tell the truth without having a truth drug Meehan?' The defence could cite many other occasions when they felt the court was less than impartial.

The sensational trial was over but ahead lay years of wrangling between lawyers, journalists and the legal establishment who fought hard and dirty to defend this injustice. At the head of the campaign to free Meehan was the famous legal eagle Joe Beltrami (this is also discussed elsewhere in this book as part of Beltrami's own story) and he soon got things underway.

From his solitary cell in Peterhead, Meehan wrote to the TV broadcaster and writer Ludovic Kennedy and got him interested in what was to become a long-running saga. Kennedy looked into the matter and his investigations brought him to the conclusion that the man to blame for the crime was William 'Tank' McGuinness, a notorious Glasgow underworld figure who was known as a 'tie-up merchant'. Kennedy believed that Waddell had accompanied McGuinness into the Rosses' house.

As is often the case in the Glasgow underworld, strange connections are frequently made and the same names seem to keep cropping up and, in 1973, with Meehan still in Peterhead, McGuinness entered the story. Over the years, McGuinness's persistent involvement in crime had led him to become one of Joe Beltrami's regular clients. In his excellent book of 1989, *A Deadly Innocence*, Beltrami says that McGuinness had told him several times that, along with another man, he was responsible for the Ross murder. But this was not the good news for Meehan that it appears to be because Joe Beltrami was adamant that solicitor–client relationship meant he could neither investigate it nor make his knowledge public while McGuinness was still alive. In later years, Meehan took exception to this but, as a working lawyer, Joe has consistently defended his stance. However, he has written that having to keep such information secret was a crushing burden for him to bear.

In March 1976, there was a dramatic change in the circumstances. The papers, always on top of what was happening to the shady characters in the city's underworld, reported that Tank McGuinness had been found beaten and unconscious in **JANEFIELD STREET**, Parkhead. Thirteen days later, he died in the Royal Infirmary without regaining consciousness. Beltrami, free from the constrictions of the solicitor–client relationship, was sure the death was simply the result of a drunken brawl. But Ludovic Kennedy told an English newspaper that the underworld had killed the real Ayr murderer. Then came a sequence of deaths and trials the like of which has seldom been seen – even in Glasgow. The last man to have been seen with McGuinness was John 'Gypsy' Winning, a notorious figure who, in the parlance of the underworld, was said to be a 'friend' of Tank. He was eventually arrested in a pub in the **GALLOWGATE** and charged with the murder.

At the trial, the indictment was withdrawn because of lack of evidence and Lord Wheatley instructed the jury to find Winning not guilty. His freedom was short lived – he was himself murdered in a house in Fife in 1980.

Meehan was freed in 1976. Shortly after that, Waddell was put on trial for the murder of Mrs Ross and cleared. Waddell was also not going to have long to enjoy his freedom. In 1982, he met a violent death at the hands of another so-called friend. Andrew Gentle was given life for murdering Ian Waddell after the two of them had stabbed a woman to death in a flat in **EASTERHOUSE**. Gentle was found dead in his cell in 1996.

McGuinness and Waddell died sordid deaths but, in life, they were inextricably linked with the extraordinary saga of Meehan. On his release, Paddy had first been offered the miserly compensation sum of £7,500. How this was expected to be seen as fair compensation for seven years in solitary confinement for a crime he did not commit was almost beyond belief. Even when the sum was eventually increased to £50,000, it still seems far from adequate. The whole travesty of the Meehan case – which was commanding acres of space in the newspapers – compelled the then Scottish

Secretary Bruce Millan to order an inquiry under Lord Hunter.

So, at last, it seemed that justice for Meehan would be done, the loose ends would be cleared up and the controversy would be stilled once and for all. Not so. When the report was published, over five years later – a few months after Waddell's death – it ran to 500,000 words but the waters were as murky as ever. It was devastatingly anti-Meehan. Lord Hunter said that 'The theory of an initial assault by Ian Waddell and Tank McGuinness, with a follow up by Meehan and gunman Griffiths to open the safes believed to have been in the house, cannot be ruled out.'

Disgracefully, it seemed the Edinburgh legal establishment was set against clearing Meehan. However, that splendid legal campaigner Ludovic Kennedy returned to the fray. In the greatly missed *Sunday Standard* broadsheet – a newspaper that, unusually, was much acclaimed by its peers – he thundered into action. He majored on the point that Lord Hunter had made it plain that McGuinness and Waddell were the men who broke into the bungalow and assaulted Mr and Mrs Ross – an attack that resulted in her death. Kennedy claimed that this clearly meant that Mr Ross had been mistaken in his identification of the voice he had heard as belonging to Meehan. He felt that this was a result of the police tipping off old Mr Ross as to Meehan's position in the line-up. Kennedy added:

> Why continue to bother about Meehan you may ask [and I too am always being asked] – a man who, for so long, was such a pest to society and who Lord Hunter has called, not without reason, a glib and inventive liar? There are two reasons. The first is that, having served seven years, been granted a pardon and since gone straight, Meehan has fully discharged his debt to society. The second is that the case is now less about a person than a principle. And the principle is that justice is, and should be, indivisible.

It was stirring stuff and few would disagree with it. Campaigner

Kennedy was also of the opinion that the establishment tendency to continue to throw suspicion on Meehan was an attempt to deflect claims that the police had been guilty of planting evidence. Along with other members of the campaign team, he issued a statement saying that the suggestion that Meehan had taken any part in the crime was without evidence.

There was disappointment too because Lord Hunter had seemingly breached his terms of reference. These stated that he was expressly forbidden to comment on Meehan's guilt or innocence.

In the continuing media hullabaloo, the accusations of police planting evidence would not go away and Meehan, by now a well-known character in the city and friendly with journalists with whom he liked to slake his thirst, joined the campaign to clear his name fully. The grit from roof felt said to have been found on Meehan's shoes and the pieces of paper in Griffiths's coat were the things that were considered particularly suspicious. Nicky Fairbairn added some petrol to the fire with his observation that the report criticises people who had fought for seven years to overturn an injustice while the policemen who had brought it about were absolved.

Hunter was a pill that many, including some politicians, just couldn't not swallow. And, when the Scottish Grand Committee discussed it in 1982, they heard the allegations that the Ayrshire police had planted evidence against Meehan. These accusations were supported by a former assistant chief constable of Strathclyde, Arthur Bell. He was a man who was respected for both his integrity and his skill as a detective. He told Mr Allen Adams, the Paisley Labour MP, that the planting of evidence had taken place. The committee heard that the police had taken no action after Mr Ross had told them he had discovered watches and rings had been stolen. Mr Adams said, 'There is little doubt that, if these matters had been inquired into, there could have been other arrests. These could have affected the case against Meehan.'

In the actual debate, it was said, by the Tory, George Younger, in defence of Lord Hunter, that he had been castigated for various shortcomings – for imputing guilt to Mr Meehan, for not finding him innocent and for not being able to conclude with certainty whether or not he had been involved in the crime. He was reported as saying:

> The fact is that Mr Meehan received a free pardon based on the doubts of his conviction in October 1969 of murdering Mrs Ross. This fact is not affected by Lord Hunter's findings, which were directed at the performance of the authorities who investigated the murder.

It has also been suggested that Lord Hunter, in stating that a possibility was that the crime in Ayr might have been the work of four men, including Mr Meehan, exceeded his terms of reference and the idea that this was the case was quite unsupported by evidence. Mr Younger then claimed that Hunter's remit required him to examine the whole circumstances of the murder inquiry. Lord Hunter's comments flowed from his investigation of the role of the authorities, including the action of the police. Younger claimed that 'far from being a breach of his terms of reference, this was an essential part of his remit'.

'If this was a cover-up, I can't imagine what an exposé would have been like,' said Peter Fraser, the Solicitor General. Those who have followed the case closely will tend to agree with the pungent put-down of Labour MP John Maxton who wryly retorted to Peter Fraser's uncertainty with 'The truth.'

Paddy Meehan's final years of freedom were tainted with bitterness at the great injustice that had been done to him. In profitable spells as poacher turned gamekeeper, he drifted in and out of security jobs. He was not the murderer of old Mrs Ross but there was no doubt that he *was* an expert in breaking and entering and in springing open safes that had a tempting hoard of ready cash. He was a notorious public figure recognised wherever he went. He enjoyed this infamy up to a point and liked the company of journalists who were always ready to buy him a pint on expenses and listen to his theories on crime. He also helped write many articles on the crime topics of the day with his media friends. And, in the end, he told his version of events in a curious book, *Framed By MI5*, which was written after he had moved south to Port Talbot to be close to his family.

In it, he spewed out his bitterness over his feud with Joe Beltrami and gave his side of the Ayr story. His bizarre theory was that he had been framed by the secret services, the victim of an elaborate conspiracy concocted to keep him quiet over what he described as his role in the escape of the Soviet spy George Blake from a London prison in 1966. And he was still banging on about his old obsession – the 'truth drug'. He wanted to be given it on TV so that he could be questioned publicly about his allegations regarding the secret services. It never happened. He died of throat cancer in Swansea at the age of sixty-seven. His career was full of question marks and lying. But there is no argument that, like Jessie McLachlan and Oscar Slater before him, he was the victim of society's lust for a villain and the desire for swift retribution whenever a high-profile crime catches the attention of the public. The seeds of his wrongful conviction lay in the desperate attempts to find the brutal killer of Mrs Ross at all costs – attempts that led to the wrong man spending seven years in solitary in Peterhead Prison.

MESSAGES

To the non-criminal community, the phrase 'going the messages' harks back to the days before the supermarkets and internet home delivery. Back when housewives shopped for food and household supplies every day, they'd say they were 'going the messages'. Or, if the family had run out of tea, butter, sugar or whatever, a youngster would be sent to the corner-shop grocer for the 'messages'. But, for those in the underworld, it doesn't mean going on an errand to the local shop – there is a more sinister connotation.

Many an old villain, confronted with the doings of one of the current batch of hard men, will dismiss the upstart with the remark, 'He once ran messages for me.' These 'messages' did not involve sugar or tea. In this context, it could mean torching a car as a warning that a debt had to be paid. Sometimes the violence would get a little more personal than destroying a cherished 'motor'. Or, maybe, the message would be the delivery of a gentle caress with a razor to remind the forgetful to pay their protection money. Or, perhaps, it would simply take the form of a whack on the face for someone who had angered the gang boss. The better you were at running such messages, the greater your chance of, one day, becoming top dog in the world where the fist and knife ruled.

MILLER, Tony

This unfortunate youngster became the last man to lose his life on the gallows in Barlinnie. Aged just nineteen when he died, he became known as 'the boy killer'. He was convicted on 16 November 1960 of the murder of John Cremin, a middle-aged homosexual, in the **QUEEN'S PARK** recreation ground, on the south of the city – an area that was known to be a haunt of homosexuals.

Miller and a young accomplice had been charged with the murder of Cremin who had been hit on the head with a piece of wood and robbed of his watch, bank book, knife and £67. Both boys pleaded not guilty but the accomplice claimed Miller had struck the fatal blow. At the time, there was a huge groundswell of public opinion against the death penalty and, considering the details of the case, it seems odd that the ultimate penalty was carried out. Miller's lawyer, the redoubtable Len Murray, recalled, in a book in 1995, that one of the grounds of an appeal made by Miller was that the judge, Lord Wheatley, had failed to offer the jury the option of culpable homicide – an option that did not carry the death penalty. The Court of Appeal, however, refused to act and the sentence was set to be carried out a couple of days before Christmas.

A petition was launched to save Miller and no fewer than 30,000 signatures were collected. The petition tables became a familiar sight to Christmas shoppers in the city centre and they signed them in their droves. But all the support of folk on the street, who were appalled by the thought of putting a teenager to death, was to no avail. The petition was sent to the then Scottish Secretary John S McLay who replied that, with regret, he was unable to find sufficient grounds to justify him advising Her Majesty to interfere with the due course of the law.

Inside the Bar-L, just yards from the infamous hanging shed, Miller was resigned to his fate. His mother visited him every afternoon but he refused to talk about the crime. 'It's too late now,' he said.

N

NOLAN, John

Nolan was a police constable who played a major role in the Easterhouse Project, which is dealt with more fully elsewhere in the book, helping to run the group from 1975 to 1982. The success of the project in giving the kids of this vast housing estate something to do and things to be proud of is, mainly down to the level of cooperation between the police and the lay volunteers. According to the *Evening Times*, John Nolan was a 'banjo-playing pied-piper figure' who ran the **WESTERHOUSE ROAD** Nissan Hut Centre. Nolan had a history of community involvement. He had run a youth club in the equally difficult area of **BLACKHILL** and, when he was offered a full-time secondment to Easterhouse, he jumped at the chance. He said, 'Easterhouse folk have a distinct sense of humour – and they need it.'

Before this truly community-friendly cop left Glasgow to go to the States with his American-born wife, he explained the reason behind the nickname of the Nissan Hut Centre being known locally as 'the Bears' Disco'. 'Why not?' he said 'After all, it is the bears who attend – or at least they were bears when I first got involved here.'

Before he left, Chief Constable Sir James Robertson, who had bent the odd rule or two to help get the project started, made a special presentation to Nolan.

NORVAL, Walter

Generally accepted as the city's first true Godfather of organised crime, rather than merely the leader of one gang faction, Norval was a ruthless hard man with brains and a talent for meticulous planning in his criminal escapades, especially bank robberies. Born in **FERGUSON STREET** near **GARSCUBE ROAD** in February 1928, in the 1960s and 1970s, he was a dominant figure in the Glasgow crime scene and was tagged the 'King of the Twilight Zone'. In his teens and early years, the population of the Garscube Road area, called the High Road by locals, was similar to that of other parts of the city like Bridgeton, Tollcross and the Gorbals. There was a mixture of hard-working, friendly folk who looked out for each other and made the best of a bad hand given to them by fate and desperate men always on the wrong side of the law. Amid the smoke-blackened tenements, the street bookies, the shops and pubs, there festered a hard-drinking violent gang culture. The role of the pub in the life of the Glasgow hard man can't be underestimated. In a map that Norval drew for me for, *Glasgow's Godfather*, my biography of him, there was a pub on almost every street corner – a total of thirteen in the short stretch from **NEW CITY ROAD** to the **ROUND TOLL**.

Norval led a lonely early life and began thieving when still in short pants. His father was away from home for long spells as a sales representative for a confectionery firm and his mother had rented flats and other businesses which took up much of her time. The youthful Norval was often left to his own devices. He would gaze down from the window of his Garscube Road flat at the regular battles involving glasses, bottles and razors, as patrons of Scott's pub, across the road, spilled out after closing time to continue booze-fuelled feuds and wars that had started earlier inside the hostelry. There was a learning curve here – dramatic demonstration that, in the world of the High Road, you had to take care of yourself.

Before he was in his teens Norval was well known to the police of the Northern Division who could see that here was a figure who would almost certainly cause them trouble in the years ahead. They were right – his crimes escalated from stealing from sweet shops and fruit merchants to moneylending, protection rackets, armed robbery and attempted murder. His early life makes rewarding study for those interested in the nature-vs-nurture debate. It could not be claimed that there was much in the way of nurture shown to him in his early years – except perhaps by street fighters like Foy and O'Hara, the legendary Kings of the Garscube Road. They quickly saw something of themselves in this tough, cocky, little Cagney-like kid who was always ready, with fists, knife or boot, to take on anyone. In the young Norval, they recognised the makings of a natural gang leader.

In many ways, they exerted more influence on Norval than his own family did, getting him to run errands for them and sometimes letting him into the rough Tower Ballroom where they were bouncers. They were his hard-men mentors. He looked up to them and they soon became his role models. As well as being fascinated by the street battles that took place below his tenement window, he enjoyed the mixture of violence and gambling that was also on his doorstep. On the nearby banks of the Forth and Clyde Canal, bare-knuckle gang fights and pitch-and-toss schools were regular occurrences. All this provided an ideal apprenticeship for his life ahead, a life that led to years behind bars in jails – army and civil and both north and south of the border – that made him something of an expert in penal matters.

He started to develop his expertise in crime and violence at an early age. His mother had a little cottage in the attractive Argyll village of Lochgoilhead and, during the Second World War, Norval was packed off there to avoid the German bombers and to experience rural life. Along with his suitcase, he took the mores of the Garscube Road with him and he was barely in Argyll before the peace of the mountainous countryside was broken. He organised a gang and got into scrapes that included fights with the locals and helping boys who had escaped from an approved school to hide from the police. Not for the first time, he was quickly collared by the law and his father was summoned to take this troublemaker back to the city. There, he continued to get into trouble, dodging school and running wild on the streets with like-minded tyro gangsters in an outfit known as the Wee Mob.

It is interesting that Norval, an undoubtedly intelligent man, if lacking in respect for the law, managed to grow up not only without much parental control but also with more or less no input from the Scottish educational system because of his systematic truancy. Would it have made much difference if he had had more of an education? Who knows? But he acknowledges that, when he first became a gang leader at a tender age, it was an initial step from which it was hard to draw back. He believed that, having taken control, any sign of backtracking would be dangerous and so the pattern of his life was set. He protected his authority with violence from his days in short pants to his heyday as a seasoned and infamous bank robber.

Almost from the time when he was a toddler, he was one of the usual suspects in an area seeped in crime – petty and otherwise. And, year by year, his villainy was racked up a notch or two. After all the early scams, there came the first armed robbery. On this occasion, the gun was fake but, later on, the weapons were real – and deadly. The next stop, after a guilty verdict following a raid on a shop in the city centre, was Polmont Borstal where the wannabe gangster tasted serious incarceration for the first time. This particular borstal was noted for the brutality of its regime and the cruelty of its warders at that time and Norval suffered under the full force of both. But he emerged toughened rather than chastened, enjoying the notoriety of a boy who had survived the worst borstal could throw at him. He wore the respect that this gave him on the streets like a badge of pride. But he was not back on his home patch for long.

This was the time of National Service and he soon found himself in the army. His career in uniform was distinguished by the fact that only nineteen days, of the around two years expected of him, were spent as an ordinary soldier – the rest of the time, he was in army jails for deserting, stealing or assaults. In the end, he was discharged 'with ignominy'. To Norval, this was just another medal signifying that he was a man destined for a long criminal career. He actually revelled in the word 'ignominy'. Many of his Garscube

Road friends, whose bad behaviour had led to them being kicked out of the army, were merely 'discharged'!

Back in Glasgow, he was soon back in trouble. The most serious charge against him was the attempted murder of Mick Gibson, a man who Norval believed had designs on taking over his burgeoning criminal empire. Norval lost part of an ear in a backcourt fight with Gibson. It was bitten off, in Mike Tyson fashion, by his enemy, leaving a scar he carries to this day. This scar is his only one and that is what Norval considers another mark of his 'success' as a Godfather. He describes the various chib-marked faces that are still around as 'losers'. The winner, in this dark world, inflicts the scars rather than suffers them.

The initial backcourt fight with Gibson was to lead to a second, more serious affair in which Walter Norval used a knife with almost deadly effect on his enemy and the attack resulted in him spending years behind bars. It came perilously close to murder which would have meant even more time in jail but his victim pulled through despite his horrible injuries.

The experience of a long-term prison sentence and the fact that he'd almost killed somebody did little to deflect Walter Norval from his chosen way of life. On his release, he began his reign as a true Godfather. In his heyday, the crime reporters who kept a careful eye on his career considered him something of a Glasgow Al Capone. It was a comparison that he found not unflattering. He dressed well and he liked champagne, gambling, fine cigars, big cars and the sweet life generally. When he took some of his ill-gotten gains on his frequent holidays in the Spanish sunshine, it was in the company of an attractive blonde mistress. His wife stayed at home.

In what he calls his 'business' life, there were other similarities to the American gangsters of Chicago, New York and St Paul. Norval and his boys started to make forced amalgamations with other Glasgow gangs. Once it had been organised, the larger gang he created used its muscle and his brains and knowledge of what was going on in the city to plan a spectacular series of robberies that brought in tens of thousands of pounds. The robberies also baffled the police for long periods. One of the best books on the Glasgow crime scene is *Such Bad Company* (Edinburgh: Paul Harris, 1982) by legendary city reporter George Forbes and the late Paddy Meehan. In it, they say that, at the peak of his career, Walter Norval only occasionally took part in the actual robberies – just to show that he was still a force to be reckoned with. For the most part, he contented himself with selecting targets and planning the raids with military precision. His style and his flash life helped him recruit tough youngsters from areas like **MILTON** and **GOVAN** to work as the foot soldiers in these criminal expeditions. But, if any young buck had overdosed on the brave pills and found the courage to step out of line, Norval was ready with his fists to remind him exactly who was in charge.

At this stage in his career, he had an army of informers to alert him to possible opportunities for robberies. These insiders could give him the details of how money was moved around by banks and firms, the details of hospital payroll deliveries and such. He paid well for such titbits. When a target was selected, no detail was too small to overlook. Gang members disguised themselves as workmen to study what was going on. Escape routes were researched and dummy runs took place. Where to park the getaway cars, the route of any cops called out, what false trails could be left – it was all meticulously planned. The amount of violence needed to get the cash into their hands was also carefully calculated and there was a secret arsenal, kept hidden in a garage, from which the robbers drew all that was needed – masks and gloves, revolvers, shotguns, hammers, axes and knives.

For a while, it all ran like clockwork but there was a certain consistent methodology involved in the bank raids that troubled the cops. They were puzzled by this succession of well-planned raids that garnered huge sums of ready cash for the robbers. For months, they hadn't a clue but, eventually, it began to dawn on them that this could only be the work of one gang with one mastermind. And, on their patch, there was a flamboyant character that fitted the bill as the organiser, a man who threw his cash around and led something of an exotic life as a womaniser – Walter Norval.

Arriving on the scene of one robbery that showed all the hallmarks of the current crop of raids, the cops chased round to storm his house. They were a tad late as Norval had beaten them to his home by minutes. He dived into the shower and, when the doorbell rang, he appeared wrapped in a bathrobe and dripping wet. He pointed out he had just risen and was set for his breakfast rather than leading a wild bunch on an early morning hospital payroll seizure. His loyal wife confirmed this fanciful tale and off he went on holiday to Tenerife – with his mistress.

But that was to be something of a last dalliance with the sweet life. On his return, he had one stroke of luck when he collected insurance money on the demise of his stepfather Joe Kotarba, a notorious vice king who had been stabbed to death. But his good fortune was beginning to run out. Another robbery pointed to his involvement and, this time, the police were not to be thwarted so easily when his home was raided yet again. The Godfather had to switch off the telly which was showing horse racing – a lifelong passion – and go down to the local station.

He tried to explain away his wealth as a result of his skill as a punter on the horses but he was in bother when a weapon was found in his luxury car. Norval always claimed that this was planted by the police. In particular, he believed a detective called Norman Walker who has been accused of similar plants in other cases had done it. (Walker was involved in the Ice-Cream Wars saga.) Norval also said the car belonged to his son, not to him. But the cops were determined to get their man. Many of Norval's associates were interviewed and one, Philip Henry, talked. He provided the police with enough evidence to send Norval and his henchmen behind bars for long stretches.

Henry was that most detested of criminals – a supergrass. As a favour to one of the gang members, he had been taken into the gang when he was on the run for another crime and, in the end, he squealed so loud, he brought the gang down. Of Henry, Norval says:

> He was a coward, a number one rat who wanted to do the crime, reap the rewards but couldn't do the time. He shopped the whole organisation – the men who helped him when he was on the run. How low can you get?

To this day, Norval believes that it was only this betrayal that resulted in him being jailed – his crimes were so carefully planned that few clues that could have led to his conviction were ever left.

It was indisputable though that Norval's big-time days were over. But before the XYY gang, as they were to become known, were behind bars, there was to be another spectacular chapter in the city's criminal history.

On a bitterly cold night, at the end of October 1977, a motorist passing the High Court thought he saw smoke coming from the building. He phoned the Central Fire Station and, within minutes, a dozen fire engines and sixty firefighters were in action trying to save the famous old building. They used turntable ladders and pumped water from the nearby Clyde in a battle against a blaze so powerful that it lit up the sky around and could be seen from miles away. The firefighters won – the North Court was almost destroyed but the South Court was saved.

Daybreak saw the arrival of a team of fire investigators. The conclusion was that the blaze had been started deliberately by petrol bombs that had been lobbed through a skylight window. Strangely, this had happened on the eve of the trial of Walter Norval and twelve others who were charged with a series of raids on banks, post-office vans and hospital payrolls! It did not take a genius to deduce that the idea had been to destroy papers and other evidence to be used at the trial. But, even if the fire had succeeded, it would not have prevented justice taking its course – the documents and other exhibits to be produced at the trial were stored deep in the basement and officials told me they would probably have survived even if the firefighters had failed to save the building.

Emergency repairs got the South Court back into action within a few days and, with the ashes of the adjacent North Court barely cold, the trials went ahead. But, until the High Court building was given a £5 million facelift in 2000, lawyers, public and press could still glimpse fire-blackened wood that was evidence of the dramatic attempt to destroy one of the best known and most historic buildings in the city.

The slightly delayed trial lasted sixteen days and attracted enormous media attention. After the firebombing had signalled the dangers inherent in dabbling deep into the city's violent underworld, the court precincts were turned into a virtual fortress. Armed police swarmed around the court and nearby areas. The crowds who flocked to the trial and to watch the comings and goings of the accused and the legal establishment were searched for weapons.

It had been reported that some key witnesses had been threatened with being shot if they spoke out so they were hidden away at secret addresses, guarded by police escorts. The threat of violence was so serious that the two trial judges, Lords Kissen and Cowie, and four prosecuting counsel, who were involved in four separate trials involving the gang, were given special protection. The firebombing had raised the stakes and there were fears that lawyers could be kidnapped or worse. The movements of witnesses and lawyers were carefully organised, with guards always at the ready. In the evenings, the lawyers were escorted back to the security of a city-centre gentlemen's club.

As if this highly visible armed operation wasn't enough of a sensation, the trials had another unique aspect. Since several of the accused were involved in more than one of the four separate trials, it was ruled from the bench that newspapers, TV or radio could not identify them till all four trials were completed. So it came about that the readers who lapped up the trial reports, day after day, heard Norval and his connections described as Mr X, Mr Y or whatever. This is how the gang got its nickname of the XYY mob.

In the end, sentences totalling seventy-four years were handed down and it was said at the time that Norval and his associates had created Scotland's first big-time crime syndicate. Norval got fourteen years but his was not the longest sentence handed down at those trials – John 'Plum' McDuff got twenty-one years. Norval had recruited McDuff, a henchman he had met in Peterhead, to his enterprise many years before and he had played a major role in carrying out the operation. Joseph Polding, aka 'The Mallet', got eighteen years and other lesser members got shorter stretches. The supergrass Henry escaped with a light sentence of just four years but Norval swore vengeance on the turncoat and he lived his years in jail in fear. There was the odd incident involving boiling water but Henry survived and disappeared on his release. If he is still alive, it would be unwise for him ever to return to the city.

This sensational trial had a follow-up that was to prove almost as dramatic. This was the trial of 'The Frighteners' as the papers had dubbed them. Norval, known in the tabloids as the good-time bad guy, may have been behind bars but the events that preceded his trial were still making headlines. Four people faced court in the aftermath of the trial – his daughter Rita Norval or Gunn, Billy Gunn, David Garvie of **TEMPLE** and John McNeil of **GOVAN**. It was said that 'knowing that Walter Norval and others had been indicted and were to stand trial at the High Court of Glasgow on charges including assault and robbery and contraventions of the Firearms Act, they conspired to defeat the ends of justice by intimidating witnesses'. The Gunns were accused of intimidating two detectives in Walter Norval's house in **MILTON**. They were reputed as saying that they had a surprise 'of an explosive nature' in store for the police and, thereby, putting the detectives in fear. It was also alleged that, on the eve of the trial of Norval and the others, Billy Gunn and Garvie climbed on to the roof of the High Court and set it on fire with bottles of petrol. Rita, a somewhat glamorous young woman who the tabloids tagged the Godfather's Daughter, was further charged with conducting herself in a disorderly manner at the High Court on 2 November and putting two detectives in fear for themselves and their families. It was also alleged that, on the same day, she attempted to suborn George Sinclair and his wife Rosemary, both of **MARYHILL**, into giving false evidence at the trial. Further charges alleged that Billy Gunn and McNeil conspired to intimidate Mr Sinclair to give false evidence at the trial of Mrs Gunn, who, as has already been reported, was charged with attempting to suborn the Sinclairs. McNeil was accused of telling Mr Sinclair that there was a contract out for him and of attempting to intimidate him into absconding. Billy Gunn was also on a similar charge.

At the end of this trial, McNeil got four years and Billy Gunn got five – basically for telling a Crown witness that he would be filled full of holes if he gave evidence against the gang. Rita Norval and David Garvie walked free. Rita was cleared of intimidating the police and the Crown witnesses who gave evidence against her father. The case against Garvie of setting the court on fire with petrol bombs was found not proven. Rita, Billy Gunn and Garvie were also found not guilty, on the direction of the judge, Lord McDonald, of conspiring to destroy the High Court on the eve of Rita's father's trial.

The Norval saga was finally played out, the Godfather had been deposed and the XYY team behind bars.

NOT PROVEN

Almost every time someone writes about this unique feature of Scottish law, it is referred to as 'that bastard verdict'. The phrase was coined by no less a figure than Sir Walter Scott and the verdict itself has been in use in the Scottish courts since the 1720s. It offers a jury a third option in addition to a straightforward not guilty or guilty. If the jurors are unconvinced that the prosecution or the defence has established guilt or innocence beyond reasonable doubt, they can declare the case against an accused 'not proven'. Not proven, like not guilty, is an acquittal verdict – the accused is freed and cannot be tried again on the same charge. This, it seems to me, is the major cause of the public unease at the verdict. The critics tend to see it as a verdict that means the accused is guilty but the law just can't prove it. And, even if some time in the future, new evidence of guilt emerges, it cannot be used to retry the accused.

Calls for its repeal are made with stunning regularity but supporters of retention of the verdict believe that, by having this option, once again, Scots Law is superior to most other legal systems. The verdict is unique in that it allows shades of grey to be painted around a case. In the rest of the world, it is a black and white matter – simply guilty or not guilty. However, real life is not as clear-cut as that!

Madeleine Smith's not proven verdict in 1857 is, perhaps, the most famous one to have been recorded but it has always been a controversial conclusion to a court case. The campaign to abolish 'that bastard verdict' was raised a notch or two in 1992 when the trial of Francis Auld, accused of killing a Lanarkshire teenager, ended in a not proven verdict. The media went to town on this one and much was made of the campaign which was led by the victim's parents. They argued, with some force, that the verdict was unsatisfactory for both the prosecution and the accused who would have to live with the stigma of being unable to prove his innocence beyond that reasonable doubt.

In recent years, there has been much questioning of the verdict whenever it has been delivered in a high-profile murder case. The whole controversy over this unique verdict was still making headlines as recently as June 2004 when the case against a self-confessed sadomasochist, George Johnstone, who was charged with killing prostitute Jacqui Gallagher, was found not proven.

The differences in the standards required, as far as proof goes, between criminal and civil law have been highlighted in cases where victims' families have sued for compensation in civil cases and won.

O

ORR, Sir John

His immediate predecessor as chief constable of the Strathclyde Police Force was Leslie Sharp and, when Orr took up the job in 1996, it was considered another successful appointment to one of the toughest police jobs in Britain. On his retirement, Andrew Sloan, who had also held the post, said that, in his opinion, about five years in the job was enough – any longer than that and the chief ran the risk of becoming stale.

Despite this, Sir John was so well thought of that he was asked to extend his term to seven years. However, in the event, he only agreed to a further six-months' extension to his five-year contract. He underlined the strains of the job and the effect it can have on the post-holder's private life as reasons for his reluctance to stay on any longer than that. 'It's like twenty-four hours a day sometimes. You cannot do this job any other way.' He found that, instead of going home, he was spending large periods of time in the flat above the police HQ in **PITT STREET** in the city centre.

Incidentally, the HQ also has a splendid private dining room where the chief of the day can entertain local bigwigs. The luncheons held there can be productive to the police in giving them insights into the way the folk who don't wear the blue uniform and chequered caps are thinking. These occasions are also a chance for the top men in the force to get over their point of view in an informal way and usually there is a touch of humour on the menu as well as a nice steak.

Sir John was succeeded by Willie Rae and, coincidentally, both men had an involvement in the handling of the aftermath of the Pan Am jumbo jet crash at Lockerbie. John Orr was joint head of Strathclyde CID at the time and he was drafted in as the senior

216

investigating officer into the wicked murder of 270 men, women and children on that fateful night. The expertise he acquired in this international investigation resulted in him having to increase his already heavy workload. Much of this extra time was spent lecturing on disaster planning, administration and the investigation of major incidents.

On the streets – and that's where he liked his coppers to work, when possible – he was a great believer in robust, high visibility, interventionist policing. In the early 1990s, the innocent, as well as the guilty, were well aware of the yellow-jacketed squads who dropped in, uninvited, on pubs and restaurants during his Spotlight Initiative. The audiences of passers-by and quiet pint quaffers were able to watch a hard-line attack on the weapon carriers and drug dealers.

At this time, no one in the city could doubt that the police were taking the job seriously and the visibility of the operation had an effect on the villains. But, although it looked as if the police were tackling the bad guys mob-handed, the fact was that John Orr, like every chief before him, could have used more manpower. Other campaigns in his reign included a Safer Scotland which was inspired by the Spotlight Initiative. There was another catchily labelled drive called Know the Score which saw millions of pounds' worth of drugs being seized.

On taking retirement, Orr indulged his lifetime passion for Kilmarnock Football Club, eventually taking the elevated post of chairman. But the law-and-order scene can still pull strongly on any ex-cop – policing is a hard drug to kick! So it was no surprise when he came back into the public eye in mid 2004. The old controversy surrounding sectarian marches came back to prominence in the press. Catholics complained of intimidating marches and the Orange Order talked of freedom rights. The 'right to march' was much debated. In the old pre-war Glasgow, the marches of the Orange Order were charged with mounted police – the so-called Sillitoe's Cossacks – when they strayed off agreed routes but, these days, more carefully considered actions are required.

In June 2004, the Scottish Executive's communities minister, Margaret Curran, tasked Sir John, now aged fifty-eight, with the tricky job of reviewing the procedures for allowing marches and parades in Scotland. His review was to take account of those who want to march, the communities and the authorities. It was also to look at the length of notice that was required to be given by parade organisers to councils and communities. On entering this minefield, the ex-chief constable was diplomatic. 'I am aware of the high level of interest this issue generates. I will be approaching the review with an open mind.' There is no doubt that Sir John's reputation as a fair cop was valuable.

Jim Slaven, Scottish national organiser of Cairde na hEireann, an umbrella organisation for republican groups, welcomed the appointment. Robert McLean, the spokesman for the Grand Orange Order of Scotland, supported Sir John's involvement too. He said, 'We look forward to meeting Sir John and hope he will take a balanced view of the issue.'

P

PATRICK, JAMES

This is the pseudonym used by the author of one of the most insightful studies of Glasgow's gangs. In 1973, when Patrick's *A Glasgow Gang Observed* (London: Eyre Methuen, 1973) was published, the author was working as a lecturer in educational psychology at an English university. It was the result of remarkable undercover work done during an intensive period between October 1966 and January 1967 and its findings are, in parts, as relevant today as they were when they first appeared. Patrick, who was a teacher in an approved school, was invited by one of his charges to join a gang on the streets of **MARYHILL** in order to gain a better understanding of what made young gang members the way they were. It took courage to take up the invitation and inevitably there would be considerable controversy about a teacher in an approved school going out on the streets with members of a gang. Indeed, when the book first appeared, the then assistant chief constable, William Ratcliffe said, 'It is nonsense that someone on the staff of an approved school should run about with a gang.' The leader of the gang, Tim, knew who Mr Patrick was and this was bound to have an effect on the boy.' This may have some validity but to go on to say, as Ratcliffe does, that the book added not one iota of information about the sum total of knowledge about gangs in the city seems, to me, to be plain wrong. The book was studded with interesting insights into the psychology of gangs and, if some of it was already known to the cops, then so be it. The general reader was given a touch of understanding of gang culture that could only help in the battle against young thugs.

Patrick was also criticised for using a pseudonym. He denied that not using his own name was a piece of sensationalism that was designed to shift more books off the shelves. The author's riposte to the criticism was to point out that, since he had ceased to associate with the gang, two boys had been murdered. 'That is not melodrama – it is tragedy. I have a family and relatives in Glasgow. I must protect them as much as myself,' he said.

Then, as now, gang members often shy away from the use of the word 'gang', preferring to call the group a 'team'. Maryhill, in the late 1960s, had many gangs and perhaps the best known was the Maryhill Fleet. But, on taking up his pupil's invitation, it was the Maryhill Young Team that Patrick found himself mixing with.

The chalk-splattered tweeds and battered cords of the approved school teacher were not appropriate for this undercover research so Patrick donned 'a midnight-blue suit, with a twelve inch middle vent, and a light-blue handkerchief with a white polka dot (to match [his] tie) in the top pocket.' He allowed his hair to grow and his fingernails became rough and dirty. On his first night out with the team, he had to intervene when his new friends mindlessly attacked a man in pub, hitting him on the head with a bottle, kicking him in the stomach when the was on the floor and 'running like fuck' to escape. This was the reality of life on the streets. This was a first-hand view of the sort of behaviour that ended up with youngsters in an approved school like the one Patrick taught in. It was more valuable, one suspects, than gazing out at a sea of disinterested faces, waiting for the lunch break.

One surprise for Patrick was the amount of time the boys spent just hanging around street corners, looking for trouble. The rumbles in pubs or dance halls punctuated the long periods of boredom. Just as they had been in the 1930s, 'Mars Bars' – scars – were worn with pride. There was also plenty of evidence to support the theory that, once a youngster was known to the authorities and had a reputation amongst his mates as a troublemaker, it could be difficult for him to break away from an existence that revolves around the gang and take up a life of respectability. Youngsters released from approved schools for a weekend on the streets were under heavy pressure to conform to their image as a tough guy – this was something that was not perhaps fully appreciated by the folk who ran the schools.

It would seem to me that there is scope for a programme to help first offenders, particularly the young, get back into a normal way of life by giving them real support to break with the old ways. Time after time, gang members have told me that crime becomes a way of life – that, once they have the bad-guy label round their neck, they respond to the expectation society then has of them by continuing to misbehave.

Patrick found that, for the Young Team, one of the main driving forces was marking out and protecting territory – and this was in the days before drugs became the major problem. A successful foray into the territory of another gang was a source of great satisfaction – even it only meant daubing a slogan on the walls of someone else's patch.

It took guts for an academic to join a 'team' on the streets and, despite the hostility directed towards such an undertaking, it provided valuable lessons for all concerned.

PEDDIE, Reverend J Cameron

Rev. Peddie was one of the most remarkable figures in the history of fighting the gangs in Glasgow. As is told elsewhere in this book, the kirk ministers, the Rev. J A C Murray and the Rev. S H R Warnes, had considerable success in the 1930s, in **BRIDGETON** and the east end generally, with youth groups and football leagues. Their pioneering work in giving young gang fodder outside interests was a forerunner of the Peddie's work after the Second World War.

Peddie was minister of **HUTCHESONTOWN** Parish Church in the Gorbals for around thirty years. His work was chronicled in the old evening paper, *The Evening Citizen*, by a fellow cleric-turned-newspaperman, Duncan Campbell. As is the way of the papers, Peddie was labelled by the *Citizen* as 'The man who *really* broke the Glasgow gangs'. Such headlines are understandable when Peddie's full story is told but, of course, no one – not even that much celebrated gang-buster, Chief Constable Percy Sillitoe – totally curbed the gangs. There have been moments of great success – and the work of Peddie is one such episode – but gangs are still with us. It is interesting to look back all these years and get an insight into what life on the streets of the city, particularly the Gorbals, was really like. Duncan Campbell spelled it out in an introductory article to his newspaper series on Peddie. The start to this piece was arresting.

> Alarming scenes in **CROWN STREET** when three gangs came into conflict were described in court when four youths appeared charged with being members of a gang known as the 'South Side Stickers', that they did form part of a riotous mob of evil-disposed persons. The shopkeepers 'live in a state of terror' said a witness. 'I saw one of the accused leading a crowd of fifty young men. He was brandishing a stick, cursing, swearing and shouting. The melee lasted about twenty minutes.'

This is a dramatic word picture of life in the late 1940s and early 1950s of the last century. The now defunct evening paper (at one time Glasgow had three evening papers – *Times*, *News* and *Citizen*, as the newsvendors shouted) saw the behaviour of these youths as symptomatic of the Glasgow of that era. It was a time when 'citizens were afraid to walk the streets alone after dark and beaten-up shopkeepers refused to talk'.

This was the kind of climate of violence that Peddie lived and worked in. It contributed to the fearsome reputation that the Gorbals in particular had of being a hell on earth – a reputation that spread around the world and was often commented on in other cities where, in fact, the slums were much worse than anything in Glasgow. However, Duncan Campbell used masterly understatement to record that 'Glasgow had a bad name' at the time!

Peddie's story is an uplifting one. After an early career of academic success in which he gained bursaries and attended Aberdeen University, he started his ministry with a post in Barrhead. Being so close to Glasgow, he became intrigued with the newspapers of the time and their lurid tales of crime and gangs. This quietly spoken man of God wondered if he could do anything to help sort out some of this mess. So he moved to the Gorbals and discovered the other side of that much-maligned place. His congregation was made up of friendly folk who were just trying their hardest to live decent lives, despite the slums, deprivation, unemployment and sometimes desperate hopelessness that were all around them in that gloomy, smoke-stained industrial environment.

Life in the Gorbals has spawned many memoirs in which the legendary friendliness of such places features strongly. These were folk who lived up a close and had the 'we are all in it together – let's make the most of it for each other' type of attitude. It is something of a cliché that life in such primitive housing was no easy mark. Maybe a decent inside toilet, a bath and some running hot water would have been better than the camaraderie but, like all clichés, there is truth in it. However, as well as its good folk, the Gorbals, in those days, had a hard core of ne'er-do-wells too.

Peddie studied the bad guys – the youngsters who were never out of trouble with the police and who threatened the shopkeepers and merchants and fought bloody battles on the street of a night. His studies produced a thought that has driven many a man wanting to do some good in this, at times, benighted city – idle hands find the devil's work. Peddie was convinced that many of the young thugs were little more than 'mischievous youths with no outlet for their high spirits'. This was very close to the analysis of Warnes and Murray. But his studies of the young gangs did produce one surprising conclusion.

Unlike gang membership in many other areas of the city, the membership of the two main Gorbals gangs, the Stickers and their rivals the Liberty Boys, was not defined by sectarianism. Both had

Catholics and Protestants as members. Peddie also noted that conventional church clubs were unlikely to do much good in such an area and in such a violent atmosphere. This observation was amusingly underlined when he approached one particular group of young tearaways about joining a church club only to be told succinctly, 'We're no' wantin' any o' yer ping-pong.'

In the face of such attitudes, some of what the politicians these days call 'blue-sky thinking' was called for. Peddie's solution was to create clubs where the potential troublemakers entertained themselves and ran the club themselves – they were not asked to join existing clubs with pre-set agendas. And it was to be no wee group of just a few lads – Peddie helped get no fewer than thirty clubs started and, at their peak, the membership of them stood at around 4,000. Dealing with this number of youngsters – youngsters who were definitely no angels – took guts. And, in an area where fist, knife and bottle were ready weapons in any dispute, it is interesting that, despite verbal threats to him, Peddie was never physically attacked.

But he never dodged a dangerous encounter. He told, for instance, of one street-corner meeting with a bunch of boys who confessed to being members of the Stickers. He approached them with his somewhat radical idea of them starting a non-political, non-sectarian club with their own committee to run it. (Incidentally, Peddie stuck to his belief that the members themselves should make their own rules and he was mainly a figurehead as the honorary president of each club.) As a way to getting this club started, he asked for their names and addresses but, as you might expect, the street-corner boys gave false ones to get rid of the 'do-gooder' and failed to turn up at a meeting that had been arranged. Undeterred, the minister again took to the streets to try to find them. Some were now on 'holiday', a euphemism for being in the clink. Others told him of a more pressing matter – an impeding battle between the Stickers and the Liberty Boys who had upset the Stickers by attacking one of their members.

The peacemaker invited them all to a meeting in the kirk vestry.

Around forty turned up with an amazing assortment of weapons, including a sword, jemmies and razors – well, after all, this was the Gorbals. Equally surprising was the fact that the cleric talked them out of that particular fight and nudged them in the direction of eventually starting a club. Tobacco, now rightly a top social enemy, played a positive role in these less enlightened days. One of the favourite tasks of the clubs was to organise 'smokers' – concert evenings with singers, musicians and comedians entertaining the smoke-wreathed gang members. Other ploys were to hold fish-and-chip-supper nights, singsongs, boxing nights and dances. This was new and positive thinking in the Gorbals. The local folk responded by donating gifts of equipment and the press and police were also on side.

Keeping order in these clubs could have been a major problem. Peddie's idea was that drinking, betting and bad language were banned. Many of the clubs had a printed syllabus and their main principles were brotherhood and good citizenship. The accepted rule was that, in disputes, any decision made by the leader was to be regarded as final. Further insight into the thinking of the times came when various members of the clubs, finding an intelligent and helpful listener in the minister, told him of their 'holiday' breaks away from the Gorbals. This was generally a spell in a borstal or prison. One young lag told Peddie that sixty days in the Bar-L was as good as a three-month holiday 'doon the watter'. This was not a totally absurd comparison since inside the Big House in the east end, the inmates had food, rest and regular hours. They were also kept away from the demon drink.

The police, of course, always took a close interest in what was going on in this valuable experiment in reforming tough nuts – at least the boys in blue knew where the villains were at any given time. Peddie recognised a particular danger and guarded against it. He was always very careful not to be an informer or spy on his young friends on behalf of the police, no matter the temptation. He was, however, able to work with the lawmen when it suited him.

An example of this was the occasion when he found the Stickers in a particularly gloomy mood one Friday night. There was a big football game the next day and their star man was languishing in the cells. Peddie turned his verbal skills on the cops for a change and managed to talk the errant footballer out of the cells for one day to play in the game. The Stickers won and the youngster returned to police custody to face the music in court on the Monday.

Many of the generalities and beliefs attached to gangs worldwide were confirmed in Peddie's attack on group misbehaviour. The concept of 'honour', so important to the Mafia and to many veteran gang members in the city to this day, was discussed in those far-off days in the Gorbals. Peddie wrote:

> The first thing that impressed me deeply about the boys was their amazing loyalty to their class. Supposing, I asked them, 'Someone is killed in a gang fight and one of your men, though innocent, is charged with the death and you know the guilty man to be one of the other gang. Would you not save your own man by giving away the name of the guilty person?' 'No,' they replied. 'If you are to mix with us, sir, you must understand we never give anyone away – this is the first principle in our code of honour.'

This chilling attitude drove Peddie to remark, 'I resolved never to let any of them down. I never gave away any of them and they knew it.' He then added a postscript that would find agreement from the hundreds of good people, down the years, who have worked with such young gangs – 'What a magnificent spirit they had – if only they had turned to other channels.'

Part of the secret of the success of the clubs was the fact that meetings were not held in church halls – the club the Stickers formed met in a disused factory and their meetings were particularly successful. But, although things were going well, there were still incidents. One gang used to shout through the windows of the old factory, 'Come out and fight, you minister's boys!' and sometimes they did just that. On one occasion, Cameron Peddie was patrolling the dangerous streets of the post-war Gorbals at 4 a.m., trying to stop fighting. Brave man. The respect he was held in by the hard men of the time is shown by the fact that Billy Fullerton, leader of the Billy Boys, admitted in later life that Peddie had had an effect on members of his wild, dangerous and infamous bunch.

Peddie never rammed religion down the lads' throats and, indeed, there was some minor trouble with his congregation over meetings that were held in the kirk halls. Peddie took the view that his job was to urge the lads to be true to their own faiths, be they Jew, Catholic or Protestant.

After some time, the experiment was moved up a notch or two. Recognising that unemployment was at the root of some of the area's problems, Peddie started various schemes to keep the lads occupied. One such venture was the Lightening Distribution Agency which delivered items such as handbills and samples of goods round the doors. The boot-camp brigade of today might have thought some hard labour would have been more in order but it is significant that Peddie ruled out labouring. His reason for this was that most of the club members were 'underfed, pinched, stunted in growth and just did not have the physique' for it.

Gradually, like all such enterprises, the project simply ran out of steam. The gangs are still with us but, in his day, a Christian visionary like Peddie must have kept hundreds of youngsters away from a way of life that would have seen them end up in Barlinnie and would have further blighted the already-scarred area. It is the mark of such a man that, despite all his years in the Gorbals and all his experiences with knife men and gangsters, his basic faith in human nature was not destroyed. The *Citizen*'s old minister-turned-reporter, Duncan Campbell, could note that, twenty-five years after starting his clubs, J Cameron Peddie was 'still a believer in his fellow man and there was not trace of toughness of cynicism in his make-up.'

PENNY MOB

This is the name of the first gang to come to the attention of writers and newspapers. First mentioned in the 1880s, they managed to survive, in one form or another, until the Sillitoe era in the 1930s. The name came from their habit of each member chipping in a penny a week to pay for fines and other gang expenses. They were a gang of hooligans whose original territory was **TOWNHEAD** and one newspaper report noted that 'they were for long a source of serious annoyance in the community'.

Even in those days, reporters tried to infiltrate the gangs in search of exclusives and, in the early part of the last century, one writer who was successful in forging close contact with the Penny Mob reported that one of their chief activities was street fighting with other gangs. Their main rivals appear to have been boys of the Wee Doe Hill and the Big Doe Hill gangs. Another 'opposition' group was a gang that styled itself the Drygate Youths of whom a contemporary newspaper report said, 'While holding high revel, they fell foul of the police and a battle royal ensued.' This particular stramash ended with the arrest of an individual described as 'chairman of the gang'.

Interesting insights into the early days of the Penny Mob emerged in the 1930s when an unusual character called Robert Earle May returned to Glasgow on a visit. May had left the city in the 1880s to make his fortune in America, an ambition in which he seems to have succeeded. Indeed, he was wealthy enough to be able to raise, what was for those days, the huge sum of $15,000 to erect a statue of Robert Burns in Boston, Massachusetts. Back in Glasgow on holiday, he sought out a reporter to chronicle his thoughts on his return and to listen to some tales of the old days. Not surprisingly, he 'found gang and sectarian violence still flourishing'. And the same can be said today!

He showed his reporter friend articles he had written in the US. These were publications containing personal memories of the days when he had helped the Penny Mob harass certain sections of the city. He recalled the street fights with the Big Doe Hill gang and others when the ammunition was broken whinstone from the railway tracks that were then being constructed round the city. Paling staffs and wash-boiler lids made useful swords and shields and belts and bare fists also came into play. When not fighting other gangs, the Penny Mob, for a spell, specialised in being chuckers-out at political and other meetings. But they became so enthusiastic and violent in their efforts to give the speakers a 'fair' hearing that the organisers of the meetings decided that this was one aspect of gang life that should no longer be encouraged.

After their demise the Penny Mob were not quickly forgotten and their infamy lived on in a verse in a ditty once sung by the Bridgeton flute bands of the thirties. Angus Yule, now a kirk elder in Stepps, grew up in Parkhead and remembers hearing this verse in his youth:

> Many years ago, the Penny Mob,
> They guarded Brigton Cross.
> Now they have gone and we deeply feel their loss,
> But Brigton's still as Protestant –
> So let your heart rejoice,
> And we'll give three hearty cheers,
> For the Brigton Billy Boys.

That feeling of 'loss' would be far from universal.

PRITCHARD, Dr Edward William

A medical man, of **SAUCHIEHALL STREET**, he turned to taking life rather than saving it. His favoured method was poisoning and it led to him making his mark in criminal history as the last man to be hanged in public in Glasgow. These days there are still plenty of folk braying for the return of the rope. You can't help wonder if they have something of the bloodlust in them – the same kind of bloodlust that led to the remarkable figure of between 80,000 and 100,000 people, according to reports at the time, turning up to see the grim spectacle of the doctor dangling at the end of a rope.

Pritchard breathed his last on 28 July 1865. There used to be an old saying in Glasgow that, if you did wrong, you would die 'facing the monument' – that is, you would be hanged for, in those days, the scaffold faced Nelson's Monument at Glasgow Green and that would be the last scene the victim would see. This was to be the fate of the strange Englishman who came to Scotland and apparently took pleasure rather than profit from murder.

Pritchard became known as 'the human crocodile'. The derivation of this unlikely sobriquet seemed to have been long forgotten but, according to Jack House in his *Square Mile of Murder*, it came about as a result of the fascination in the Glasgow of old with what were called 'penny poems'. These works tended to have important public occasions as their subjects and the putting to death of Pritchard was just that. One Alexander Allan penned a poem called 'Dr. E W Pritchard turned into a Pillar of Salt' and it was so successful that he followed it up with another called 'An Hour with Pritchard, the Prince of Poisoners'. This last epic had the subtitle 'A full confession with the murderer's motive, a dialogue in verse, interrupted occasionally by voices from the lost! And a demoniac song!'. In one of the poems, Allan wrote some lines that stuck in the public memory:

> And men condemn the murderer to die
> But when a wretch in secret hate and guile,
> A foul cold-blooded human crocodile,
> Plots calmly on for months, from day to day,
> To take his fellow creature's life away –
> (and that the wife that in his bosom lay) –
> Counts out the grains of poison it requires
> To do the deed his hellish heart desires.

The 'human crocodile' attracted great public hatred when the extent of his crimes and hypocrisy were finally in the public domain. Some contemporary accounts have it that, at the time of his wife's death, he had the coffin opened and kissed the corpse of his victim with a tear in his eye. This public show of grief was a spectacular sham, for the doctor had, in fact, slowly poisoned his wife and mother-in-law. Not that sham was anything new to him as, having bought his medical degrees, he wasn't actually a doctor at all – although he did have some medical experience which he gained during his navy service.

After some shady amorous adventures in the south, he had come north with his wife but he was soon up to his old womanising tricks. He had an affair with a servant girl who died in a fire at his house in **BERKELEY TERRACE**, not far from **SANDYFORD PLACE**. The girl's body was horribly charred and suspicion hung around the doctor that he had murdered her. There were certainly inconsistencies in the reports of her death. However, despite the whispers of his enemies, Pritchard continued to walk around the Sauchiehall Street area and indulge in a curious habit of handing out picture postcards of himself to passers-by.

A couple of weeks or so after the fire, the Pritchards moved to **ROYAL CRESCENT**, on the other side of Sauchiehall Street. But it was far from a happy family time. The doctor who was both a bit of a charlatan and a ladies' man started an affair with another servant. This was Mary McLeod who entertained Pritchard sexually while his family went down the coast to Dunoon for a holiday. She was not to pay for her involvement with the shady medic with her life but, instead, she was to find herself in grave trouble when the doctor accused her of the poisoning of his mother-in-law.

A tip-off, from an anonymous source, had aroused police interest in the activities of the 'human crocodile'. Along with chemists, they investigated and their inquires turned up the fact that the doctor was piling up dangerous poisons at a rate far in excess of the needs of even the most conscientious of doctors. In an intriguing connection with the Madeleine Smith case, Pritchard had bought his poisons from, among others, Murdoch and Currie's in Sauchiehall Street – a source of supply that Madeleine had also used!

By being poisoned with small doses, over a long period, Pritchard's wife and mother-in-law must have suffered hellish deaths. The prolonged administration of small quantities of poison resulted in agonising illnesses before they finally passed away. Because of the nature of their deaths, the Pritchards' neighbours and a doctor colleague of Pritchard suspected poisoning might be involved. The authorities received an anonymous letter to this effect and it sparked a police inquiry that led them to Pritchard. He was sentenced to hang and, in a life that had had few redeeming factors, he at least took time in the condemned cell to pen a final confession that cleared the unfortunate servant Mary McLeod.

His final hours made for a grisly scene. Crowds had started to gather at the Green on the night before the execution and, on the morning, six ministers addressed groups of spectators at various points. At 7.30, the hangman, William Calcraft, who was also known as the 'London Hangman', arrived to make sure all was well with his scaffold. The crowd recognised him and he was greeted with a combination of cheers and hisses – though the papers seemed to think that the cheering was the stronger! Soon after, a procession appeared from the prison with Pritchard immaculate in a suit of mourning that he had also worn on the day of his arrest. He wore one white glove and carried the other in his hand. A showman to the end, he wanted to be allowed to address the crowds but was dissuaded. The Edinburgh *Courant* reported:

When he appeared on the scaffold great commotion prevailed amongst the crowd. Exclamations were heard to proceed from every quarter, which were such expressions as, 'How well he looks!', 'He's very pale!', 'That's him!' and 'Hats off!'. Mr Oldham read a short written prayer, while Calcraft adjusted the cap, put aside the long hair and beard to allow the rope to be rightly placed and tied the legs. Calcraft, after putting the rope around the prisoner's neck, and drawing the cap over his face, steadied the wretched man by placing his hands on his back and breast. On a signal being given by the culprit, the bolt was drawn and, at ten minutes past eight o'clock, he was launched into eternity. As soon as he was seen dangling on the rope, a loud shriek arose from the crowd, and many turned their heads away from the horrid spectacle.

That was the last time the 'human crocodile' was seen – until many years later when workmen, building a new high court at the site of the South Prison, uncovered the murderers' graveyard. Under a stone simply marked 'P', they found the skeleton of Dr Edward William Pritchard.

Q

QUINN, John

A highly experienced and respected reporter, news editor and boxing expert, he is the man credited with inventing the name Bible John, for Scotland's cruellest serial killer to remain uncaught. (There is, however, now a theory that the murders were copycat killings and not, as most believed at the time, the work of one man so this assessment may yet prove inaccurate.)

Why Bible John? John Quinn denies that it was a flair for the dramatic that made him give the murderer this tag. He says:

> Well, it is simply this. There seemed no more appropriate name for a man known to be John whose calling card of death was a fixation with the Bible and his habit of quoting from the Good Book. I meant it merely as the seemingly perfect tag to jog the memory of those whose paths may have crossed the dapper dancer of death who made criminal history by being the first man to have his identikit picture issued with the approval of the Scottish Office.

John Quinn, digging energetically for background on a story that dominated the Scottish newspapers for months, got valuable info on the killer from the famous city detective 'Elphie' Dalglish who was working on the unsolved murders. Dalglish told the reporter:

> The man is thought to be called John and may speak of being of a family of two and having a sister. He may also speak of a strict upbringing and of a strict parental attitude to drink.

The man may also speak of having a strict religious background and make references to the Bible.

'What more could a reporter ask?' said John Quinn, as he looked back at that exciting day. After this hard-earned briefing, the reporter ran to the office radio car – this was before the cushy days of mobile phones and laptops! – and started to dictate to the copy-takers who, in those days, sat with their headphones on and typed out the copy phoned in from out-of-office reporters. It was then the custom to give the news editor a call first to let him know something of the strength of the story you were about to file. When John Quinn did this, there was some discussion on what to call the suspect now that the press had more inside info on him. 'Let's just call him "Bible John",' said the reporter and history was made. It was an inspired tag that was picked up by every newspaper, radio and television station.

R

RAMENSKY, 'GENTLE' JOHNNY

One of the most remarkable characters in the history of crime in Scotland and a Glasgow legend, he was the most famous of the 'petermen', a name given to skilled safe-breakers. He died in prison, aged sixty-seven, after a career on the wrong side of the law that had started in the 1930s and which led to him spending more than fifty of those sixty-seven years in jail. When not behind bars, he lived for a time in **EGLINTON STREET**.

His nickname was derived from the fact that, when caught, he always went, as they say, gently. He was seldom involved in violence, using his skills with gelignite and safe-breaking tools to crack open the strongest of strong boxes, the best that the security firms could dream up. This undoubted skill was also put to good use in the Second World War when he was recruited by the British Secret Services to be parachuted behind enemy lines. His mission: to break into the German army's most secure safes, in search of secret plans.

It is said that this brave man had great success in his military career but, sadly, when peace broke out, he went back to breaking in. The lure of the excitement of creeping across darkened roofs and of pitting his skills against the safe manufacturers was too much for him to resist. It is perhaps understandable – since he had been a youngster, dodging the cops had become a way of life for him. And the high regard in which the criminal community held his services also played a role in flattering his ego. He found it hard to say no to a ploy to get some easy cash by way of a bit of 'can opening'.

His final sentence came when he was found hiding on a rooftop in Ayr with intent to steal. Taken ill in prison, he was swiftly transferred to hospital but died. His final exploit had been a low-key affair compared to his secret service days and the scrapes he got into pre-war. Incidentally, it is said that the services apparently failed to honour his war-time service in any significant way.

In his heyday, Ramensky was so skilled that, when detectives investigated a crime and found that the safe-breaking was particularly sophisticated – he did not believe in blowing safes to smithereens – suspicion inevitably fell on Johnny. Usually, he was guilty and, with the cuffs on yet again, he went quietly to do his time.

He also made his mark on Scottish prison history. When Scottish Office files were opened to the public in the mid 1990s, it was revealed that Ramensky's efforts to escape from jail in the 1930s had, on one occasion, resulted in him being thrust into iron shackles to prevent any other attempts to jump the wall. When the then Scottish Secretary heard of this inhumane treatment of Gentle Johnny, he ordered a review of the Prison Service's use of leg-irons as a restraint and the practice was banned.

Ramensky's concern that his exploits only extended to relieving the innocent of hard-earned cash rather than putting their lives at risk was underlined when he was in prison for a safe-breaking job. He wrote to the governor suggesting that 'care was taken' in handling one of the safes he had broken into on that particular job. He was worried that some gelignite that had been left behind could injure an innocent party.

His wartime skills may have been given public acknowledgement and praise but a chance to use his criminal experience for the good was turned down. Records released in 1994 showed that an Edinburgh professor of forensics requested permission to have Ramensky's safe-breaking skills recorded on film for posterity. He wanted to use the film as a weapon in the fight against crime but his request was turned down by the Lord Advocate.

REDSKINS

Theirs is an important name in the history of the gangs but it is one that is largely forgotten today. The name, presumably a nod in the direction of the popularity of cowboy tales early in the last century, peppers newspaper reports on crime in the city with great regularity, during the First World War and after.

In June 1916, amid the headlines charting how the war was going for the allies, there are others about a different sort of violence. A *Herald* piece, headlined 'Hooliganism in Glasgow', is typical:

> A display of rowdyism, fortunately unattended by serious consequences, occurred in the **BRIDGETON** district of Glasgow on Tuesday night. The crowd which numbered thirty or forty youths shouted and yelled as they passed along several of the leading thoroughfares to Bridgeton Cross. Crying 'We are the f****** Redskins!', they jostled and otherwise interfered with a number of people including a gentleman who declined to give the police his name and address, saying he was afraid his assailants might victimise him.

Such rowdyism wasn't particularly desperate and a couple of the youths involved were given the option of a fine of £1 or fourteen days as a guest of the king.

The Redskins, however, could get involved in more serious matters. A classic example was a case where they demanded money from a bookie at the old **CARNTYNE** dog track. When he unwisely refused to pay up, he was given a kicking and had to be rescued by spectators. And it was to get a tad more serious than that. The bookie reported the assault to the police and, the next day, he was in **MAIN STREET, BRIDGETON** with a fellow bookie when a gang of Redskins spotted them and another kicking followed. Worse was to come the day after. This time, the Redskins who spied the bookie were armed with a gun and, after it was fired, the bookie had to escape up a nearby close where he hid behind a door till the police arrived.

One of the most dramatic of the Redskins' exploits was to take 'possession' of a Glasgow tramcar in **DALMARNOCK ROAD**, not far from **FARME CROSS**. The newspapers of the day quaintly declared that, on this occasion, the Redskins had been 'in conflict with some other combination' and, when the two rival gangs stormed the tramcar, the passengers fled for their lives into the street. A huge crowd then gathered to watch this tramcar rumble between the two gangs. Apparently, at the heart of the dispute was an argument about which group had booked a local dance hall for a Sunday night event. Eventually, the police arrived and delivered the tram back into the hands of the Corporation. Redskins who were arrested were said to be in possession of dangerous weapons although there were no details of what these weapons were.

In an assault by gang members at a football match in **SOUTH-CROFT PARK**, a steel baton was used and a revolver fired. The old notion that the gangs only took it out on each other did not seem to apply to the Redskins who often caused mayhem that led to innocent people being caught up in their violence in what was called 'their happy hunting ground' in the east end.

The Redskins, according to contemporary reports, had around 1,000 members during the First World War – a sizeable army of hard cases who, you can't help feeling, would have been better employed in the trenches. The gang was well organised with its own hierarchy of command. In times of difficulty, gang members used a peculiar whistle to call for assistance from their fellows. With some restraint, the *Bulletin* newspaper, now no longer published, called them 'a nefarious organisation'. Extortion was their main object and it wasn't just trackside bookies turning a dollar or two at the dogs who suffered – they also preyed on shopkeepers in many parts of the east end.

ROBERTSON, James

In a case of 1950 that had many interesting features, Robertson, a policeman, was convicted of murdering his mistress, a Miss McCluskey, by means of a rather unusual weapon – a car. Initially, when the mangled body of this once-attractive woman was found at the roadside by a taxi driver and some tramway maintenance workers, the belief was that it was a hit-and-run incident. But the first cops on the scene were experienced in such matters and soon realised something was wrong about this 'accident'.

Normally, you would expect bits of broken glass and other debris on the road. There was nothing in this case. And, to the experienced investigators, the tyre marks on the road indicated that the body had been run over several times, at least. A post-mortem also raised question marks and suggested that the victim had been knocked unconscious with a blow on the head before being hit with the car. This was clearly a murder and not a hit-and-run.

The killing took place on the south side, on **PROSPECTHILL ROAD** near the junction with **AITKENHEAD ROAD**. Robertson's mistress lived in **NICOLSON STREET** in the **GORBALS** and she had told friends that her paramour was a policeman called Robertson and that he was the father of one of her two illegitimate children. It was, therefore, no hard task for the police to prove Robertson's link with the murdered woman. He paid for the crime with his life when he was put to death by Albert Pierrepoint in the infamous Barlinnie hanging shed.

According to lawyer Laurence Dowdall, if Robertson had been more truthful in the dock, he could have saved his life. Many years later, in an interview looking back at his long career, Dowdall told *The Herald*:

That was a sad, sad case. His wife knew well he had been conducting this liaison, but he said he was not going to let her down in public. If he had told the truth and admitted he had this illicit liaison with this woman McCluskey, he would have got off. The very first question the prosecution asked him was 'What was this Miss McCluskey to you?' He replied, 'A casual acquaintance.' Prosecution counsel used this like a knife; every time he mentioned the phrase 'casual acquaintance', he turned the knife. It was dreadful to see.

Had the court known of the relationship, they may have viewed the killing in a different, more sympathetic light. There could even have been a lesser charge or sentence. But, at the trial, Robertson would only allow the jurors to see him as the cold-blooded killer of a 'casual acquaintance' rather than a man in a tortured relationship with a wife and a mistress. As Robertson awaited his fate in the condemned cell, Dowdall had one last meeting with the policeman. It was an emotional farewell to a man who could say, 'I know I am going to hang in three or four days' time, but I am still glad I didn't let my wife down in public.' The meeting and the case had a lasting effect on Dowdall, a man of great humanity.

The Robertson case also made some telling points in the debate on capital punishment. And it converted one of the top men in the Scottish Prison Service into a lifetime opponent of the grim ritual of killing in the public name. As a trainee officer in Barlinnie, Bill McVey accompanied James Robertson on his fateful last walk from the condemned cell to eternity. He stood at attention beside Robertson as Pierrepoint placed the noose round his neck and opened the drop. As he left the spot, McVey vowed he would never again take part in an execution. 'It turned me against capital punishment for all time. And I believe calls for the return of capital punishment are rubbish.' Bill McVey climbed to the top of the prison service, becoming Deputy Director (Operations). His point is an important one that also highlights the fact that those who bray loudest for the return of the rope have no experience of it in practice.

ROBERTSON, Sir James

This chief constable of the old City of Glasgow Police Force retired in 1971. He had a lifelong interest in the welfare of the youth of the city. A most successful chief constable, he was far from the image of the hard-man commander of hard cops. On his death, Joe Beattie, one of the most respected and best-remembered detectives in the city, said, 'I can't say a bad word about him. He was a gentleman through and through. Sometimes I thought he was too nice to be a chief constable. He was too humane!'

Robertson's interest in youth was underlined with his work on the Easterhouse Project in the late 1960s. At one stage, this pioneering enterprise ran into difficulties with a proposed amnesty involving the youth gangs of the scheme. The police were not too happy about this and the entertainer Frankie Vaughan, one of the driving forces behind the project, wrote to the then prime minister, Harold Wilson, asking for help. Wilson, ever the wily politician, said police operations were a matter in which he could not intervene. But he said the Scottish Office had been in touch with Sir James and he had heard that Robertson had agreed to the proposal. It happened.

And, in other ways, the humane chief constable subtly bent the rules to give this imaginative scheme to help offer deprived youths every chance to get out of the bind of gangs and street battles.

ROLLER, Pat

One of the most famous by-lines in Scottish newspaper history, it was a rather obviously invented name that was used by a succession of late night reporters covering the crime scene for the *Daily Record*. And it has recently been revived for a new column with a more light-hearted touch on after-dark happening. Stairheid rammies, muggings and all sorts of minor crime featured in the original column, which ran for many years. Not much was missed by the *Record* hacks and it was required reading for the criminal classes.

S

SHARP, SIR LESLIE

A chief constable, he is perhaps best remembered for Operation Blade in 1993. Being in command has the privilege of letting you indulge a bit in pet projects. Leslie Sharp, like most chiefs before and after him, was almost overwhelmed by the statistics concerning the number of knife attacks in the city. It seemed that every ned on the street had a blade secreted about his person and had no inhibition in using it in a dispute.

The open razor may be something of a memory in the twenty-first century but the knife is still with us – despite the success of Operation Blade. The history of crime and policing in the city is peppered with similar initiatives. When the police, whose resources are generally stretched too thin, concentrate on one particular aspect of the crime scene to the exclusion of others, it is possible to make a major difference, albeit temporarily. But, eventually, the need to police all aspects of lawbreaking leads to the eye coming off the ball and events swing back.

But Operation Blade did have some spectacular success. It was a well-thought out manoeuvre. There was a catchy slogan – Bin the Knife, Save a Life – the newspapers were well briefed and the message was a powerful one. In the pubs where there was a culture of knife-wielding – the 'stab inns' as crime reporters called them – the initiative was the talk of the bar so the neds were well aware of what was going on. Part of the strategy was a month-long amnesty for handing in dangerous weapons. And a stop-and-search operation was mounted by the police.

In the first four days of this campaign, 1269 people suspected of carrying weapons were inspected. Forty-two people were arrested and charged with being in possession of offensive weapons, twenty-eight of which were knives. The haul included a Samurai sword, various styles of kitchen knife, survival knives and a machete. This campaign ran alongside Operation Eagle, an anti-drug campaign. They were sparked off by the release of alarming crime figures in 1991 and 1992 when crime rose by 9 per cent. There was a rise in the number of murders and armed robberies rose even more spectacularly. Literally thousands of attacks on policemen, involving weapons were recorded. Like Blade, Operation Eagle was a huge, if short-lived, success. All this took place at a time when police budgets were being cut because of financial shortfalls caused by the non-payment of the poll tax. None the less, 6,000 people were arrested in Operation Eagle and more than 30,000 children were given anti-drugs awareness talks.

Maybe it was the familiar complaint about lack of numbers in the force that caused Sharp to become a champion of closed-circuit TV. In 1995, with Sir Leslie about to retire, CCTV was costing £250,000 a year. It seemed like a lot of money but many credited it with cutting crime and making the city centre a much safer place to be after dark than it had been in the past. Leslie Sharp took on board much of the civil liberties lobby's concerns and created a code of conduct for CCTV.

Sadly, the temporary nature of special blitzes – be they on knives or drugs – has been underlined by recent statistics. In 2003, the Scottish National Party asked the Lib Dem's Jim Wallace to release the current details of convictions for carrying offensive weapons. The figures showed an enormous rise but the government pointed out that at least some of this was due to the lawmen having the numbers and powers to deal with this sort of crime. Jim Wallace pointed out, too, that the culture of binge drinking was a big part of the problem. Top policemen also alluded to the fact that – as Leslie Sharp had realised some years before – if you carry a knife, the odds are that, at some time, you will use it. The latest statistics show that, no matter how many knives were taken out of circulation by Operation Blade, there are still plenty around to spill blood on the streets.

A few years after Operation Blade, the Spotlight Initiative also got the press involved in a new blitz on weapons carrying. But its success was also short term – as the questions relating to knife carrying in the Scottish Parliament showed. The level of the modern problem is truly awesome. Research by Professor Neil McKegney of Glasgow University showed that one in three boys and one in twelve girls have carried a knife at some time. In the Spotlight Initiative, blades were found hidden inside mobile phones and a child's lollipop stick was rigged up with carpet knife blades. A sword and a pig splitter were taken from youths and a flick-knife was disguised as a cigarette lighter.

Perhaps, all these years after Sir Leslie Sharp's Operation Blade, the lesson is simply that, yet again, we need more cops and resources if such special initiatives are to have success in the long term.

SILLITOE, SIR PERCY

Recruited from Sheffield, where he had added the word gangbuster to his CV in 1931, Sillitoe remained with the Sheffield force until 1933. There he had met violence with violence, making sure the forces of law and order won. But he was much more than this image of tough-guy cop suggests.

Apart from the innovative use of radio cars, his Glasgow force was one of the first to have an underwater squad. These officers were always ready to search the dark muddy waters of the Clyde, or any sizeable pond in the city, for bodies, weapons or a piece of evidence that could help solve a crime. He also pioneered the idea of police 'intelligence units' infiltrating the gangs and getting solid info about where clashes were going to happen in order to allow the police to lay ambushes and stop the trouble on the streets dead.

The 1930s was the period when the slum gangs were most prominent and, by the time he left, Sillitoe had won many victories against them but, of course, gangland activity was to make a comeback big-time after the Second World War, albeit in a different form. A complex character, Sillitoe was not a single-issue cop. Alongside his legendary and bloody battles with gangs such as the Billy Boys and the Norman Conks, he attacked official graft in the old Glasgow Corporation. He was proud of his victories in this area, particularly remembering the jailing of a councillor who was convicted of trousering a tenner to let a pub licence go through unopposed.

That he thought deeply about the role that a police force has in society emerged in 1991 when wartime police reports were made public for the first time. Later in his career, after leaving Glasgow, he was to become Director General of MI5 but he was still in the city during the early years of the war. The new information released to the public showed that he was opposed to the police compiling intelligence reports for the Scottish Secretary. He wrote to the politicians in St Andrew's House, saying:

> There is a great danger that such a practice would be construed, in the present circumstances, as the beginning of the institution of a secret police organisation of the kind which the British people have always prided themselves they are free from.

His social concern also showed in a report he produced about the activities of children during the war. It highlighted the fact that, by October 1939, half the number of children who had been evacuated, to make them safe from the anticipated Nazi bombing of civilian areas, had returned to their homes and that there were not enough schools left open to cater for them. With no schools to go to, working-class children were running wild and stretching the resources of the police. It was something of a rerun of what had happened during the First World War when, with so many fathers at the front and mothers working in munitions factories, children were left to their own devices and took to forming gangs and creating trouble.

But it was his battles with the gangs that wrote this remarkable man deep into the folk history of Glasgow. His appointment was controversial – recruiting an Englishman from an English force to take command of the war with Glasgow thugs was met with some opposition. But the situation was so bad that it required drastic action. In the early thirties, gangsters swaggered almost unopposed through the streets of the east end and the Gorbals. Bicycle chains, open razors, knuckle dusters, hatchets, swords, bottles and weapons improvised from bits and pieces of metal from the shipyards and steelworks were in the hands of people prepared to use them. Street fighting was a regular occurrence. Extortion was rife. And the practice of illegal moneylending was growing.

It was far from true that the gangs only fought among themselves. They blighted the lives of thousands, putting shop-keepers and decent hard-working folk in fear of their lives. Sillitoe did not underestimate the problem and he tackled it head-on, often meeting force with force and using methods that would horrify the politically correct of this day. He rightly surmised that the police needed their own 'gang' – the cop on the beat had no chance of controlling well-armed mobs of thugs. To stop hundreds battering the daylights out of each other required policing of a different kind, so Sillitoe created his so-called 'Untouchables'. He searched the police force for the most fearless of officers, the fittest men in the force, men who could take on the gangs and dish out some of their own medicine. His son later wrote in *The Herald*, in 1992, about his methods, saying, 'My father, "Gangbuster" Sillitoe, would not be amused by the reports of street warfare in Glasgow. He solved the problem years ago by enlisting tough cops, mainly Highlanders, to club first and ask questions afterwards.' Such tactics won him the respect of both the public and his men who nicknamed him variously 'The Captain' or 'The Big Fellow'. The real flavour of what this war against the neds was like is brilliantly described in a book Sillitoe wrote about his time in Glasgow.

In the years between the wars, **MAIN STREET, BRIDGETON** was a focus for much of the sectarian squabbling in the east end. It was peopled with families who had come from both sides of the

247

religious divide in Northern Ireland to Glasgow, seeking work in the city's factories. And they brought their religious bigotry with them. I remember my own Aunt Meg, a fine person in most other ways, whose greatest delight was to hang out of her tenement window at 293 Main Street on 12 July, watching the Orange parades. She would glory in the colours of the marchers and the music of the flute bands, oblivious to the blind hatred that was bound up in it all. For her, the twelfth was a day that took her back to her roots – to the sights and sounds of the old family home in Keady, County Armagh.

It was such a parade, in the mid 1930s, that was to mark a turning point for Sillitoe in his war against the Billy Boys in particular. On Catholic holy days, the Billy Boys would organise a drum and flute band and march through **NORMAN STREET** (home of the Conks and many of their supporters) playing inflammatory tunes. Sillitoe wrote:

> As soon as the offensive music was heard by the Norman Conks, they manned the upper windows and even the roofs of their streets and, when the Billy Boys' band went to march past, it was met by a downpour of bricks, missiles, buckets of filth and broken glass. If the Norman Conks could have used boiling lead, I am sure they would not have hesitated to do so. It was certainly all that was needed to complete the picture of a medieval siege.

The police moved in on this particular march with force and Sillitoe felt it was at this moment that the Billy Boys' power began to wane. The charge against the marchers was led by the mounted police, nicknamed 'Sillitoe's Cossacks', and they successfully broke up the parade. It was a bloody affair. Sillitoe commented that, 'Only one of the Billy Boys escaped injury. He was Elijah Cooper the big drum player. When the police charged, Elijah dived into his drum and used it as shelter till he could surrender peacefully.' A battle may have been won but the war was not really over – it still isn't. Violent Orange parades followed in later years and sectarianism is still a problem for the city.

After his stint in Glasgow, Sillitoe's career took some curious twists and turns, with his spell in MI5 ending in various disputes. For a time, he was also involved with the mysterious De Beers Consolidated Mines and his role was to set up an international diamond security organisation to buy valuable stones from illicit diggers. This problem, incidentally, like the problem of the Glasgow gangs, is still with us today as millions of pounds' worth of precious stones leak out from Sierra Leone and affect the prices on the legitimate markets.

As he was nearing the end of his life, when he knew he was dying, Sillitoe wanted to fly to Moscow to confront the traitor Guy Burgess with the names of others whom he was convinced were equally as guilty as Burgess. His wife put a stop to this plan and he died of leukaemia in 1962.

This colourful character, who had such an impact on Glasgow gangland, left another marker on history. He was no 'fashionista' but he is credited with introducing black-and-white checked bands to police hats and uniforms. I like to think that perhaps this was something to do with helping you recognise your friends in the middle of a battling mob. In any case, it is another innovation that Sillitoe, Chief Constable of Glasgow, came up with and it spread round the world.

SLASHING

There is something of a climate of denial in Glasgow on the subject of razor slashing. It mirrors the denial, by many who should know better, of how serious the gangland problem has been in the city. It is partly a result of some lightweight politicians' belief that, if the problem is highlighted in the media, investment and tourists are driven away from the city. But, for more than a century, Glasgow has had a gang culture and it is something that still exists today. That it festers on is evident in the recent rise in knife carrying – of much concern to the new Scottish Parliament in Edinburgh – and the cult of the blade in drug- and booze-fuelled feuds.

But the use of the open razor as a weapon and the city's historic reputation as a haven for slashers are particularly emotive issues. Nowadays, the preferred weapon is likely to be a firearm or a knife but, for years, the razor was king. A study of the newspapers of the 1930s reveals case after case making headlines. The fact is that, for years, razor attacks were commonplace. In no way has the use of this weapon been exaggerated.

It is said that the victims of the slashers wore the criss-cross stitched scars on their faces as a mark of pride – razor wounds become the sign of the hard man. But there was a bit of fantasy in that. The *really* hard man avoided the ritual of Saturday night stitching that went on in all the big hospital casualty departments. Further evidence of this comes in the nickname 'seconder' which was given to some gang members. It was a reference to them coming off second best and being scarred in a fight. But some clung on to the belief that scars equated to toughness.

The cut-throat razor was often known on the streets by its rhyming slang name of Malky Fraser – sometimes shortened to just Malky. Its use as a weapon goes back to the nineteenth century. Part of the equipment of the early policemen in the city was a leather neckband whose purpose was to protect the officer from attack from behind with a razor. The attractions of the razor were that it was light but lethal and could easily be hidden up a sleeve or in a pocket. In a split second, it could be pulled out to inflict a long hideous wound or, if aimed at the throat, it could cut the jugular and kill an enemy. Even after the safety razor was invented, the thin blades could kill and maim and they were often hidden in the rim of a cloth cap, ready to be whipped out and used at a moment's notice. Such thin safety blades could also be set into a stick to produce an ingenious and dangerous weapon.

But the classic weapon of the slasher was the cut-throat. Maybe it all started as far back as 1599 when one George Mitchell, who had been 'apprehendit for thift', was warned that, if he did not mend his ways, 'ane lug would be cut out of his heid'. In this case, it was justice that was doing the cutting!

Certainly, even the most casual reading of the crime pages of the papers, from the 1930s, 1940s and 1950s in particular, demonstrates that the razor was in daily use as a weapon and that, in addition to its use in gang fights, many ordinary folk were slashed in random acts of violence. One tale is told of a slasher who pounced on an innocent victim at the top end of **SAUCHIEHALL STREET** and then proceeded to run through the streets of the city centre pursued by a crowd to **GLASGOW CROSS** where he was finally apprehended after slashing another half dozen or so victims on the way.

Even children as young as nine, on occasion, carried a razor as the story of a **GOVAN** mother who found her son in court accused of slashing the coat of a girl aged ten evinces. Relatives of the accused explained this away by saying that all his pals also carried blades and they were a miniature gang.

There is little photographic evidence of slashing. In the heyday of its fearsome reign, the newspapers were poorly illustrated and photography very formal. In addition, much of the blood spilling happened in dark, gaslit streets where the photographic techniques of the time would have been useless. I know of only one photograph that shows a slashing actually happening. It featured on the cover of that excellent crime book, *Such Bad Company*, by Paddy Meehan and the respected reporter George Forbes and was taken by Scotsman photographer Alan Milligan in **SAUCHIEHALL STREET**. The potential victim leaps back in fear but so swift is the attack that passers-by barely notice – at first. Just ask them if razor slashing is a myth.

SLATER, OSCAR

One of the most remarkable sagas in Scottish criminal history began in December 1908 in the then highly fashionable **WEST PRINCES STREET** which runs off **St GEORGE'S ROAD**, less than half a mile from **CHARING CROSS**. And it has continued to make headlines for almost a hundred years. It is a shocking story of wrongful accusation that took Slater to within forty-eight hours of death on the gallows and left him incarcerated in prison for almost nineteen years for a murder he did not commit.

The victim was a rich eighty-three-year-old spinster, Marion Gilchrist, who lived in some style amid the flickering gaslit streets of the west end. Her wealth and eccentricity was reflected in three thousand pounds' worth of jewels – a huge sum back then – that was stashed all around her well-furnished flat. The gems were hidden behind curtains, stuffed into the pockets of clothes in the wardrobe and generally secreted in unlikely places.

After her death, wild rumours, all completely untrue, circulated that she was some sort of fence who had been done to death by a customer who felt wronged. Indeed, the intensity of the rumour-mongering of the time showed how shocked her neighbours and much of Glasgow were at such a crime. And, as is often the case in such situations, the public hunger for a quick arrest and the expectation that it was a simple crime to solve put added pressure on the police. They were soon under attack for allowing the killer what looked like a free run. The public view of the case was, as it frequently is, wide of the mark. There was no immediate clue as to the identity of the murderer and that, in itself, helped lead to the scapegoating of Oscar Slater.

The tale began at seven o'clock on a dreary, wet night, four days before Christmas. Miss Gilchrist's flat was on the first floor and, immediately beneath her, lived Arthur Montague Adams, a musician with Scottish Orchestra. He was tying up some presents in the company of his sisters when what he described as 'three knocks' were heard to come from the floor above. Fearful of burglars, Miss Gilchrist had arranged to signal to the Adams family, if she was in trouble, with three knocks on the floor. The womenfolk urged Arthur to go out their front door and up the close at the side of it to check all was in order. The outside door was unlocked, though normally it was closed, and, when he went up the stairs and rang the bell loudly, there was no reply. He rang again and again and eventually heard what he thought was the sound of someone chopping sticks so he assumed that the family servant Nellie Lambie was doing just that and returned down stairs.

One of his sisters would have none of this and urged him to go back upstairs as she was sure something was wrong. When he went back, there was again no reply to the bell. Then he heard the sound of someone coming up the stairs and turned to see Nellie. She unlocked the door and they went into the hall, which seemed to be dimly lit by a gas lamp. A man in a light overcoat appeared from the bedroom entrance on the right. Arthur said he was dressed 'like a gentleman'. The man stepped forward as if to speak and then jinked past the surprised pair and made off down the stairs at high speed. A quick search found the old gentlewoman in her dining room, in front of the fireplace, with a rug over her head and blood everywhere. The musician was a brave fellow. Leaving Nellie at the door, he legged it downstairs and made a vain search of the nearby poorly illuminated streets with their flickering gaslight.

On his return to the murder scene, he found that Nellie had summoned the police. Back in the dining room, they discovered that, despite the battering to her head and terrible injuries, the old woman was still alive – just. The nearest doctor, coincidentally also called Adams, was called but, by then, the victim had breathed her last. A bloodstained chair at the side of the body was presumed to have been the murder weapon. The arrival of Dr Adams was a strange twist – the records show that, after his first appearance, he dropped out of sight from the case. Jack House, the legendary author of *Square Mile of Murder* and an authority on the case, says, 'It was the only case that murder experts for the last hundred years knew of where the first medical man on the scene of the murder was not called on to give evidence.' At this distance in time, we can only surmise why this happened and what possible effect it could have had on the case against Slater.

The CID arrived and discovered some confusing clues at the site of the crime. When Arthur had encountered Nellie on his second visit upstairs, she was returning from going out to buy an evening paper. Nellie swore to the police that a gas lamp, which had been unlit when she left, was burning when she arrived back. A box of matches of a brand not used in the house was found. And, on a table, a wooden casket had been smashed open and papers and jewellery were lying around. Nellie said that a brooch, shaped like a diamond and the size of an old half crown, was missing. This was a significant observation and one that was to affect the whole case.

Later that night, Nellie Lambie left the house to go to **BLYTHS-WOOD DRIVE**, now **WOODLANDS ROAD**, to let Miss Gilchrist's niece, Margaret Birrell, know of the horrific happenings.

On the identification of the mystery man, the flautist from the Scottish Orchestra was vague. He had not been wearing his spectacles and the light was bad. Nellie claimed to have hardly seen him – although she later identified Slater in a rigged identification parade!

So began the fitting-up of Oscar Slater. A German Jew, with a somewhat sleazy reputation, Slater lived with his show-business mistress, Andree Junio Antoine. He was a gambler and jewel dealer who was known to the police. However, there was nothing in his background that would point to him as a suspect in a murder. The police were under enormous public pressure to find the killer of Miss Gilchrist and solve the shocking murder that had the inhabitants of the elite west end talking of little else. Slater came to the investigating officers' notice when a tip-off claimed he had tried to sell a pawn ticket for a brooch. The police found that the brooch was not the one allegedly missing from the murder scene.

But, unaware of this, Slater made a bad mistake. At short notice, he and his mistress, who was said not to be short of male company, travelled to New York, under assumed names, on the *Lusitania*. The police diligently added two and two together and came up with five – it was their theory that Oscar Slater had fled because he had read newspaper reports that suggested he resembled the man seen leaving the scene of the crime. Slater was arrested in

New York and he returned voluntarily to face trial, no doubt confident that, since he had no involvement in the crime, no judge or jury would convict him. It was a naive assumption that almost cost him his life.

Despite the fact that the police had two different descriptions of the man said to be involved, an identification parade was set up with Slater in the line-up. Indeed, it has to be pointed out that witnesses were so in dispute about the appearance of the man who fled from the scene that, at one stage, the police thought two men were involved. The fact that there were two differing accounts of what the man seen at Miss Gilchrist's flat had looked like wasn't the only thing that made the parade dodgy. Policemen in plain clothes, who looked nothing like either of the descriptions given to the police, surrounded poor Slater and the so-called witnesses pointed in his direction. But, apart from being picked out in the identification parade, there was virtually no other evidence against him. Things are rather different now with regard to ID parades and it is said that the police sometimes still use the Slater case as a classic example of how not to do it!

Being a foreigner in the city didn't help Slater and he was to be found guilty, without any real reason, by the court of public opinion. The pre-publicity, which would not be allowed today, helped feed the public anger at the crime and all sorts of false hints that pointed to Slater's guilt were dropped. Slater knew so little about the murder that he thought it had taken place on the twenty-second of December, not the twenty-first, and claimed he could provide five witnesses to corroborate where he was on what he believed to be the night of the killing. As it turned out, he actually did have a very strong alibi for the night of the crime but that was not brought out at his trial which, it has been said, verged on the farcical.

William Roughead, perhaps Scotland's most authoritative writer on criminal matters, edited a masterly account, *The Trial of Oscar Slater* (Edinburgh: Hodge, 1910), in which he forensically dissected all the many weaknesses in the case against Slater. Reviewers leapt on this tome with high praise and the verdict was that a great injustice had been done. Sir Arthur Conan Doyle attacked the verdict in *The Times* and the novelist Andrew Lang wrote that, on the kind of evidence that had been levelled against Slater, 'a cat would scarcely be whipped for stealing cream'.

But the judicial establishment, the public and the police of the day had made up their minds – guilty. Slater was condemned to death but was, somewhat mysteriously, reprieved a couple of days before he was due to face the rope.

Long years in jail lay ahead and the tale of how he eventually got his freedom is as bizarre as that of his conviction. At the centre of it all is the remarkable figure of Detective John Trench. Trench was there at the start, having been involved from the night of the murder on 21 December 1908. According to Trench, on that very night, Nellie Lambie named the man she had seen in the flat. He was someone known to her and to the victim – it was not Oscar Slater. But along came the so-called clue of the pawned brooch – which did not come from the murder scene – and the police dropped every other avenue to pursue Slater.

Trench obeyed instructions and said little of his own suspicions. But they nagged at him for years and his belief that an innocent man was in jail was hard to live with. When Slater had been in jail for five years and with thirteen still to serve until he gained his freedom, Trench tried to pass information to the then Scottish Secretary that the German was innocent. He also told a Glasgow solicitor the grounds for his belief. The result? An inquiry, almost as sham as the trial itself, was set up and the research was dismissed. The reward for this honest cop? He was dismissed from the force for passing information to an outsider.

Although he was never officially declared not guilty, Slater was freed in 1928 on a technicality. Having served in the First World War, John Trench died in the flu epidemic of 1919. Even after Slater's release, Trench's reputation was not rehabilitated but, in 1998, the detective was again back in the headlines when the issue of how badly he was treated by the force was raised with Scottish Secretary Donald Dewar. Dewar could find no statutory authority with the powers to issue a pardon or posthumous rehabilitation. A review, by the Scottish Office, found that Trench had acted with moral conviction and that his dismissal from the force was harsh. But there was no power to intervene. The political view was that Trench should have challenged his 1914 dismissal in a court of law. But the police, who had been so at fault in the original case, all these years ago, were eventually to take decisive humanitarian action. In a gesture of reconciliation in 1999, Chief Constable John Orr invited Trench's eighty-seven-year-old daughter, Nancy Stark, to a ceremony in police HQ in **PITT STREET** and arranged for a commemorative plaque dedicated to her father to be displayed in the police museum.

And what became of Oscar Slater? He lived quietly, making many friends and leading a life of respectability, until his death in 1948.

So, whodunnit? During all the years the case has made headlines, countless theories have emerged. Was the killer a member of Miss Gilchrist's well-connected family? Was this the reason for the fit-up of Oscar Slater? The maid, Nellie Lambie, was said, by some, to have been secretly engaged to someone who may have been a suspect. Was it a simple case of theft where some Glasgow bad guy knew there was easy jewellery to be had? We will never know. But what we do know is that poor Oscar Slater didn't do it.

SLAVIN, Father Willy

Slavin was, for a time, the coordinator of the Scottish Drugs Forum and, for ten years, Barlinnie's Catholic chaplain. A man who learned more than most about drugs and prisons, he was critical of the authorities. His belief was that addicts need help and should not simply be locked behind bars. He criticised the prison services for not putting enough money into tackling drug addiction in the early 1990s. A practical man, he felt for the homeless folk who wander, full of drink or drugs, through the city in the wee small hours and highlighted the fact that they need help then – not during the daylight hours. He also illustrated the kind of desperation that existed on the streets at that time by pointing out that there were kids who would not go to a casualty department even though they had bullet wounds.

SLOAN, Sir Andrew

Old-timers who say coppers are getting younger and maybe even smaller could be right! Height played a curious role in Andrew Sloan's police life. When he tried to join the old City of Glasgow police, he was rejected for not meeting the minimum height requirement and he had to move to Yorkshire to get accepted. But, after he had built a successful career down south, he was invited to come to Glasgow in the late eighties to take on the top job. This time, since the job was a 'non-operational' regional council appointment, his lack of stature was not deemed a problem. It was a wise decision that brought a good man into the city's ongoing battle against lawlessness. Sloan spent five years in the job and had strong opinions on how long a chief should stay. He said, 'Five years is probably about right. I do not think that a man can work longer at that level without becoming stale, and I believe we have been lucky in the men we have had since Strathclyde came into being.'

Andrew Sloan's watch coincided with the seminal Glasgow Garden Festival in 1988. This could have been a major public relations disaster for a city trying to build a new reputation as a tourist destination (something it has actually succeeded in doing spectacularly well in the last decade). The attractive site, on the south bank of the Clyde, drew thousands of visitors from Britain and around the world to view the imaginative displays of the latest in gardening expertise and to simply revel in the truly magnificent colour and beauty of a garden on a massive scale. It didn't matter that there was the odd day of rain – after all it was Glasgow. The event was a groundbreaking success that left many other cities that were struggling to make the transition from industrial wasteland to modern attraction extremely envious.

But it could have been so very different. Before the event, lurid newspaper headlines told the world of too much street crime and the old misconceptions about the lack of safety on the streets. What happened was a tribute to both the people of Glasgow and to the police. In five months, despite the massive influx of visitors in to the city, often in small, crowded places, the festival reported only a couple of hundred minor offences.

Mind you, Andrew Sloan's tenure was not all sweetness and light. He had several controversial battles with the council and was strongly of the opinion that the city needed more cops than it had – an opinion echoed, and probably correctly, by almost every holder of the onerous job of chief constable.

SMITH, MARTIN

An energetic media lawyer, Smith spent most of his life trying to keep newspaper editors out of court. During a career that ended with his tragic death at the relatively young age of fifty-six, early in 2004, he represented most of the major newspaper titles including *The Herald*, *The Daily Mail*, *The Guardian*, *The Observer* and *The Independent*. He was the most respected of that specialist breed, the night lawyer – men and women who work long hours alongside shirt-sleeved editors and news editors, advising just how many of the hundreds of complicated investigations and allegations it could be safe to publish. Glasgow's proliferation of gangs, gangsters and dodgy businessmen makes it a busy job with little respite from big decisions. Regardless of legal advice, the final decision, to publish or not, lies with the editor. Martin Smith's advice was ignored at an editor's peril and that happened very seldom – when it did, it usually cost the newspaper dear.

He was also a skilled court lawyer. Following in his father's legal footsteps, he was adept at defending the most hardened of criminals. Indeed, on one notable occasion, along with Joe Beltrami, he succeeded in winning damages for Arthur Thompson Snr from a newspaper that had had the temerity to call the legendary hard man a gangster, despite the fact that Thompson's criminal record was, in fact, not all that impressive. The paucity of the number of Arthur's convictions, however, may not be an accurate reflection of how many crimes he was involved in but could, instead, show just how difficult it was for the law to actually prove his involvement. Which ever is the case, winning the damages was a success for Smith.

Away from the law, he was a sports fanatic and an enthusiastic follower of Clydesdale Cricket Club and, latterly, Ferguslie Cricket Club near his home in Paisley. He was also a highly successful president of Queen's Park FC.

SPECIAL UNIT, BARLINNIE

Here, one of the most intriguing, successful, and in the end, frustrating experiments, in the redemption of hardcore troublemaking prisoners, ever attempted took place. It opened in 1973 and was controversially closed in the mid 1990s, much to the disappointment of prison reformers. Known on the street to this day as the Wendy House or the Nutcracker Suite, it had some remarkable success in straightening out troublemakers from many of Scotland's toughest jails and setting them on the path to reform. But it was far from popular with those who see prisons purely in the terms of punishment. It was a test bed for new methods of controlling violent men who had previously responded to the conventional harsh regimes of Scotland's tough prisons by attacking warders, smearing themselves in their own excrement, setting mattresses on fire and, where possible, getting on to prison roofs to throw razor-sharp slates hundreds of feet down below on to the prison officers who were trying to regain control of their own establishments.

One of the men behind the concept was an Aberdeen psychologist called Ian Stephen. He had studied psychology, which has much relevance to prison practices, at his local university but he became disillusioned and, in the 1960s, took up teaching languages at a Borders school. The experience rekindled his enthusiasm for psychology and he began working with young offenders in Glasgow. It taught him some hard truths. He told one reporter, 'If you can work with these kids, you can work with violent men.' One of the achievements of the Special Unit is that it provided respectability for the input of psychology into the prison service and, thereby, made working towards the redemption of seemingly impossible hard cases – rather than simply seeking retribution from them – a reality.

The unit had been created at a time of crisis in the prison service. There was no death penalty and the papers were full of headlines about stabbings and rioting in prisons. Remarkably, looked at from this distance in time, Ian Stephen was, at the beginning of the 1970s, the only psychologist working in the Scottish Prison Service. Of the hardcore of tough tickets then behind bars, he says, 'We thought, "We don't know what we are going to do with them – let's try and set up this different unit and see where it goes."' He remembers, at that time, the prison service was lucky enough to have some strong men amongst both the staff and prisoners – men like Jimmy Boyle who realised such a scheme was their last chance.

Stephen was of the belief that there are some prisoners who should never be released and in this category he cited the child-killer Myra Hindley who was, in fact, to die behind bars. But, in an insight into his thinking on preparing some of the toughest for release, he says, 'Most murderers kill only once but others do it for malicious intent – because of their own needs. You have got to be progressive when you can afford to be but you can't afford to be stupid.' In this particular interview, he went on to say, 'You don't change people. What you do is help them adapt, so that things that were negative for them in the past are channelled.' This sort of thinking led to Special Unit meetings lasting hours as prisoners and officers tried to resolve violence before it became physical. As Stephen commented, 'We didn't have cells, we didn't have punishment – instead we wanted to give responsibility back to the prisoners. If you took it away, they could blame the prison system for their violence.'

Right from the start, the unit was experimental and controversial. The inmates were men serving long sentences, fifteen years or more, men wrapped gloomily in the dark knowledge that freedom was a long, long way off. They were held in a secure area but faced a regime which was much more relaxed than that of a 'normal' prison. They wore their own clothes and had record players and books. Freedom, to a degree, responsibility and a certain amount of personal choice were what was on offer. Mail was uncensored and the ratio of staff to prisoners was high.

Jimmy Boyle, Hugh Collins and Larry Winters were the highest-profile inmates and they have their own entries in this A to Z. Winters died of a drug overdose and this brought a public outcry and criticism of a regime that apparently allowed drugs to circulate in a prison. There is no doubt that the 'drug paradise' stories in the more lurid papers did much to speed up the closure of an experiment that had had many success stories in turning useless and damaging lives around. But there were also tales of prisoners sleeping with attractive women who were among the hordes of social workers, lawyers and prison reformers who flocked to the unit. Collins bluntly claimed that some of the female visitors would sleep with criminals, getting a thrill from their intimacy with men of violence.

The very nature of the unit, with its relative freedoms and comforts and regular visits – the very things that could make it work – were also the things that were always liable to be taken advantage of and not just by the inmates. And, in the prison service, there had always been an army of critics who found wallpaper, sofas and paintings on the walls too much to take. It all began to climax after a 1994 report by Prisons Inspector Alan Bishop who criticised the lifestyle in the unit which then housed eight killers. There was talk of prisoners being taken on shopping trips and visiting swimming pools. Security checks on the cells –

themselves unlike the sparse tombs of other prisons – were claimed to be almost non-existent. Visitors came and stayed too long and were not searched. The concept had been stretched and stretched and now, after more than twenty years of evolution, it was near breaking point. The papers ran constant allegations of prisoners enjoying sex, booze and drugs while inside. Alan Bishop did not want the unit closed – he wanted it to be returned to its original regime and tightened up. And there seems little doubt that, at the time of the closure, things had gone just a bit too far – even for some supporters of the concept.

The publication of this report led to officialdom becoming more and more involved in what was going on. The then Scottish Secretary Ian Lang promised a wide-ranging review and Alan Bishop told a press conference that he had found no direct evidence of prisoners having sex with visitors or that drink or drugs were taken during the period of his inspection. But he could not rule out the possibility that such things had happened. He wondered, like many who followed the saga in the press, if liberalisation had not gone too far. 'But for the lockable doors, it would have been easy to forget this was a penal establishment,' he said. The writing, if not the graffiti, was on the wall.

Ian Lang said the closure of the unit was not desirable but that its future and purpose would be looked at again. However, the waves of criticism could not be swept aside. The prison service had to face the fact that the concept had been blown off course and, alongside the success, there were legitimate matters of public concern. Trust had been high on the priorities of the original management of the unit but that trust between prisoner and regime was being regularly broken and the stories of a cushy life in one little section of the Bar-L was unsettling men and women incarcerated in harsher regimes. The prison service moved on to a concept of small special units in many prisons, with regimes designed to cope with long-term violent prisoners, criminals with little hope of a reasonably speedy release and, therefore, with no incentive to behave when behind bars.

The Special Unit had lost its way. It had been at the heart of the long-running argument in society about prisons – redemption over retribution. Let a final word go to the *Herald* columnist Ron Ferguson, a former kirk minister in **EASTERHOUSE** with first-hand knowledge of the experiment. In a feature headed 'Hope Amid All the Hatred', he was trenchant. Of the unit, he wrote, 'This is an everyday tale of murdering folk, violence, venomous hatred, books, redemption and hypocrisy.' In the early days, the unit was a clergy-free zone but one of the regular visitors got Ron Ferguson an invitation inside, where he met Jimmy Boyle. Ferguson said:

> What I discovered was that there were powerful people who wanted Boyle to fail, in order to prove their own theories that the likes of him could not change. One former Moderator was vehement that the unit should be shut down forthwith. There were church people – and I choose my words carefully – who wanted him to reoffend. The sight of a notoriously violent man changing was, strangely, too much for some clerics.

He concluded his look at the unit by saying, 'In my manse, there is a special sculpture which is a symbol of hope. And there are desperate people in Easterhouse and Barlinnie who have taught me more than theologians about the meaning of that most precious word – redemption.' It was a thought-provoking comment about the end of a remarkable experiment.

STAB INN

This is the street nickname for a pub where everyone knows your name – because they read it in the court cases in the tabloids. The clients of such establishments sip their pints as they plot villainy and they tend to use a knife, blade, chib, or whatever they choose to call it, to settle scores and underline their control of their patch. Sadly, the city and its peripheral areas contain many such places where the innocent passer-by is ill-advised to drop in for a chat about the weather or the latest DVD releases. Warning signs that a pub might warrant this sobriquet are graffiti-covered walls, poor lighting and a general state of disrepair – sawdust on the floor is not quite the dead giveaway it once was.

STEWART, DAVIE

A top reporter on the old *Evening Citizen*, he later became a news-desk executive and had the confidence of King Billy Fullerton, the leader of the infamous Billy Boys. Later in his life, when Fullerton had largely put his gang days behind him, he cooperated with Stewart in many articles telling the history of the gang. Among the insights delivered to Stewart by Fullerton was the story behind the founding of the Billy Boys.

In 1924, Fullerton was playing in a football match on Glasgow Green when he committed the ultimate mistake – he was brave enough to score an important goal against a team comprised of members of the Kent Star, a rival gang. Fullerton's teammates were just a bunch of Bridgeton lads who, at that time, didn't have a name for their group. Playing football was enough. The goal angered the Kent Star so much that their response was to attack Fullerton with hammers. The goal-scorer survived this vicious attack and vowed revenge.

Following the tradition of gangland, Fullerton, as the hardest of the hard, became the group's leader and the Billy Boys were formed. Depending on which theory you choose to believe, either Fullerton himself or William of Orange was the source of the 'Billy' part of their name – or perhaps it was in honour of both of those King Billies!

STREET BOOKIES

It was far from the most heinous crime in the city but, at one time, before betting shops became legalised, placing a bet with a street bookie took both punter and bookie on to the wrong side of the law. Today, the city is peppered with chains of betting shops which are often brightly lit and attractively decorated. This creates a magnet, especially for punters who are retired or unemployed. Such folk come in out of the rain for a heat and a modest flutter. Of course, the big-money betting comes from those with hot phone lines in their offices to the bookies or online internet betting accounts. But, inside these glossy high-street palaces of dreams, you'll find some people with ample time on their hands between races to plan a little illegal manoeuvre or two with their mates.

It's a bit different from the old days when placing a bet was itself illegal and there was little time to plan much other than how to find the bookie's runner at the street corner and how to avoid the cop who was also looking for him. The street bookie's premises have also undergone a transformation. Back then, there were no bright lights or central heating. The bookie's 'office' would be in a rain-sheltered spot in a muddy backcourt or, at best, in a bedroom or kitchen up a close. The punters used noms de plume and bookies lived on their wits, using as much brainpower to dodge the cops as they did to calculate the odds.

The legions of bookies' runners, employed to take the punters' betting lines back to the bookies, were often made up of the unemployed. Indeed, the practice was an attractive way for many who were down on their luck to turn a bob or two.

Lookouts were also employed to warn of the approach of the boys in blue. One famous lookout in the **GARSCUBE ROAD** area was a remarkable character called Maggie Purdon. She played the saxophone and had only one eye – something of handicap for a lookout, one imagines. The story is told of one cop who sneaked past on her blind side but was still spotted and pounced on by her before he could collar the bookie in question.

Laurie Venters is one of a large number of street bookies still remembered on the north side of the river, though there were street bookies to be found on most major thoroughfares throughout the city's tenement areas. The big league bookies didn't just trust to the Maggie Purdons of this world – they often had friends in the

266

police ready to tip them off about a raid. Venters had a routine for this eventuality. He would assemble half a dozen or so fake punters who were paid a pound for their services – there was always a queue of willing would-be helpers – and, when caught, they were taken to the police station and fined. The cash, of course, didn't come from the pseudo-punters' pockets but from the bookie's satchel. Those lifted always had fake lines and care was taken when the heat was off to pay out on genuine bets. The bets were collected by many different people and the lines themselves were identified by the noms de plume but it was not always possible to put a face to every nom de plume and a degree of trust was involved.

Bookies, of course, had access to large sums of cash and were often drawn into laundering the proceeds of robberies or some illegal moneylending. During the war and the years immediately following it, when clothing and food shortages were common and rationing was a part of everyday life, having ready cash to buy into all the scams that were going on was handy. But some of the old backcourt bookies had a reputation of being good to their neighbours who helped them in their games of cat-and-mouse with the police. The occasional bit of back rent was paid and a loan or two handed out to folk who found themselves in financial trouble. It all helped to grease the wheels of the illegal gambling. And, of course, there were plenty of hard men around to work for the bookie. If it turned out to be necessary to convince someone that it might be a wise move to pay any debts owed on their gambling, the hard men were called in. A good 'doing' from them was the reward for the punter who welched, after betting money he didn't have on losers.

T

TERRITORY

The root cause of much of the gang warfare in Glasgow, as in other great metropolises of the world, comes down to disputes over who controls certain areas of the city. Here, as in New York and Chicago in particular, gangs tend to have their own clearly defined territories which they defend in blood and often to the death. The expansion of the territory you control is a driving motive that applies both to the teenage gangs, for whom street fighting is an end in itself, and to the more mature groups, whose major concern is being in control of drug distribution, moneylending and extortion. It has been like this for more than a hundred years. The very earliest gangs in the city marked out their areas clearly and dealt with interlopers harshly.

The Penny Mob, perhaps the first real street gang in the city, were mostly active in the Townhead area. The Billy Boys and the Norman Conks, in Bridgeton, fought each other for both sectarian and territorial reasons. Their home streets were no-go areas to other gangs. In the Sillitoe era, in the late 1930s, gangs like the Parlour Boys, from the streets around the Parlour Dance Hall on the verges of the Gorbals, and the Kent Star, from Calton, were territorially based, as were the Redskins and many others. A territory could be a few streets or a whole district but, whatever its size, the defining lines were known to all.

There were certain advantages for the police in these strict geographic demarcations. Since the cops themselves were usually locally based with stations peppered around the city, often near known trouble spots, it was a great help in getting intelligence about what was happening, or about to happen, on the streets. After the Second World War, the huge schemes built on the outskirts of the city, such as Drumchapel, Castlemilk, Easterhouse and Pollok, became the homes of gangs ready to fight incomers or to travel to other areas in a show of strength. Many of these gangs continue to this day despite the partial 'gentrification' of some parts of the schemes with houses for sale and the belated addition of public swimming pools, libraries and pubs. The seeds of the territorial violence, that were sown so long ago, can still produce evil fruit.

THOMPSON, ARTHUR, SNR

This was the man some call the last of the Glasgow Godfathers – an optimistic claim as who knows what lies round the criminal corner! Ironically, Thompson hated the term Godfather and had instructed his legal representatives – usually Joe Beltrami – to sue whenever the newspapers hung that particular tag round his bull neck. Beltrami, The Great Defender, was, surprisingly, of much the same opinion, writing that Thompson was never a Godfather in the Mafia sense. Those who suffered at the hands of Thompson and his many hard-men lieutenants would tend to disagree. A man with strong physical presence, Thompson certainly strutted the public stage with the air of Godfather and anyone in his company quickly realised it was wise to step warily. His preferred pose in later life was that of a retired businessman and he affected the style of sharp suits and silk ties.

But this was a gloss over what was a remarkable life of crime and violence that often brought him to the attention of the crime columns in the newspapers and made him instantly recognisable in the public meeting places of the city – bars, hotels, expensive restaurants and the like. Such was his power at the height of his career in crime in the 1970s and 1980s that, when he was around, there was always a touch of fear in the air. The extent of his effect on crime in the city is underlined by the fact that some experts believe that inter-gang violence and the drug wars of the early years of this new century date back to the early 1990s. This was when major fights for the control of the massive Thompson empire broke out following the murder of his son Arthur Jnr in 1991 and Thompson's own death not long after that.

Old Arthur may have looked the part of a businessman but few businessmen have his string of convictions for extortion, robbery, housebreaking and reset. In *Glasgow's Hard Men* (Edinburgh: Black & White Publishing, 2001), I described Thompson as wearing his fearsome reputation with the honour of a Corleone who had unexpectedly found himself in the cold north-west of Europe. One surprising aspect of this career criminal is that he did so few long sentences for his crimes, mostly escaping with relatively short spells behind bars. This allowed him to have continuity in controlling his criminal associates and no doubt consolidated his gang's grip on crime in the city. By contrast, when his predecessor as Godfather, Walter Norval, was finally brought to justice, he spent long years away from the streets, banged up in Peterhead, and this undoubtedly hindered the ongoing activities of the gang he had built up. The fact is that, in the thirty years before his death from natural causes, in the spring of 1993, Thompson Snr did not face a jury.

His funeral became an east-end legend. It had all the trappings of a Hollywood Mafia send-off – mountains of flowers and streets lined with sharp-suited men, with chib-marked faces, paying their respects. There were also armies of detectives mingling with the mourners in search of snippets of information on who or what would fill the vacuum in the underworld left by the death of the big man. The traffic police were in action as well – to control the crowds on the streets leading to the cemetery.

The final farewell to this criminal legend took place at Riddrie Park Cemetery and the old mobster was buried in the family plot alongside his murdered son Arthur Jnr and his daughter Margaret. It did not pass without incident. There was a bomb scare and, for a spell, the police cordoned off the cemetery, close to The Ponderosa, as Thompson's home near **HOGGANFIELD LOCH** was called. After bomb disposal experts had been called in, it was decided that the alarm was a hoax – but, with the Thompsons, you didn't take any chances.

It was actually something of an achievement for Thompson to die in bed. Arguably the most prominent figure in the Scottish underworld since the Second World War, he had survived several assassination attempts. The most notable occurred in 1966 when his mother-in-law died when a bomb, that was intended to kill Arthur, blew their car apart. Twenty or so years later, he was shot by a gangland enemy but again survived and, with a nod in the direction of the Mafia's cherished omertà principle, he refused to cooperate with the police in any attempts to find the culprit. No doubt it was a more attractive proposition for him to order his own retribution. And, in 1990, he also came close to death or serious injury when a car was deliberately driven at him, breaking his leg.

Although he liked to deny it, The Godfather was not short of enemies. In a rare outbreak of humour, he told one of the reporters whose beat was to cover his activities that he had 'more friends than Hitler had an army'. The 'friends' who helped him run his various rackets, that basically started with moneylending and extortion but, in later life, extended to controlling the drug scene, tended to pitch up at his home in **PROVANMILL ROAD**, near the notorious housing estate of **BLACKHILL**. This much-altered house was nicknamed The Ponderosa and it often featured in the newspapers. However, it is doubtful whether the dubious, if expensive, taste involved in its décor would have made it to the House Beautiful type of magazine. It is not recorded if his London connections, which included the likes of Mad Frankie Fraser and the Krays, paid a visit to the Thompson home but, if they did, they would have shown respect for what was something of a criminal's fortress and HQ as well as a family home.

Thompson liked his up-and-coming lieutenants to benefit from a little touch of 'finishing school', sending them to work with the London gangs before allowing them to return home to oversee the distribution of drugs or lean on those reluctant to pay their protection money. On one occasion, he got word back from London advising him to tell one of his young men to curb his enthusiasm

271

for violence. The London contact suggested it would be wise to point out to this trainee thug that a dead punter is no longer able to cough up his dues for the security services being provided.

After the excesses of Arthur Thompson's funeral were over, the police knew that much work still lay ahead. One senior officer predicted that 'there could be bloody warfare out there. There is an empire of dough to be fought over and there are lots of neds desperate to get their hands on it. Then all hell could break loose.' It did. And that is the legacy of the Thompson clan.

THOMPSON, THE FAT BOY

His real name was Arthur but Arthur Thompson Snr's elder son was generally known as The Fat Boy or The Mars Bar Kid. There is a well-known saying in business life that a grandfather makes a business, his son ruins it and his grandson sells it. In the Glasgow Godfather stakes, at least, the second part of that old saw is true. The drugs empire built up by Arthur Thompson Snr crumbled and fell into the hands of rival villains when the reins were handed over to his son.

Aptly, for a criminal known as The Fat Boy, life quickly went pear-shaped for young Arthur. He died after being shot down in **PROVANMILL ROAD**, not far from The Ponderosa, that bizarre family home-cum-fortress. He was killed by a gangland assassin or assassins whose identity or identities are still unknown. It was a bloody end to a short career that was a shadow of that of his infamous father. And it had shown signs of going off the rails early on. After Arthur Snr went into what he called his 'retirement', he left full-scale turf wars going on. The various factions that had worked with him in the past were fighting for the rich pickings that came with control of drug distribution in a city where thousands were addicted to mind-altering substances.

Young Arthur had none of the physical presence of his father. He was overweight and podgy rather than lean and hard and he had another, perhaps more important, flaw – he talked too much.

This tendency got him into all sorts of scrapes. At a relatively young age, he found himself doing an eleven-year stretch for drug dealing. It was the beginning of the end for a boy of whom an underworld insider remarked, 'If he'd had half a brain, he could have taken over the Glasgow drug scene.' It didn't happen.

As a favoured scion of the gangland dynasty, The Fat Boy had grown up surrounded by hard men and he was always in the shadow of his infamous father. All his life, he struggled to win the respect of the dangerous men who had filled The Ponderosa and carried out his father's bidding. In a curious way, it is said that he took some satisfaction over his time in Peterhead in that, here at least, he was in the company of a pack of serious nasties who had been shipped up to the north-east from Glasgow and elsewhere. To him, this fact alone meant that he was due some grudging respect as a hard man.

But, always the talker, he whinged incessantly that he was inno-cent of the particular charges that had got him sent to prison, claiming that the reason he was there was down to police corruption and the interest of the press in everything his family did. He once complained to a Prisons Director, Peter McKinley, that he did not seem to understand that he was speaking to an intelligent man and not to some 'gas-meter bandit', as he put it. This was a tad ironic since the real criminal hard men who shared the jail with him just didn't rate him. And they had a pretty fair idea of what awaited him on the outside. After a press visit to the jail, one prisoner told the reporters that 'that slavering bastard should shut up because he is safe in here. He will not survive a day outside.' It was to be an accurate prediction.

While still in prison, young Thompson had been trying to pull the strings in the drug trade but without much success. The reality was that, outside the prison walls, men much harder than he was were fighting desperate battles to take over the evil trade of drug distribution and sale. Turf wars were going on all over the place, especially in the schemes where addicts lived miserable lives, dodging from one fix to the next and paying big money for the drugs that would, in the end, kill many of them. In the misery of the surroundings that most of them lived, a score was vital temporary relief. The sort of thinking that drove such unfortunates was illustrated in one trial when a package of heroin was described not by weight but as 'many days' happiness'.

Young Thompson surely knew what was going on and should have realised that he was safer out of all this mayhem when in jail. But he took a big risk in August 1991. By then, he had been transferred from Peterhead to Noranside Prison in Angus, a much less secure prison where proximity to the rolling countryside and a gentler regime was supposed to exercise a civilising influence on those sent there. In Noranside, The Fat Boy became eligible for a home visit and unwisely decided to take it. Maybe it was the lure of a good curry in one of Glasgow's famous Indian restaurants or maybe it was the desire to meet with his gangland associates in an effort to wield some influence on the drugs war that was going on in the city that drove him to leave his prison sanctuary. Whatever the motivation was, he went home on leave to Provanmill.

After a city-centre meal with his common-law wife Catherine, he headed to The Ponderosa for talks with his father. When this was over, he left his father's house and took the short walk to his own home. It was just before midnight. Three shots echoed round Provanmill Road. Two .22 bullets thudded into the amply fleshed back of The Mars Bar Kid and another grazed his cheek. One of the bullets that entered his body reached his heart. For a spell, he was still standing and there was no sign of blood caused by the deadly bullets. His sister Tracy had heard the shots. She ran from the house and reportedly heard her brother gasp, 'I have been shot – I am going to collapse.' He was lifted into his brother Billy's car and taken to casualty in the Royal Infirmary, a place with much expertise in patching up the gangland warriors and the innocents who sometimes also get caught up in their violence. But, even there, The Fat Boy could not be saved.

In the middle of the gang warfare that was going on that summer and autumn, it was a fearless, if somewhat foolhardy, act to take

274

out the favoured son of old Arthur – an act that was sure to have bloody consequences. Who was responsible? To this day no one knows. One Paul Ferris stood trial for the killing, an episode dealt with elsewhere in this book in some detail, but he was found not guilty and walked free. He was alleged to have acted with Joe 'Bananas' Hanlon and Bobby Glover in killing The Fat Boy but Hanlon and Glover were murdered before the trial began. They were found dead in a car on the morning of young Arthur's funeral, imparting something of a Hollywood-style touch to the whole affair.

However, the removal of The Fat Boy did not stop the killings – or the drug wars. Instead, it heralded a period of police activity that, in its intensity, clearly illustrated how serious the battle for control of the drug scene had become. Senior detectives made some controversial and unusual comments to the press when they criticised the family and friends of Glover and Hanlon for not co-operating with the investigation and 'choosing to deal with things themselves'.

In the midst of all this, the city's newspaper readers woke up one morning to read banner headlines and column after column of print on a remarkable raid. The cops made a dramatic breakfast-time swoop on the Thompson home. They were armed with more than their search warrants. A helicopter flew overhead as officers, with guns and dogs and using shields, entered the house. The street was sealed off for three hours and, in scenes reminiscent of a B-movie, officers with handguns took cover, kneeling behind walls as houses were searched. The justification for this heavy-handed approach was that the police were acting on intelligence.

Crowbars and sledgehammers were used and members of the Thompson family were held in a parked police van as the search proceeded. At one stage, Arthur's other son, Billy, was taken away, voluntarily it was said, by officers. It was no surprise that, after all this, Joe Beltrami could thunder out to the press that he had been instructed by the Thompsons to make a complaint to the chief constable 'regarding certain aspects of the police operation today'.

The searches found little of significance but they were an indication of the fevered climate in the city at the time. They also demonstrated that those who felt themselves to be above the law were mistaken. Detective Chief Superintendent John Fleming described what was happening as the product of 'an ongoing feud between regional factions'. He said:

> The drugs trade in Glasgow is controlled by major toughened criminals. Very often, they resort to acts of extreme violence to protect what they consider to be their own jurisdiction and strongly resent anyone trying to muscle in on their scene.

He also told a press conference that these criminals thought nothing of turning to arms and predicted further deaths. He did, however, point out that this was a war between criminals and that the population at large was not in danger. He revealed that he had personally warned Glover and Hanlon that their lives were at risk. His advice had no effect on their behaviour and it was not an intervention they welcomed. And a warning to old Arthur, that he too was at risk, also cut no ice with the man who had seen off three assassination attempts in the past.

John Fleming went on to give a modern version of a complaint the police have had down the years. He said that members of families who had been bereaved were openly warning other family members not to cooperate with the police. And even victims who had survived attacks would not help the police nail their assailants. Witnesses, too, were likely to fall silent when questioned. In the 1990s, the evidence the police needed to present to courts was as hard to come by as it had been in the 1920s and 1930s. It took real bravery to speak out against the gangs. It happened. But not all that often.

TONER, Big Jim

Toner was a **GARSCUBE ROAD** hard man who, with some like-minded characters, ran big-time pitch-and-toss gambling schools on the banks of the Firth and Clyde Canal near Maryhill in the years after the Second World War. The previous owner of this nice little earner for the neds was a character called Haggerty but, seeing the opportunity for easy money, Toner and Co. used their fists to take over and extract even more money from the Sunday afternoon gamblers.

TONGS YA BASS

Once the most frequent form of graffiti (apart from the ubiquitous FTP) to be seen on walls in the city, it is now less popular. The phrase was also used as a verbal cuss by young gang members.

Many theories exist about its origin. The most accepted is that it came into use around the mid 1960s when a popular film called *The Terror of the Tongs* (Anthony Bushell, 1961) was doing the rounds in Glasgow. One young gang member told the staid *Daily Telegraph* about his version of the birth of the phrase. The tongs were, of course, Chinese gangs with a lengthy history – famous long before Hollywood ever came into being. When the Chinese moved around the world, as they did when they poured into California and Nevada during the gold-rush days, they took the term tong with them – establishing it in the American consciousness – and, indeed, it is still used around the world as a generic name for a gang.

Glaswegians were quick to adopt it. There has been a Calton Tong for many years and the name was used in other areas as well – as in the Milton Tong and the Toon Tong of Townhead. According to the *Telegraph*, its universal use in Glasgow dates to the showing of the film in the city. A gory melodrama with torture and screaming, *The Terror of the Tongs* seemed to hit the spot with the Glasgow thugs and, one night in particular, the audience was raised to such a height of excitement by the violence in the film that they ran from the cinema, screaming, 'Tongs, ya bass!', breaking windows and generally creating mayhem. The war cry was soon in common usage.

TORRINGTON, JEFF

Born in **ABBOTSFORD PLACE** in the Gorbals, Torrington was, from the age of two, brought up in **LOGAN STREET**. He wrote the novel, *Swing Hammer Swing!* (London: Minerva, 1993), which won the 1993 Whitbread Book of the Year Award. The book, which was also dramatised for the stage, revisits some of the same subject matter as that of the pre-war *No Mean City* – crime and poor housing – but its greater humour and closer observation made it more to the taste of the modern reader. His unexpected success in a major literary competition brought new scrutiny to the Gorbals.

Working on the novel on and off, it took Torrington nearly thirty years to complete it. The story is set in the late 1960s when the hammer of the title had already demolished large swathes of the Gorbals. But more than the stone walls of the old Gorbals were destroyed – a whole way of life was swept away. In its place came appalling housing – bleak high-rise buildings that Torrington called 'punishment blocks'.

Torrington was critical of the slum clearance programme, saying:

> Don't get me wrong. A lot of the old Gorbals were slums and they needed to get knocked down. There is no sense denying that. But what sickens me is what was built for the Gorbals people in their place.

Maybe such high-profile comments played a role in the regeneration of the Gorbals in the new century. The hammer has swung yet again and much of the old 1960s' housing has, in its turn, been battered to the ground to be replaced with new housing and landscaping that the characters in novels such as *No Mean City* and *Swing Hammer Swing!* could not have dreamed of.

TOWER BALLROOM

The **ROUND TOLL** is a pretty nondescript place today. The policeman who once stood proudly, controlling the cars and buses, at this intersection of several of the most important roads on the north side of the city, is long gone – having been replaced by traffic lights. There is a collection of pubs, a bookie, shops and some flats. It is totally unremarkable. The only place of note to catch the eye is the tenement block that is labelled Tower Building. In that peculiarly blindingly obvious Scottish way, which gives every river a River Cottage and every hill a House on the Hill, the name reflects the architecture – it once had a tower! These days, it is a cut-down version of the original but, to a degree, the architect's idea lives on.

This landmark was once the home of one of the busiest dance halls in the city – and there is still a dance school on the premises. But, in its heyday, it was a popular, if, on occasion, tough, spot. In the 1940s, John Foy and Joe O'Hara, hardmen known as the Kings of the **GARSCUBE ROAD**, were amongst its bouncers – and a place like this had much need of bouncers who knew their business. After donning their Saturday-night finery, the dance hall's male clientele liked to have a serious 'swally' or two in the local howffs before heading to the Tower in search of 'talent'.

The entrance was less than glamorous – up a close and several flights of steps to the third floor. But, in the city where dancing was almost a way of life, its appeal to customers was strong. Colm Brogan's 1952 book, *The Glasgow Story* (London: Frederick Muller, 1952), put it this way: 'Perhaps the dancing provides an outlet for rumbustious and highly emotional people who chafe against inhibitions and conventions they hardly know how to defy.'

One famous musician who played the Tower, trombonist George Chisholm, remembers that, as the dancers slipped across the floor, they were watched by men with whom it would be unwise to disagree. To maintain what was known, in those days, as 'the best of order', these tough guys periodically cried out, 'Nae birlin'!'

Any crime or violence in the hall was usually pretty small-scale

– although, on occasion, troublemakers could make their exit via the fire escape and find themselves lying bruised and bleeding on the ground, many feet below. A tale is told of one such unfortunate who was found, many hours after his ignominious ejection, still unconscious on hard frozen ground, his flesh having been nibbled by rats.

What fighting there was would mainly be between locals and clients who had travelled from the city centre or other areas for a few hours of glamour, bright lights and sweet music. The regulars resented these interlopers who, they felt, just came to the Tower in order to steal the favours of the local girls.

The hall was a favourite haunt of Walter Norval and his Wee Mob, a gang that gave the area much grief over many years. A snooker hall, in the same building, was the place where the gang honed their skills with cue and ball and plotted many a scam.

V

VAUGHAN, Frankie

This popular song-and-dance man was, surprisingly, a seminal figure in the ongoing attempts to improve the quality of life in the vast scheme of Easterhouse. Like the building of other post-war schemes such as Castlemilk and Drumchapel, the creation of Easterhouse was a seriously flawed, if well meaning, experiment in social engineering. Post-Second-World-War local Labour politicians were appalled by the standard of housing in the city. There were too many crumbling tenements with outside toilets, primitive coal ranges, cracked porcelain sinks and muddy backcourts awash with litter.

The politicians acknowledged the part that poor housing had played in the forming of the 1930s' gangs and the high level of crime in run-down areas generally. Their solution was to take vast tracks of open countryside, on the edges of the city, and erect thousands of blocks of council flats, all with inside toilets, good heating and other touches of comfort that were undreamed of by the denizens of the old tenements. It was supposed that, at a stroke, this would wipe away much of the crime that had attached itself to the old city. There was one serious mistake – they decanted, for example, a population the size of that of Perth to one scheme, Castlemilk, on the lower slopes of the beautiful Cathkin Braes.

However, they failed to appreciate what made Perth such a pleasant place in which to live. Castlemilk, Easterhouse and the other schemes may have provided relatively comfortable housing but they had little of the other necessities for a contented life. As the altruistic, if naive, councillors forged ahead with the building plans for the houses, they forgot the need for such amenities as pubs, libraries, churches and swimming pools. The folk who moved to the bright-as-new-paint houses were sentenced to live in what one comedian called 'deserts wi' windaes'.

The scale of what was happening was almost unprecedented elsewhere in Britain. And the trouble caused by the new form of 'desert' warfare that sprang up, particularly between youths, was watched by local and national newspapers with concern. It was mainly a problem involving young folk. The older men who had been whisked to new surroundings may have appreciated the comforts of a modern house as much as their hard-working wives but, if they did get nostalgic for their old surroundings, they just took the bus into town and met up with the mates they had left behind. The teenagers, however, were more seriously trapped in the schemes and, as idle hands do, they turned to gangs and violence.

Frankie Vaughan had read quite a bit about what was going on when he pitched up for a gig at the old Alhambra Theatre. At this time, in the 1960s, he was a massive figure on the popular entertainment scene with hit songs like 'Green Door', 'Kisses Sweeter than Wine' and his theme tune, 'Give Me the Moonlight', which earned him the soubriquet Mr Moonlight. He liked to appear with a straw boater and immaculate dinner suit. He would belt out the hits, pausing only for an occasional high kick or two that thrilled the matrons who so loved his act. He was a real touch of show-business glamour but it was a manufactured and carefully crafted persona.

Frankie Vaughan had a feel for the kids he read about in the newspapers when they reported that, in Easterhouse, the youngsters were knocking lumps out of each other and making the scheme something of a no-go area. Vaughan's real name was Frankie Abelson and he grew up with a Russian grandmother in a tough area of Liverpool. His granny retained a thick accent and liked to refer to young Frankie, her first grandson, as 'my number vorn'. Casting around for a stage name, the young singer took inspiration from her accent and adopted Vaughan as a name that was, in time, to shine in marquee lights in Las Vegas. His Liverpool upbringing gave him a lifelong interest in youth work and youth clubs and, wherever he was, he liked to see what he could do to help. In 1968, in Glasgow, he played a major role, with concerned locals, in setting up the Easterhouse Project – an attempt to end or at least ameliorate the violence in the scheme.

The solution, pushed by Vaughan and the friends he had made locally, was the age-old one that is resorted to when a community is faced by unruly kids running wild in gangs – give them something to do. My research into similar problems, down the years, shows that the cynics who decry such efforts are wrong. They do help – albeit often only for a limited period.

No one suffered more than Frankie Vaughan from cynics and right-wing local politicians decrying his efforts, accusing him of courting publicity and suggesting that giving youngsters club rooms and things to do was merely pandering to them. It was all garbage, of course.

But there was a welter of criticism around the whole Easterhouse Project that, even today, leaves a nasty taste in the mouth. These were good people trying to do something constructive and they were being pilloried by politicians whose only solution was to lock 'em up and throw away the key. It is a great pity that Frankie Vaughan died before the definitive statistics were to emerge to prove the success of the early days of the project. The entertainer, always a man to give his audiences full value with an energetic belter of a show, developed heart trouble and died in September 1999 after surgery. But, in January 2000 – thirty-two years after the start of the Easterhouse Project – documents were released that showed dramatically and factually that Vaughan and the local laymen and police who helped develop the project had achieved some remarkable successes. Papers prepared by Glasgow University's School of Social Studies reporting on gang activity in the city showed that, when Mr Moonlight intervened, crime in the area dropped dramatically. The police records in the Northern Division showed a marked drop in assaults and robberies in the area. These figures were released under the thirty years' rule.

But, at the time it was set up, the Easterhouse Project sparked major controversy. It had started to make headlines when the touring troubadour made a plea to meet with the leaders of the gangs. He had the idea of parleying with the youths and hoped that, because of his fame, he could help to get the boys to settle their differences peacefully rather than with knife and club. The meeting happened and Vaughan told the press that four of the gangs in the area had agreed to lay down their weapons – swords, bayonets, sledgehammers and meat cleavers. The leaders of the gangs involved, the Drummie, Pak, Rebels (Easterhouse) and Toi, would leave their weapons on neutral ground opposite St Benedict's Hall.

The deal was that, for this sacrifice, the singer would help them set up a club or centre of their own where they could pursue pastimes of a less violent nature than in the past. Frankie Vaughan spelled out the ground rules:

We must stop the violence and I have told the lads that I will take nothing to do with them unless this is done. I will stand up for them against anyone and will come up here any time they feel they need me – but the main part is up to them.

It was all very reasonable and, no doubt, getting the gangs to deal face to face with a major personality helped. But it also fuelled the inaccurate criticism that here was a bad bunch who were being feted.

Originally, the idea was that boys would build the club them-selves with help and there was an offer of assistance from the Boys' Club of Great Britain, something the singer was also involved in. Initially, there was some concern from the police regarding the arrangements for the handing in of the weapons and they said they would not cooperate in such a public 'stunt'. Frankie Vaughan took this seriously and wrote to the then Prime Minister Harold Wilson. Wilson, ever the wily politician, wrote back to say that he could not intervene in police operational matters but, behind the scenes, there was a change of heart. Although it was pointed out that weapons could be handed in at any time at, say, a police station, the go-ahead was also given for a mass handover. The police arranged to be at St Benedict's at the appointed hour on a Saturday night. They were there to make sure the weapons did not fall into the wrong hands rather than take note of those who were handing them in. The press and TV from around the world came to watch this unconventional handover which had been brokered by a world-class entertainer. Despite this, it has to be said that the police presence was enough to make some of the gang members give their weapons to youth leaders to add to the pile – being a tad 'shy' to do so themselves. It was an unforgettable Glasgow event and, being Glasgow, it was celebrated in a good commercial way – four ice-cream vans and two mobile fish-and-chip shops turned up to add to the festivities.

The newspapers at least were grateful to Frankie. In a generous tribute *The Herald* wrote that, if a single life had been saved or an assault forestalled, it was a notable achievement 'for which the leading and ordinary citizens of Glasgow will be grateful'. Not everyone saw it that way and there were lively arguments on TV talk shows. One local politico wanted to meet violence with violence and admitted that, although it seemed brutal, he felt that was the solution! No lessons learned down the years there, then. *The Herald*, however, kept a steady hand and showed common sense in its reporting of the ups and downs of this experiment in curbing youth gangs. In a shrewd comment, it observed:

> However much one may deplore the showmanship and publicity associated with the flights to Blackpool [the entertainer had invited gang leaders to a meeting in a theatre where he was appearing] and so on, most thinking adults are bewildered by the wave of gang terrorism, the suborning of witnesses, the extortion of protection money and the stabbing of innocent passers-by in the thoroughfares of the city, the gangs are a fact of life.

The extent of such problems had been well illustrated. As is the way with all such initiatives, early success gets moderated as the years pass but there is no doubt that the **WESTERHOUSE ROAD** Nissan Hut Centre that was eventually built in the scheme kept many youngsters out of the gang culture and saved lives. In its heyday, the lads went camping, hillwalking, rock climbing, canoeing and mountaineering. There was a full programme of activities to keep them out of trouble – and out of the pub. There were discos at night and indoor sports during the day. It was not, of course, all down to Frankie Vaughan but he did help to get the ball rolling and, at the time of his death, a local councillor told the press that 'Frankie Vaughan will always be remembered by the people of Easterhouse'.

Much has changed in the last thirty years or so since the project began but a lot of the thinking behind it continues. Now Easter-house has a thriving and innovative festival and, indeed, remarkably, the scheme is to be home to a national theatre project. That is something that would have been hard to envisage, all these years ago, when Mr Moonlight sat in his star's dressing room, in the Alhambra, and read in his newspapers about the mayhem that was taking place a few miles up the road, on the outskirts of town. And, whatever else he did, Frankie Vaughan did not wring his hands and rabbit on about swingeing sentences for youngsters dumped into that particular 'desert wi' windaes' through no fault of their own. He undid his glitzy cufflinks, rolled up the sleeves of his immaculately laundered shirt and did something about it.

W

WARNES, Rev. S H R

Warnes was a pioneering **BRIDGETON** Church of Scotland minister who, along with his colleague the Rev. J A C Murray, initiated some of the first attempts to woo gangs away from the street-fighting life with the alternative of active sports. Their initiative took place against the bleak background of battles between gangs in the **DRYGATE**. The problem of gang warfare was so severe that Lord Alness, sitting at the High Court in 1930, issued the following warning: 'The time might come when use may have to be made of the lash and to revive an old statute of George IV under which the penalty of death could be imposed on those who went razor slashing'.

These two ministers, Warnes of St Francis-in-the-East in Bridgeton and Murray of Park Church, were very concerned and had the idea that the answer was to 'provide recreational facilities and substitute games for fights'. They explained their ideas to a meeting of the presbytery that had been called to look at ways to reform non-church-going youths in the east end. Coincidence had drawn the two like-minded clerics together. They made an investigation and found, remarkably, that, within a radius of 150 or 200 yards of Rev. Warnes' church, there were no fewer than ten or eleven gangs with a membership of 250 to 300 boys and men. Members of these gangs or groups ranged in age from fifteen to forty. Each of the 'bands', as the members themselves preferred to call the groups, had a territory and a name and they were well organised as far as discipline and finance were concerned.

By their own admission, the ministers approached the gangs with some timidity. But a party was taken away from the tenement canyons to leafy Hillfoot for an afternoon of football. A dance and a ramble were also arranged. Rev. Warnes considered these gangs to be a phenomenon thrown up by the depressed conditions in the area at the time. In his opinion, it was 'the economic conditions which had crowded them together in such unsanitary areas and which had produced for them an unemployment market in which there was little or no demand for their services' that led to their aggressive behaviour. These kirk pioneers were very positive in their approach and thought that, considering the conditions of life in these slums, it was surprising that the problem was not worse than it actually was. They felt that the element of gang rivalry could be turned to good use, believing that the independence of spirit and energy that the gang members undeniably displayed could be directed to matters other than territorial street fights.

All this was a long, long time ago. But, even then, a leader writer in *The Herald* remarked that there was nothing new in their thinking – the idea of getting them to kick a football instead of shins had been tried already. The leader writer also warned that there was more than a day's work in the reform of such characters. But Warnes and Murray were optimistic.

It was decided that a football league would be set up with an admission charge of a penny at the gate. In a separate initiative, tickets were sold to pay for trips into the countryside.

A new organisation was born – the Rockcliffe Parish Football League. Eight teams, from the corners that then lay between **BRIDGETON CROSS** and **MAIN STREET**, took part and games were played on Wednesday nights and Saturday afternoons on vacant ground near **SHAWFIELD PARK**. The Playing Fields Association provided a secretary and Bailie Alexander Munro, no less, of **DALMARNOCK** Ward, was one of a group of honorary vice presidents. This was a modest start for what went on to become the Churches League, at times a mainstay of amateur football in the city. Like many similar ideas, it didn't stop gang warfare but it played a role in keeping many a youngster out of trouble.

WILLIAMSON, PETER

One of the most remarkable, but largely now forgotten, gangs of the 1930s was the Beehive and Williamson was its leader. Although he was a major figure of the time, he is less well remembered than Fullerton of the Billy Boys or Bowman of the Norman Conks. Unlike many of the other gang leaders back then, he was said to have been well educated and from a respectable family – indeed, he seems to have been a genuine black sheep.

A fluent speaker, with mental agility and a knowledge of the law, he was in the habit of sacking lawyers and defending himself in court – and he made a pretty good fist of it too. His gang had originally been called the Beehive Corner Boys, tacit acknowledgement of the fact that this group was built up around men who had time on their hands and would hang around street corners, looking for trouble. Housebreaking was the main activity of the gang and they were noted for it – though they could also turn their hand to street fighting and intimidation. Williamson made a powerful impression on gang-buster Chief Constable Percy Sillitoe who records in his book on his time in Glasgow that the leader of the Beehive was especially adapt at fooling police officers about his identity and purpose. On the arrival of the cops at the scene of a fight or disturbance, where the injured would be lying bleeding in the streets and on the pavements, they'd find Williamson, in the thick of things, apparently trying to separate the two sides and playing the unlikely role of peacemaker. It was a tactic that worked for a while until his face – and the fact that whenever he was around there was always trouble – became too familiar with the boys in blue.

Williamson was a good leader and inspired great loyalty in his sidekicks. Indeed, one lieutenant of this feared gang, Harry McMenemy, was so in his thrall that he once pled guilty to an offence committed by his boss. The rationale was that, since McMenemy had fewer previous convictions, any sentence was likely to be lighter than that handed down to the leader and, therefore, less damaging to the activities of the gang. Despite his education and background Williamson was well able to scare his enemies and control his men with his ability as a one-to-one fighter with both fist and weapon.

WINTERS, LARRY

Winters was one of the celebrity inmates of the Barlinnie Special Unit which, in the parlance of the streets, was also known as the Wendy House or the Nutcracker Suite. Winters also spent much time in Peterhead where he was a continual problem to the staff. Some prisoners, faced with a long stretch, get their heads around it and get on with smoothing life behind bars as much as possible, staying clean till time for release eventually comes. Not so Winters. He got involved in the rioting that, for a time, was a regular occurrence in Peterhead and he attacked warders. He was such a handful that, when the Special Unit became a reality, he was sent south to join it.

Experts there confirmed that this man – who had murdered a barman over a fiver – was extremely intelligent. He was said to have an IQ of 160. But he had a violent streak that could show itself even in the relatively civilised atmosphere of the Special Unit. One psychologist who visited him in prison told of being threatened by Winters. Armed with a pair of scissors, Winters said, 'Do you realise I could cut your throat? I have done this to better people than you. How do you feel?' Presumably the answer was scared. But violent criminals are nothing if not unpredictable. On this occasion, Winters laughed and threw the scissors down.

Almost everyone in authority who met Winters remarked on the dangerous mixture he presented – he was an extremely clever man with extremely low self control. Winters' life, like that of fellow celebrity inmate James Boyle, sparked a film. *Silent Scream* (David Hayman, 1990), starred Iain Glen and was directed by the renowned actor David Hayman who had a successful association with Glasgow's internationally respected Citizen's Theatre.

Other celebrity inmates like Boyle and Hugh Collins left the

Special Unit to build new lives in the arts and to prove to some at least that prison can reform the hardest of cases. Not Winters. He was found naked, on a chamber pot, dying of a drugs overdose in the Special Unit. How those drugs got there is part of the story of the demise of the Special Unit.

X

XYY GANG

This was the name given to a group of bank robbers led by legendary Godfather Walter Norval. The name came about during and after the complex trial of Norval and his associates in the High Court in 1977. Thirteen men faced a series of charges in four separate trials lasting three weeks. The charges covered bank robberies, armed theft of hospital payrolls, an attack on a post-office van, illegal possession of explosives, including nitro-glycerine, and, of course, possession of illegal firearms. Some of the accused were involved in each trial and, in order to stop newspaper reports of one trial prejudicing another during the ongoing proceedings, the robbers were referred to in the newspapers as Mr X and Mr Y and so on.

So complex were the charges that it took more than an hour to sentence the seven who were eventually found guilty. Before leaving the bench, the judge, Lord Cowie, said that he was deeply grateful to the press for their restraint and discretion in reporting the cases which were of great interest to the public – something of an understatement! He then withdrew his legal restraint on the reporting of the trial and, for the first time, the public, who had followed every twist and turn in the case, learned the true identities of Mr X, Mr Y and company. They were an evil bunch whose success in a series of spectacular armed thefts had caused the police much grief over many months. But they were to pay the price for their crimes – sentences totalling seventy-four years were handed down to the gang.

Z

Z CARS

Many people, picking up a book of this nature, go straight to 'Z' to see what ingenuity – if any – has gone into digging up an appropriate item – items would usually be asking too much! – to go under this notoriously difficult to fill alphabetical section. So, here it is and it's something of an exclusive.

Even some ardent fans of this 1960s–1970s TV cop series often don't know that Glasgow, not Liverpool, was originally proposed as the setting for Z Cars, which was to feature police patrolling a city in fast vehicles – the 'Z' of Ford Zephyr, giving the show its title. For it was here in Glasgow that PC Plod first stopped pounding the pavements and got himself some decent wheels to police the mean streets. The cars and the two-way radio system that was introduced around the same time meant that the cops could get to the scene of any action fast.

And Glasgow's fleet of radio patrol cars was just one of a number of innovations thought up by Sir Percy Sillitoe, the most famous and most effective of a long list of powerful chief constables to rule the city's boys in blue.